The
Development
of
Social
Understanding

The Development of Social Understanding

Edited by
JOSEPH GLICK
City University of New York

and **K. ALISON CLARKE-STEWART**
The University of Chicago

GARDNER PRESS, INC., New York

Distributed by Halsted Press Division
John Wiley & Sons, Inc.
New York • Toronto • London • Sydney

Gardner Press, Inc.
19 Union Square West
New York 10003

Distributed solely by the Halsted Press Division
of John Wiley & Sons, Inc., New York

Library of Congress Cataloging in Publication Data
Main entry under title:
The Development of social understanding.
    (Studies in social and cognitive development; v. 1)
    1. Socialization—Addresses, essays, lectures.
I. Glick, Joseph. II. Clarke-Stewart, Alison,
1943- III. Series.
HQ783.D48   301.15'37   77-25044
ISBN 0-470-99367-7

Printed in the United States of America

Series
Preface

This volume begins a series of books dealing with problems of human socialization. Based on the notion that some degree of "end-state" analysis of how to be a culture member should inform our attempts to derive a developmental theory of socialization processes, while at the same time an end-state analysis uninformed by developmental processes is likely to be inadequate, the series brings together the work of developmental psychologists with that of cognitive and social psychologists, sociologists, and anthropologists. It is our hope that this juxtaposition of disciplinary and individual perspectives, in a context of theoretical integration and substantive synthesis, will illuminate the development of human social behavior in ways not achieved by current academic journals. We intend for each volume, over the years, to occupy a leading-edge position in the field, by reflecting not so much what is being done but what is important and yet to do. Ultimately, perhaps, the series will help to identify and define a new field of knowledge, giving clearer and more coherent meaning to the term "social development."

JOSEPH GLICK
ALISON CLARKE-STEWART

Contributors

Aaron V. Cicourel, Department of Sociology, University of California—San Diego, La Jolla, California.

K. Alison Clarke-Stewart, Department of Education, University of Chicago, Chicago, Illinois.

Joseph Glick, Graduate Center, City University of New York, New York, New York.

Barbara Davis Goldman, Department of Psychology, University of Waterloo, Waterloo, Ontario.

Denis Newman, Graduate Center, City University of New York, New York, New York.

Hildy S. Ross, Department of Psychology, University of Waterloo, Waterloo, Ontario.

Elliot Turiel, Merrill College, University of California, Santa Cruz; and Institute of Human Development, University of California, Berkeley, California.

Gilbert Voyat, Graduate School, City University of New York, New York, New York.

Contents

The

Development

of

Social

Understanding

1 Cognition and Social Cognition: An Introduction

JOSEPH GLICK

Developmental studies of social cognition have grown in recent years to the point where this area is one of the more popular topics of developmentalists' concern. Shantz (1975) in a recent review of work in the area indicates that a great deal of the impetus for studies of social cognition has stemmed from extensions of the cognitive developmental theory of Piaget (e.g., Piaget, 1970) and Werner (e.g., Werner and Kaplan, 1963). The basic research strategies in the area utilize some measure of cognitive capacity, such as perspective-taking, as a model for the processes that are likely to be involved in knowing others— which is taken to be what social cognition is all about (Selman, 1971, Flavell et. al. 1968, 1974).

The present volume brings together researchers who have begun to study social cognition from an interactive perspective, which treats the social domain of knowing as one which may be in conflict with, or at least different from, the classical developmental models of cognitive knowing. From this point of view, the simple translation of cognitive processes as applied in the object world to the social world is an enterprise that must be undertaken with great caution. The studies presented here tend to start with considerations about the dynamics of social interaction and ask questions relevant to cognitive theory from a viewpoint grounded in the particularities of engaged social behavior. Reasons for this approach can perhaps best be located in a characterization of the distinction between knowing objects and knowing people.

While cognitive developmental theories tend to stress the range and organization of activities a knower uses to gain access to a "to be known," the "to be known" is usually treated as either an aspect of the physical world or some logical operation, which is in turn derived from interactions with the physical world. Within Piagetian theory, the physical object stands at the receiving end of a variety of organismic activities (the application of action schemes) which define the meaning of the object (assimilation). The object, moreover, because it is a physically constant thing, serves as a stable substrate supporting an integration of all those actions that somehow converge upon it. In this manner thought achieves its characteristic coherent form, since the integration of common actions allows for abstractions about the *form* of activities which are distinct from the particular *objects*. This cognitive model requires a stable substrate so that stable integrations and hence stable knowledge structures can develop. This stable substrate is well afforded by the physical world.

The application of this developmental scheme to the social world may be difficult since it remains a distinct possibility that people do not behave as objects do. On the most superficial level it is clear that objects do not move unless moved. Their movement is predictable from a knowledge (or a perception) of the physical forces exerted upon them. There is then a direct tie between the action exerted on an object and the movement of the object. People move in other ways. People tend to move themselves, and it is only in some loose sense that the action of one is directly contingent upon the actions applied by another. Thus the person as the recipient of an action scheme acts differently from the object as recipient. This difference is precisely in the critical area of predictability and stability. Given the Piagetian scheme of things, this must have consequences for the kind of knowledge afforded by the social world and suggests a basis for the possibility of different cognitive structures in the social domain.

The differences that account for object and people movements have ramifications for the types of theoretical knowledge likely to emerge in the social and physical domains. Physical events are *in principle* specifiable because they are stable and involve determined reactions to identifiable forces. Accordingly, they afford the development of logical systems which allow for knowledge that transcends physical particulars. Social events, on the other hand, display less stability *in principle* and hence should involve knowledge structures of a more probabilistic sort. Social knowledge therefore should be more uncertain and more sensitive to current informational conditions (contexts) than physical knowledge. Following this line of reasoning, we might also expect characteristic differences in both the type of information processed and the manner of its processing in the social as opposed to the physical domain.

The inherent uncertainty of social knowledge and its concomitant context sensitivity implies that social knowledge is oriented toward a wide range of features of the social environment. Social actors not only react to actions upon them but act by themselves as well. Further, the reaction of a social actor is likely to be largely governed by internal states which are difficult to know. In this manner the same action may have different consequences at different points in time, if the internal state of the reactor has changed. Accordingly, cues to internal state and the reaction potentiality of the social object become important for gaining some sense of predictability in the social world.

This process is all the more complicated by the fact that socially significant cues are displayed at many levels, from minute facial gestures and gross bodily movements to verbal messages which are themselves complexly interpretable. In some cases, moreover, these cues are contradictory (c.f. the double-bind hypothesis of Bateson, 1972), and if not simply contradictory, at least indicative of subtle "keyings" (Goffman, 1974) of the form of relationship and sense in which the current social interchange is to be taken.

Given the complex structure of the stimulus domain potentially relevant to social understanding, we might expect social information to be processed in ways that differ from the manner in which information about the object world is processed. Normal object relations involve closed sets of information constraints which are in principle determinable. Information-processing strategies might then be adapted to this information field and display a systematic logical form. Such strategies have been identified for both adults and children by such researchers as Bruner, Goodnow, and Austin (1962), Gholson, Levine, and Phillips (1972), and Moss (1976), with respect to sets of concept acquisition material defined by combinations of various geometric dimensions. There is evidence, however, that when stimuli using socially relevant materials are constructed to logically parallel geometric sets, one finds different information-processing strategies. Bruner, Goodnow, and Austin (1962) found, for example, that socially relevant materials led to the strategy of testing out intuitive guesses, while geometric materials of the same informational complexity and logical form led to strategies that isolated dimensions one by one and then tested their relevance for concept definition. More recent work in social psychology (Abelson, 1976; Nisbett et al., 1976; Schank and Abelson, 1977) has demonstrated a similar phenomenon. When individuals are given concrete, socially relevant materials, ideal information-processing strategies are eschewed and more intuitive strategies are employed.

We might venture that socially construed situations, no matter what their actual informational structure, are *conceived* as being informationally rich and beyond complete specification. Accordingly, we might expect that these situations would lead to strategies of knowing which attempt to short-circuit complete informational testing. We should then expect social knowledge to be referenced to devices which would reduce informational complexity while yet providing some basis for social action. This is precisely the kind of mechanism that Abelson (1976) and Schank and Abelson (1977) refer to as social scripts. Paradigm cases and shared scenarios are apparently used in cases where complete informational analysis is impossible and coherent action sequences must be carried out.

D'Andrade (1972) has recently summarized evidence bearing on this point. He has adduced evidence which suggests that in the social domain people tend to operate with stored "cultural belief systems," which may in fact override presently available information. In one study reviewed, three judgment conditions were contrasted. In the first situation subjects rated group interactions by means of the Bales category system as interactions were ongoing. A second condition involved ratings based on the memory of a segment of interaction. There were near zero correlations between the concurrently rated and retrospectively rated scores. A third condition involved a hypothetical rating of the interrelationships within the rating scale itself. Using only the rating scales and seeing no behavior, subjects were asked about the expected covariation of various scales (e.g., aggressiveness and intrusiveness of questions). Comparison of this rating (which was designed to expose the operation of pre-exposure beliefs about what can possibly be seen) and both the concurrent and retrospective ratings yielded near zero correlations with concurrent ratings and moderately high correlations with retrospective ratings. This study suggests that, at least in memory, stored schematic representations of social scenarios act to override and restructure an informational display. At this point one can only speculate about results that might be obtained should the rater be an actual participant in the social situation rated (which is the norm in "real life"). One might expect, for the reasons offered above, that actual interaction would be more guided by the kind of structure that characterizes memorial representation. (Ongoing studies by my students are attempting to test this implication.)

We have thus far built an argument that seems to indicate that social knowledge in fully rational form is most likely unattainable, dealing as it does with a shifting and subtle object in an informationally rich and unanalyzable world. Locked in a world of this complexity, we seem to have no choice but to indulge in social fantasizing. To leave the argument here, however, is not only uncomfortable, but also probably wrong. We got here by fully trying on the analogy between cognitive achievements in the physical world and those in the social domain. We have treated the social knower as an observer and theorizer about the world as it is displayed for analysis and prediction. Yet in trying on this analogy we have been forced to neglect one of the fundamental facts of social existence. The social world is not only "known about," it is acted within. In fact, it has been argued in some quarters that our sense of a social world is *interactively maintained* (Garfinkel, 1967). It is to this approach to the problem of social knowledge that we now turn.

The main problem of social life is not necessarily to emerge with a "theory" of social actors. It is rather to maintain and sustain coherent courses of action which are related coherently to an interactive context. Much the same point has been made by cognitive anthropologists who have supplanted the goal of ethnographic description of a knowledge domain by the goal of behaving in a situation as a native would. The latter goal would be a trivial change if "acting as a native does" were fully equivalent to "knowing what a native knows." It is not. Knowledge for an actor is governed as much by its conditions of application (Glick, 1975, 1977) as it is by its structure as a known field of information. Two bodies of knowledge must intersect: knowledge of a domain of information and knowledge of the domain of application. Yet it is likely that application rules are obeyed and not "known" as a cognitive object. In much the same way that we use appropriate syntax without being able to talk explicitly about grammar, or follow rules of conversational sequencing (Sacks, Schegloff, and Jefferson, 1974) without being able to describe them, we probably know about sociability without that knowledge being explicit. In fact, in the social domain it is most likely that tacit knowledge (Bransford and McCarrell, 1974; Franks, 1974; Turvey, 1974) is pre-eminently important.

By this formulation, tacit knowledge is seen as some sort of invisible groundwork of coherent action, not specifically cognizable in and of itself but present in and underlying the possibility of coherence. It is knowledge that may be "displayed" and retrieved by an analyst working to uncover the grounding of coherent action, but it is not known under ordinary circumstances in any explicit way. Particularly in the social domain it is important to distinguish between rule-regulated and rule-recognized behaviors (Glick, 1975, 1977). Rule-recognized behaviors conform to our understandings of formulable cognitive knowledge. Rule-regulated behaviors are those which are bound into systems of recognized coherence, but where the regulatory rules are obeyed and not formulated.

Ethnomethodologists such as Garfinkel (1967) have adopted specialized classes of inquiry procedures to make visible some of the invisible structures underlying social cognition. They have found that our sense of social reality is in fact based on an elaborate structure of presuppositions which are sometimes elaborately maintained in action but which normally escape explicit formulation in social psychological and developmental accounts of social life.

There are two classic approaches to the analysis of the interactional maintenance of social life. One approach draws an analogy between the social object and the physical object, while the other is rooted in an approach to the sociological conditions of knowing. Both approaches are discussed in this volume.

The object analogy is most often pursued with respect to a hitherto unremarked-upon feature of human social objects—they can speak and in other ways contingently react to a social actor. Hence, one might construct, as does Piaget (discussed in the chapter by Voyat), a model of social action which looks to the feedback-producing characteristics of a social actor for those conditions of stable action that should allow for some degree of coherence and hence provide the possibility of social knowledge properly construed. In this manner, then, either through language or contingent action, the social actor provides "object stability" by having himself a determined mode of interaction. By thus being stable as an object-to-be-known, this determined social actor takes on the characteristic of a stable object in classical cognitive theory. This approach depends heavily on the ability to characterize human actions as being, if not rational, at least determinable in some consistent manner, and clear, if not univocal, in their expression.

Turiel's chapter confronts the extension of cognitive developmental models to the social domain by attempting to show that an extension of cognitive models focusing on problems of logical form (as the moral development literature has tended to do) may be inadequate to the task of specifying social judgment. A heavy loading of concrete social knowledge may be required in the social domain, and developmental sequences fundamentally different from logical sequences may be found there.

Clarke-Stewart's chapter, too, speaks to some of the complexities in social readings that are often glossed in experimental studies of social understanding. What is particularly interesting is the evidence presented here which suggests that the child is able to read through scripted social interactions, and the subtlety of the distinctions about social events that determine young children's social behaviors.

Cicourel points out what is perhaps one of the fundamental problems in the "feedback" interpretation of social interaction. Human communicative functioning involves the use of "interpretive and summarization procedures" which give name and form to a lived-through interaction. Often we are not in a position to know, either as social interactors or as social observers, the form in which such interpretation and summarization proceed. Thus, while acknowledging feedback, one must at the same time recognize that the feedback itself is filtered through a system of interpretations. Hence it is not as much feedback from others as it is feedback from oneself about others. Depending on how heavily we stress this aspect of the problem of social understanding, the goal of objective clarity in social doings approaches or recedes.

Clarke-Stewart's chapter deals directly with the complexity and subtlety of social readings which must be incorporated into a viable model of social cognitive development. Taking the well-researched area of children's reactions to strangers, Clarke-Stewart demonstrates a range of phenomena that speak for the great complexity of social understanding that even young children display. In the social domain we are confronted with subtlety of relationship as a primary fact.

The remaining chapters in the book focus on the interactional approach to the analysis of social understanding. The chapters by Newman and by Goldman and Ross detail some of the particular mechanisms that give coherence to children's social interactions. They point the way to a form of analysis which may characterize the future in social cognition research. The attempt is to find those mechanisms existing in concurrent, ongoing interactional sequences that can provide coherence to children's interaction even though they may not yield a cognitive interpretation of the meaning of the social situation or a typification of the social interactor. The eventual problem will be to find the way from engaged interactional competence (or incompetence) to those mechanisms that eventually allow for some form of social rationality.

The authors of this volume do not all speak with one voice. There are paradoxes presented and some hard methodological grounds to be worked through. What the chapters do share is some sense that simplified models of social understanding are not enough and that any form of simple extension of theory and technique from other domains of inquiry will encounter resistance in the social domain. Perhaps nowhere else does the inherent complexity of human behavior and the concomitant necessity for subtle and powerful means of understanding stand in such clear relief.

Note

1. This project has been supported in part by a grant from the National Institute of Child Health and Human Development (5T01 HD 00231).

References

Abelson, R. Script processing in attitude formation and decision making. In J. S. Carroll and J. Payne, *Cognition and Social Behavior*. Hillsdale, N.J.: Erlbaum Associates, 1976.

Bateson, G. *Steps to an Ecology of Mind*. New York: Ballantine Books, 1972.

Bransford, J. P., and McCarrell, N. S. A sketch of a cognitive approach to comprehension: Some thoughts about understanding what it means to comprehend. In W. B. Weimer and D. S. Palermo, *Cognition and the Symbolic Processes*. Hillsdale, N.J.: Erlbaum Associates, 1974.

Bruner, J. S., Goodnow, J. J., and Austin, G. *A Study of Thinking*. New York: Wiley, 1962.

D'Andrade, R. Cultural belief systems. Unpublished manuscript, 1972.

Flavell, J. H. Botkin, P., Fry, C., Wright, L., and Jarvis, P. *The Development of Role Taking and Communication Skills in Children*. New York: Wiley, 1968.

Flavell, J. H. The development of inferences about others. In T. Mischel (Ed.), *Understanding Other Persons*. Oxford, England: Blackwell, Basil, Mott, 1974.

Franks, J. J. Toward understanding understanding. In W. B. Weimer and D. S. Palermo, *Cognition and the Symbolic Processes*. Hillsdale, N.J.: Erlbaum Associates, 1974.

Garfinkel, H. *Studies in Ethnomethodology*. Englewood Cliffs, N.J.: Prentice-Hall, 1967.

Gholson, B., Levine, M., and Phillips, S. Hypotheses, strategies and stereotypes in discrimination learning. *Journal of Experimental Child Psychology*, 1972, B, 423–466.

Glick, J. Cognitive development in cross-cultural perspective. In F. D. Horowitz (Ed.), *Review of Child Development Research,* Vol. IV. Chicago: University of Chicago Press, 1975.

Glick, J. Functional and structural aspects of rationality. Paper delivered to the Jean Piaget Society meetings May 21, 1977.

Goffman, E. *Frame Analysis.* New York: Harper and Row, 1974.

Moss, A. The developmental effects of irrelevant information on problem solving strategies. Unpublished dissertation, City University of New York, 1976.

Nisbett, R. E., Borgida, E., Crandall, R., and Reed, H. Popular Induction: information is not necessarily informative. In J. S. Carroll and J. W. Payne (eds.) *Cognition and Social Behavior* Hillsaale, N.J.: L. Erlbaum Associates, 1976.

Piaget, J. Piaget's theory. In P. Mussen (Ed.), *Carmichael's Handbook of Child Psychology.* New York: Wiley, 1970.

Sacks, H., Schegloff, E., and Jefferson, G. A simplest systematics for the organization of turn-taking for conversation. *Language,* 1974, *50,* 696–735.

Schank, R., and Abelson, R. *Scripts, Plans, Goals and Understanding: An Inquiry into Human Knowledge Structures.* Hillsdale, N.J.: Erlbaum Associates, 1977.

Selman, R. Taking another's perspective. Role taking development in early childhood. *Child Development,* 1971, *42,* 1721–1734.

Shantz, C. The development of social cognition. In E. M. Hetherington (Ed.), *Review of Child Development Research,* Vol. 5. Chicago: University of Chicago Press, 1975.

Turvey, M. Constructive theory, perceptual systems, and tacit knowledge. In W. B. Weimer and D. S. Palermo, *Cognition and the Symbolic Process.* Hillsdale, N.J.: Erlbaum Associates, 1974.

Werner, H., and Kaplan, B. *Symbol Formation.* New York: Wiley, 1963.

2

Cognitive and Social Development: A New Perspective

GILBERT VOYAT[1]

Though cognitive and social development are interdependent aspects of the child's development, the study of the relationship between the emergence of cognitive operations and processes of socialization has not received stress within the Piagetian paradigm. One of the reasons for this neglect may stem from Piaget's primary emphasis on classically defined epistemological problems: a focus more on the forms of scientific intelligence than on their affective and social surround. It is important, however, to bear in mind that the child never exists in a vacuum and that it has never been Piaget's design or descriptive style to interpret the child in this way.

The relationship between cognitive developmental issues and forms of social thinking and social influence bears some examination in detail and will be the object of this chapter.

The Sociological Problem

The proposition that cognition is socially determined has been defended by many authors. The extreme protagonist of this view is undoubtedly Durkheim (1924). According to Durkheim, individual thought derives from the group because, thanks to language and to the pressures of one generation on the other, the individual is at all times subjected to the integration of present knowings with past acquisitions, transmitted through the "external" channel of education in its various forms. Individual intelligence is limited, in his view, to practical knowing. In contrast, the interplay between concepts, categories of knowledge, and rules of thought leads to "collective representations" which are the products of continuous social life and the "stuff" of social knowledge. This totality is an entity which constrains and modifies individuals and remains, in a sense, independent of individual consciousness.

In opposition to Durkheim, Tarde (1903) maintains that cognition, and logic in particular, fulfills two functions common to individual activity and social interactions. First, it has the function of equilibration: cognition consists in a coordination of beliefs which eliminates contradictions and assures synthesis between reconcilable positions. Second, cognition tends to ever-increasing certainty and thus contributes to replacing fragile with more solid beliefs. Individual knowledge is thus a source of coherence of beliefs within each individual consciousness, while social knowledge is a source of beliefs within society. Societies can be conceived of as an interplay between these sources of knowledge. In autocratic and fascist societies there is a subjugation of individual knowledge to social beliefs; the reverse is true in democratic societies. It is important to note that these two forms of knowledge rely on different categories. Theological, spiritual, religious notions are part of the social framework while "rational" notions are part of the individual realm.

The Durkheim-Tarde controversy illustrates the extreme positions from which the relationship between individuals and society can be conceptualized. In Durkheim's case, society, in effect, defines and imposes knowledge on its members, whereas for Tarde, society is merely a collection of beliefs, and rationality remains the property of the individual (see Nisbet, 1965).[2]

An interactionist position, such as that adopted by Piaget, takes a different stance on these issues. From this perspective individual consciousness and social knowledge are treated from the point of view of their interrelationship. Accordingly, the burden of an interactionist analysis would be to attempt to characterize the forms of interaction that can exist between an individual and his[3] social milieu in a search for the joint contribution of organism and environment in the process of the socialization of thought.

In order to proceed with this kind of analysis, I shall first briefly treat Piaget's characterization of cognitive development in its major stages, and then attempt to apply this general analytic scheme to developing a means of analyzing the relationships between individual thought and socialization.

The Cognitive Development View

Let us analyze first, artificially and only for the sake of my task, the individual as a closed system, simply open to interactions with the *physical* milieu, without the intervention of interindividual factors. From this perspective, cognition appears as a form of equilibrium of actions. Cognition becomes a system of internalized actions which follows laws common to all groupings: reversibility, composition, identity, and combination (Piaget, 1964, p. 54). For Piaget, to think is to reunite or to differentiate; to think is to carry out actions on objects, actions of the most general nature either concretely or mentally, and to group these actions according to a principle of progressive, reversible composition.

The developmental origin of these operations is to be found much earlier than the moment at which the child is capable of symbolization. The child achieves concrete operations around 7 years of age, and in order to developmentally understand their construction, Piaget constantly insists one should follow their path from the early sensorimotor coordinations themselves. Furthermore, he observes on the one hand a functional continuity of development, when it is interpreted as a progressive path toward equilibrium, and on the other hand a discontinuity of the successive structures marking the stages of a general process of equilibration. This dual proposition of discontinuity and continuity is essential for grasping his interpretation of the development of cognition.

Before the emergence of the symbolic function, the infant comes to construct from primitive perceptual and motoric structures a sensorimotor intelligence which is sufficient to lead to the discovery of the schemas of permanent object, of space and displacements, and of elementary causality. This process can be summarized as the constitution of a "logic of actions" (Piaget, 1936). During the preoperational period of thought, actions become mediated through the symbolic function which allows for the ability to represent actions mentally, although egocentrism will remain an important source of disequilibrium for the child. This period of intuitive thought heads toward a more stable equilibrium. At the concrete operational period of thought, conservation and reversibility assure the stability of the cognitive operations which Piaget formalizes as groupings. But between 7 and 11 years, these operations remain understood at a concrete level, that is, under the condition of being accompanied by effective or potential manipulations. The constraint of concreteness partially disappears with the acquisition of the formal level of reasoning. This period is formalized by a new logical grouping: the INRC group (Inhelder and Piaget, 1955).

This brief overview leads to the following consideration: if one conceives of the individual and his relationship with the physical milieu as a closed system, one understands the development of cognition as a progressive pathway from actions to operations. From this framework, Piaget interprets concrete thinking and cognition in general as the form of equilibrium of the actions in which reversibility and conservation are the two main criteria.

The Interindividual Sphere

It is useful now to analyze the individual from an interindividual framework. Here the problem is: if cognition consists in an organization of operations which, in the final analysis, are nothing but internalized actions, is it conceivable that the child achieves this organization alone or is the intervention of interindividual factors necessary to explain the development I just summarized?

In order to answer this question it is pertinent to analyze the main aspects of the development of socialization of the individual. The reason comes from the fact that only after such an analysis is one in a position to decide if socialization can be the cause of this development or its effect, or if the relationship between the two is of a more complex nature.

It is clear that the main stages of cognitive development correlate with stages of social development. At the level where the infant is entirely dependent on external support, it is difficult to talk of true social exchanges, let alone their gradual internalization. Similarly, during the sensorimotor period, one can hardly talk of a socialization of the intelligence. In a sense, sensorimotor intelligence is principally an individualistic intelligence. Furthermore, developmentally the child learns to imitate before he learns to talk, but he only imitates, at this time, movements and actions that he knows—in general, things that he already knows how to execute by himself.

In the preoperational period, deferred imitation, which occurs around the end of the second year, is the true initiator of the internalization of social exchanges. Thus, preoperational thinking represents a very significant moment for socialization. This period reflects, in effect, a transition between the individualistic aspect of the sensorimotor period and the possibility of a social input to knowledge. The reasons are numerous.

First, from the point of view of the means of expression, language derives very much from the complex system of collective signs that the external milieu offers to the child. But those verbal signs are not all understood immediately and are accompanied as well as completed by a rich world of individual, private symbols. Piaget was certainly one of the first to insist on the creative aspect of symbolic play (Piaget, 1937, 1946).

Second, as for attribution of meaning which refers to a cognitive point of view, one observes that interindividual exchanges between 2 and 7 are characterized by an egocentrism which remains midway between the social and the individual. Piaget (1923) globally defines it as a lack of differentiation and coordination between points of view. The child talks as much to himself as to the other; the child does not really know how to discuss, how to present his thought in some systematic order; in collective play he largely stays on his own without group coordination. In brief, all the features arising from the lack of groupings and all the characteristics of an idiosyncratic reality define and determine this intermediary situation.

It is important to note the existence of a strict relationship between the egocentric character of the thought processes during this period and the intuitive character of these interindividual exchanges. On the one hand, preoperational reasoning centers on static configurations and implies a primacy of the immediate, subjective, personal point of view. Egocentric thought implies a centration on objects which are the focus of the activity of the child at any given time. Furthermore, the intellectual constraints exercised during this period by adults are assimilated to an egocentric mentality and will only superficially modify the true preoperational thinker.

At the concrete operational period of thought, a new process in socialization occurs: the child becomes capable of concrete cooperation. This implies that he will no longer think only from his own point of view but that he will be able to coordinate points of view, will be able to discuss, reflect, organize the exposition of ideas; in other words, common rules will underlie collective activities. Above all, he is truly understandable to peers, parents, teachers, and society in general. The mastery of the concrete relationship of reciprocity demonstrates the generality of these new attitudes as well as their connection and interactions with reasoning itself.

Thus, from a Piagetian perspective one can infer a real correlation between the development of cooperation and cognition. Furthermore, socialized thought progressively favors the resolution of contradictions; it is much easier not to correct oneself when one thinks for oneself in a private way. It is much harder to contradict ourselves when our peers are there to remind us of what has been said before and what has been agreed upon.

On an intellectual level, reversibility and conservation are in opposition to the appearance of things. They are abstractions from objects. They are deduced from manipulating them. The corresponding operations begin to become more stable when they can replace objects by signs and symbols, in short, when they are mediated by an achieved system of collective expressions. This observation implies Piaget's interpretation of groupings as a system of concepts encompassing a coordination of points of view. For the formal level of thought, this interpretation is even more evident. Hypothetico-deductive thought is above all, according to Piaget, a reasoning which has, as metastructure, a common, mathematical language. The point is that from a Piagetian point of view, progress in cognition goes hand in hand with the advance of socialization.

If such is the case, should one endorse the proposition that the child becomes capable of rational operations *because* his social development leads toward cooperation, or should one accept that individual cognitive acquisitions allow him to understand the other and thus lead him to cooperation? Since these two types of progress are so intimately related, the question seems without solution, except that these two phenomena are both aspects of one and the same social and individual reality. Yet an attempt at answering it can prove useful.

The Individual, Society, and Cognition

According to Piaget, then, cognitive operations reach a form of equilibrium when they are grouped under laws of totality. But social cooperation also concerns a system of actions, undoubtedly of interindividual actions, but actions nevertheless. Consequently, they should also be subject to the laws of totality and groupings. Thus, social actions that lead to cooperation will also be governed by laws of equilibration. In this case, they will attain their equilibrium under the condition of reaching the status of a reversible system. In short, the laws of groupings should apply equally to cooperation and to individual actions dealing with the physical world.

The individualistic position, as we have seen with Tarde, consists in affirming that knowledge is constructed within individual activities and, once achieved, allows the establishment of cooperation. But it is in cooperating with the other and not before that the individual constructs his cognition. Durkheim's sociological proposition presents another interpretation: social relationships constrain the individual to develop cognitively. This is only possible if social relationships themselves contain such a logic. The latter proposition should then be expressed through laws of groupings similar to those of cognition with, among others, a criterion explicitly encompassing reciprocity as a parallel to reversibility. In this respect it is useful to mention that an autocratic or externally imposed point of view does not necessarily generate a great deal of cooperation and reciprocity, whereas free exchange has a better chance to lead to reciprocity of judgments and, in the final analysis, to objectivity.

The problem here is in fact to understand how social relationships can lead to cognition. From a Piagetian point of view, one finds here the same solution as on the developmental level: the actions of the individuals upon each other, which are at the root of any society, can create a system of cognition under the condition that they too can reach an equilibrium analoguous to the one attained within cognitive structures. Thus social relationships, equilibrated under the form of cooperation, constitute a system of totality, exactly in the same way that the actions exercised by the individual upon the external world lead to cognitive structures (Piaget, 1928).

The burden of analysis here then consists in demonstrating that the social exchange of thoughts is an exchange comparable to any other, belonging to the same scheme of qualitative exchanges, yet a scheme which does not necessarily deal with objects.

Within an exchange between individuals one can distinguish four different moments which can be expressed qualitatively as follows: (1) The individual exercises an action on the other. (2) The other experiences a positive, negative, or neutral effect. (3) This effect creates a feedback on the initiator of the exchange. (4) This feedback in turn leads either to a positive, negative, or neutral effect on the other. This cycle is clearly of a heuristic and recursive nature.

In these terms the conditions of equilibrium among qualitative exchanges are the following: first, it is necessary that between two partners an implicit common value system exists which will allow for a reciprocal assimilation of the respective effects in terms of their experienced and felt meaning. Second, an equilibrium will be reached when closure is achieved. Third, this equilibrium will be reversible.

The sharing of a common value system implies that the partners agree on the meaning of the words that they use and, generally, implicitly or explicitly, agree on the definitions of the concepts which constitute their system of exchanges. This common level has two complementary aspects: first, it contains a language comparable to the system of signs and symbols present in intellectual life. For instance, political or emotional exchanges suppose a level of reference that individuals can share. Second, it entails a system of defined concepts either entirely divergent or partially convergent but always with a key allowing the translation of the concepts from one partner to the other.

The first feature fulfills some of the conditions of an equilibrium and it is worth clarifying their status. A first condition is one of similarity or identity, implying that the two partners can agree or disagree on the same proposition or facts which justify their difference of opinions. This condition supposes also that the individual will feel himself obligated by the propositions he has recognized as valid. In short, the individual cannot contradict himself at will, solely according to his views, ideas, beliefs, or feelings of the moment. A second condition implies that the individual attributes to propositions a validity which can be preserved and conserved beyond an immediate context. A third condition is one of implicit trust and thus coherence between individuals. This "trust" involves a shared reference system and an engagement in processes of mutual clarification.

In short, it is clear that an equilibrium within an exchange of thoughts presupposes a common system of signs and definitions, a conservation of valid propositions which compels the individual, and a reciprocity of thought between the two partners.

The problem is now to understand if these conditions can be fulfilled by any type of interindividual exchanges or if they imply a particular type of relationship. This leads me to the problem of disequilibrium from the point of view of social development. One can distinguish two types of disequilibrium: those resulting from egocentrism and those due to social constraint.

Socialization and Egocentric Thought

One source of disequilibrium during the preoperational period may be simply that the two partners do not succeed in coordinating their points of view. This is what systematically occurs among truly preoperational children who conceive of things and persons according to their own activities. But it also can be observed at any age when interests, motivations, emotional judgments, or simple intellectual immobilism are prevalent. From a developmental point of view, during the period of egocentrism the conditions of equilibrium can never be truly fulfilled. In the first place, there is not yet (or there is no more) a common level of reference because the partners use terms with flexible and different meaning or refer to largely private, idiosyncratic symbols. Lacking common or sufficient homogeneity in their concepts, they lack a true, lasting intellectual exchange. In the second place, there is not, at that time, the possibility of sufficient conservation of previous propositions because of a lack of felt obligations between partners.

In a sense, nothing demonstrates more clearly the role of factors of obligation and of intellectual conservation in the equilibrium of exchanges than listening to discussions between truly preoperational children who achieve some communication but rely, in a very large measure, on unsocialized symbolism. The subject forgets what he has recognized as valid an instant before, contradicts himself many times without taking notice of it, etc. Everything looks as if an essential mechanism of social reasoning is lacking, a mechanism which, as a regulation, would oblige the individual to take into account what he has admitted or said, to conserve its value during subsequent exchanges.

Finally, there is no presence, at that time, of regulated reciprocity. Each partner, departing from the implicit position that his point of view is the only one, constantly refers to it, without the possibility of feedback from the other.

Socialization and Social Constraint

A system of exchange which is mainly determined by externally imposed, unified collective systems of thinking is of a different nature. Such a system reflects itself particularly in the preoperational child who fluctuates, from this point of view, between egocentric thought and the imitation of adults.

In a first approximation, the formal aspect of a situation of constraint seems to present optimal equilibrium. It appears as lasting and can even be conceived as crystallized in the case of traditions or mores.

Yet it is fundamental to distinguish between a stable, reciprocal equilibrium and a unilateral equilibrium, externally defined and imposed on individuals. From this perspective, it is clear that a system of collective thought, crystallized through the transmission from previous generations, progressively leads to a common level of intellectual values, in the form of a relatively homogeneous language and of general concepts with relatively fixed definitions. What is important here is that in those cases the underlying structure, instead of being the result of free and spontaneous exchanges, tends to be equilibrated through constraint.

For instance, the rules of family life bring about constraining laws between individuals, and in the final analysis it is the state which decides on its stability and criteria. Suicide, to take another striking case, although by definition an individual act, can be legally condemned, no matter what its internal, individual "rationality."

These types of notions are not constructed as a result of interindividual, mutual feedback (although it might have been so initially). What is crucial is that they are actually imposed through the authority of mores and traditions. Within this constraining framework, there are three possibilities for an individual-social dialectic. Either the individual thinks on his own terms but does not question the constraining external value system. Or the individual, who is not in a position to interact in a reciprocal way with his social system, comes to an implicit, internal disequilibrium which may or may not result in external manifestations. Finally, the individual may find himself in agreement with the nature of the external constraints.

What is important is not what the individual can or cannot do within such a paradigm, but the fact that the concept of internal obligation will last only as a result of the constraint itself and not as a result of the construction of a mutual and reciprocal network of social commitments.

In reality, this type of dialectic leads to an absence of equilibrium not because there is no exchange or interaction, but because there is no reciprocity in the system of obligations. Within this framework Kohlberg's (1969) stages are interesting to interpret because their final dialectic shows a synthesis of a reciprocal nature, between an individual's internal principles and his social interactions.

What is important to stress here, too, is that a logic of constraint is in effect not reversible and thus cannot truly lead to operatory structures. As such, it can hardly serve as a tool of formalization for the interactions between the individual and his social system. Furthermore, the conservation of propositions in a system of constraint does not consist in invariant agreements resulting from a succession of reversible transformations, but in a body of already constructed beliefs whose solidity and permanence rely on their rigidity and which are transmitted in a unilateral way. This rigidity is in fact comparable to what characterizes the difference between the egocentric thought structures and the operatory ones.

Socialization and Cooperation

The resulting form of an equilibrium based on reciprocal systems of social exchange is interesting to analyze. Within a paradigm of reciprocity and cooperation, a common level of concept will in fact consist in a system of conventions which can be conceptualized as hypotheses, as occasions for intellectual search. Thus they allow for progressive constructions encompassing these notions which are not under the matrix of external constraint. In this case agreement is possible under the following conditions: two individuals have necessarily different and not interchangeable perceptions; ideas are exchanged in terms of verbal judgments dealing with perceptions which can lead to adjustments of points of view of one or the other. The same observation holds for actions that different individuals execute upon objects, for the mental representations and images that they have about objects and persons, etc. In brief, the whole spectrum of concepts remains private as long as it is not translated into socialized terms.

The conventions fixing the meaning of the words thus take the form of communication in terms of judgment or reasoning. As long as those judgments are not of an operatory nature and as long as they rely on an intuitive, egocentric referent, the equilibrium will remain unstable. Operatory agreement will only be achieved when the child is capable of reconstructing and repeating the same operation for himself. Thus the sense of obligation implies also an internal construction which results from assimilation, mainly guided by strong external accommodations inherent to this form of communication.

Adaptation and organization in terms of the construction of an internal hierarchy of values have thus both a social and an individual counterpart. From a Piagetian point of view, the implication is that the structural law of intellectual organization will not only be valid in the framework of individual development but also from the point of view of the process of socialization.

A Perspective

The actions of the individual on the external world are directed by laws of equilibrium and equilibration. They have a reversible form and consist in operatory groupings. Social relationships which result from true exchanges of thought lead to reciprocity. This observation in turn implies similar structural laws; cooperation becomes part of a system of operations effectuated in common, with a differentiation and a coordination of points of view.

Can one then infer that the cognitive operations achieved by the individual make cooperation possible, or should one deduce that the operations encompassed by reciprocity and cooperation determine logical groupings? It is clear that in this form the question loses its meaning because groupings as logical structures represent forms of equilibrium and equilibration (Piaget, 1975) and as such necessarily apply to the overall process of development.

The problem could perhaps be more efficiently phrased as follows: Does the individual by himself achieve an equilibrium which takes the form of groupings, or is cooperation and reciprocity necessary to this effect? On the other hand, can society reach an equilibrium without taking the particular form of the classic Piagetian scheme of structuration of individual actions?

From the point of view of individual development the question is twofold: Is the individual able to construct for himself a system of stable definitions constituting what could be symbolized as a system of autoconventions? Furthermore, once he has mastered such a system, will he be able to make use of it through his operatory structures? Achieving this implies reversibility as defined by Piaget and consequently the rigorous conservation of the totalities. But above all it should apply equally to this system of autoconventions. This condition means that one interprets the individual as making conventions and agreements with himself, as relating his actual thoughts with his anticipations as if there were two distinct individuals. Yet in observing how much the child in the process of socialization constantly changes the meaning of the concepts that he uses, one can hypothesize that an operatory agreement with oneself will only emerge as a result of internalized social interactions. Thus concrete reflective dialogue or hypothetico-deductive thinking will always clearly benefit from progress in socialization.

Sensorimotor processes are notoriously insufficient in themselves to explain the emergence of operatory reversibility. From a Piagetian point of view, operational reversibility always supposes some form of symbolic representation. Only through potential or possible reference to absent objects can the assimilation to the schemas of actions and their respective accommodation result in operatory, stable, equilibrated structures, governed by reversibility. The egocentric referent of the preoperational child is far too fluctuating to produce this result.

In effect it is language, as a system of arbitrary, socially determined signs that carries the plain effect of social factors, and, as such has been correctly identified by Piaget as a necessary, although not sufficient, condition of the development of socialization (Piaget, 1923). Furthermore, reason, objectivity, and the necessary coherence of an operatory system implies cooperation. In order for the individual to be able to construct operatory structures, one has also to attribute to him all the characteristics of the socialized personality.

On the other hand, it is clear that cooperation cannot in itself lead to the construction of the cognitive structures because of the progressive impact of socialized language on the development. The main reason derives from the fact that cognition is not the result of language alone; it is also the result of the internalization of sensorimotor co-ordinations. It is not surprising then that no matter how one considers the problem, individual and social functions must be invoked to explain the necessary conditions for the construction of logical equilibrium.

Finally, actions which become coordinated and come to be cognitively structured reflect substitutions of two types: within the individual it reflects his cognition, interindividually it reflects operations of cooperation and reciprocity. These two types of resulting possible substitutions and combinations reinforce the case for a general dialectic, simultaneously individual and social, which would characterize the form of equilibrium and equilibration common to cooperative and individualized actions. The axiomatization of such a system is obviously far from being achieved because we are touching here the very foundations of the dialectic of development itself. It is equally clear that the wealth of research such a perspective opens is far from being exhausted even within a Piagetian paradigm.

Notes

1. This chapter has been supported in part by a grant from the Office of Education (Bureau for the Education of the Handicapped) (RF-02907-02977).
2. As Nisbet (1965) indicates, "The controversy between Durkheim and Tarde (more intensely between the students of each) kept French so-

cial science in ferment for a quarter of a century. Durkheim's criticisms of Tarde are to be found in his *Suicide* (1951). Tarde's criticisms of Durkheim in his *Études de psychologie sociale* (1898)."
3. In order to avoid making this kind of writing unduly distracting I use "his" rather than "his or her" and ask for the reader's indulgence.

References

Durkheim, E. *Sociologie et philosophie* (1924). Translated by D. F. Pocock as *Sociology and Philosophy*. London and Glencoe, Ill.: Free Press, 1953.
Durkheim, E. *Suicide: Étude de Sociologie* (1897). Translated by J. A. Spaulding and G. Simpson as *Suicide: A Study in Sociology*. New York: The Free Press of Glencoe, 1951.
Inhelder, B., and Piaget, J. *De la logique de l'enfant à la logique de l'adolescent* (1955). Translated by A. Parsons and S. Seagrim as *The Growth of Logical Thinking from Childhood to Adolescence*. New York: Basic Books, 1958.
Kohlberg, L. "Stage and sequence: The cognitive-developmental approach to socialization." In D. Goslin (Ed.), *Handbook of Sociolization Theory and Reserach*. Chicago: Rand McNally, 1969.
Nisbet, R. A. *Makers of Modern Social Science*: Emile Durkheim. With Selected Essays. Englewood Cliffs, N.J.: Prentice-Hall, 1965.
Piaget, J. *Le langage et la pensée chez l'enfant* (1923). Translated by M. Gabain as *The Language and the Thought of the Child*, London: Kegan Paul, 1926.
Piaget, J. Logique génétique et sociologie. *Revue Philosophique*, 1928, *53*, 167–205.
Piaget, J. *Le jugement moral chez l'enfant* (1932). Translated by M. Gabain as *The Moral Judgment of the Child*. New York: Harcourt, 1932.
Piaget, J. *La naissance de l'intelligence chez l'enfant* (1936). Translated by M. Cook as *The Origins of Intelligence in Children*. New York: International Universities Press, 1952.
Piaget, J. *La construction du réel chez l'enfant* (1937). Translated by M. Cook as *The Construction of Reality in the Child*. New York: Basic Books, 1954.
Piaget, J. *La formation du symbole chez l'enfant* (1946). Translated by C. Cattegno and F. M. Hodgson as *Play, Dreams, Imitation in Childhood*. New York: Norton, 1951.
Piaget, J. *Six études de psychologie* (1964). Translated by A. Tenzer as *Six Psychological Studies* with an Introduction, Notes and Glossary by D. Elkind. New York: Random House, 1967.
Piaget, J. *Genetic Epistemology*. Translated by E. Duckworth. New York and London: Columbia University Press, 1970.
Piaget, J. *L'équilibration des structures cognitives; problème central du développement*. Paris: Presses Universitaires de France, 1975.
Tarde, Gabriel. *Études de psychologie sociale*. Paris: Girard and Brière, 1898.
Tarde, Gabriel. *The Laws of Imitation*. Translated by E. Clews Parsons. New York: Holt, Rinehart and Winston, 1903.

3 The Development of Concepts of Social Structure: Social Convention

ELLIOT TURIEL

An aspect of experience central to children's social development is their participation in social groups and social organizations. The developing child, from an early age, participates in social systems, be it in the family, the school, or with peers. It follows, therefore, that individuals form concepts about social groups and systems of social interaction. Little research, however, has been done on the development of the individual's concepts of social systems. One reason for the paucity of research in this area may stem from the emphasis students of social cognition have placed on the moral domain. By focusing on the obviously important topic of the development of moral reasoning, study of the individual's understanding of the nonmoral aspects of social interactions has been largely ignored.

A second reason research on the individual's societal concepts has been limited may stem from the emphasis traditionally placed on the influences of *specific others* on the child's social values and behavior. For instance, although psychoanalytic and social-learning theories postulate somewhat different psychological mechanisms, each puts great emphasis on the role of caretakers, particularly in the familial situation. Parents (or parent-surrogates) are seen both as instrumental

in the acquisition of values and as causal agents in changing the child's
social concepts and behaviors. Thus, a common presumption is that
children acquire social standards through modeling or through an
identification process (Aronfreed, 1968; Bandura and McDonald,
1963; Burton, Allinsmith, and Maccoby, 1966; Freud, 1921; 1923;
Mischel and Mischel, 1976; Sears, Maccoby, and Levin, 1957; Sears,
Rau, and Alpert, 1965; Whiting, 1960). These theorists pay little attention to the effects of the child's interactions with more general
social environments or social organizations. Even when Freud (1927,
1930) considered the role of society in moral development, he assumed that societal standards were transmitted to children through
the mediation of parents.

In our perspective, however, it is assumed that the child's social
development is influenced not only by specific others, but also by
interactions with patterns of social behavior and with social organization. To understand the development of social concepts, it is necessary to consider the individual's symbolic interactions with the social
environment. In this chapter we discuss research with children, adolescents, and young adults on the development of an integral aspect of
social systems: social conventions. In addition to presenting theory
and research on social convention, we shall show how some of the
research on moral reasoning and on the socialization of the child
relates to an understanding of the development of societal concepts.

Social convention in here defined as behavioral uniformities that
serve the function of coordinating the actions of individuals participating in social systems. Social conventions are thus part of all
systems of social organization, including small but stable social units
(e.g., specific types of social organizations) and those at the general
level of society. As coordinative of interactions within social systems,
convention constitutes shared knowledge of uniformities in social interactions. Social-conventional acts are arbitrary in the sense that they
represent regularities that achieve social coordinations. Conventional
regularity is based on mutual expectations, accepted usage, and uniform standards that coordinate social organization.

Our research has shown that children form concepts of social
organization, which structure their thinking about such conventional
issues as family patterns, forms of address, dress codes, and national
order. We have found that the development of concepts about these
types of social-conventional issues forms an age-related sequence of
seven levels. Throughout these levels judgments about convention are
based on concepts of social structure.

These levels and the research on which they were based will not be discussed until a later section. It is first necessary to consider several issues related to our definitional and developmental bases for research on social convention. One major issue to consider is the difference between social convention and morality. We are proposing that concepts of social convention are structured by underlying concepts of social organization. Thus, social convention forms part of the individual's *descriptive* understanding of systems of social interactions and thereby should be differentiated from moral *prescriptions*.

Social convention is an aspect of what we label the *societal* domain, which refers to concepts of social groupings and social structure. Our thesis is that the societal domain forms a conceptual framework distinct from that of the moral domain. Social-conventional acts, in themselves, do not have an intrinsically prescriptive basis independent from the coordination of social interactions or from the symbols of social organization. Social-conventional acts are part of social order, but they do not prescribe behaviors related to the welfare of others, protection of rights, or avoidance of physical or psychological harm to others.

The distinction we are making between convention and morality implies a narrow definition of morality as justice. It is proposed that children develop concepts of justice which apply to a relatively limited range of issues, such as the value of life, physical and psychological harm to others, trust, responsibility, etc. In contrast to convention, which involves the coordination of actions, morality is defined by factors intrinsic to actions: consequences such as harm inflicted upon others, violation of rights, effects on the general welfare. On this basis we can distinguish between (a) convention, which is part of social systems and is structured by underlying concepts of social organization, and (b) morality, which is structured by underlying concepts of justice (though concepts of justice may be applied to social organization, they are not defined by it).

Social convention and morality, however, generally have not been treated as distinct by students of social development. It has been assumed that convention and morality are part of one domain and that they do not develop independently of each other. The failure of psychological theorists to deal with the moral-conventional distinction is evident in the predominant theoretical approaches to moral development. Recently, there has been considerable controversy between those who view moral development as an internalization process and those who approach it from a constructivist perspective. The debate takes the following general form. On one side, it is argued that moral development is the learning of socially acceptable behavior and the internalization of transmitted values. Moral development is therefore conceived as a process of enculturation or socialization of the child by caretakers such as parents or teachers. In viewing social behaviors and values as the incorporation of externally determined and imposed content, theorists taking this view make no conceptual distinctions between different social behaviors. As a result, our *two* categories—moral and conventional—are treated as one category. On the other side, it is maintained that moral development is not an internalization of values, but the construction of universal judgments of right and wrong or good and bad. In this case, it is presumed that moral judgments of right and wrong may apply to any form of social behavior. Consequently, the conventional is treated as a subclass of the moral.

These antithetical orientations to morality and to its development have been prevalent in much of the research conducted during the past 15 to 20 years. The dialectic is not new. In fact, the same sort of "debate" among social scientists occurred in the 1920s and 1930s. Two of the principal opponents at that time were Durkheim (1924, 1925) and Piaget (1932). Durkheim defined morality as a generalized respect for society and a specific adherence to the authority, norms, and rules of the collective system. Piaget's research and theory on children's moral judgments directly opposed the internalization position. Thus, explicitly contrasting his research findings with Durkheim's theoretical assertions, Piaget claimed that the child's social interactions produce a morality of autonomous principles of justice. From this perspective, moral development is directed not toward constraint and conformity, but toward social relations of cooperation and mutual respect among equals. To Piaget, such development represents the triumph of principle over convention—or stated another way—justice over society. As we detail later, in that formulation convention is viewed solely as an inadequate form of morality.

In the rejuvenation of this dialectic in recent years the neobehaviorists (Sears, Maccoby, and Levin, 1957; Whiting, 1960) and social-learning theorists (Aronfreed, 1968, 1976; Grinder, 1962; Mischel and Mischel, 1976; Sears, Rau, and Alpert, 1965) have adhered to the internalization position, while the structural-developmental theorists (Kohlberg, 1963, 1969, 1976; Lickona, 1976a; Rest, 1976; Selman, 1976; Turiel, 1969) have maintained that moral judgments entail autonomous principles regulating social interactions. Neither in the 1920s nor in recent years has either side identified the moral and societal domains as distinct from each other. It is our contention that both these orientations require modification to include the study of the development of concepts about social groups and social systems.

The proposition that children form distinct conceptual frameworks in the societal and moral domains is directly related to propositions about developmental processes. The hypothesis is that children construct different conceptual frameworks out of different forms of individual-environment interactions. In the next section we outline the developmental assumptions underlying our approach. In that context, we consider evidence for the validity of the proposed distinction between the development of social-conventional concepts and the development of moral concepts.

The Source of Development: Individual-Environment Interactions

A fundamental assumption of our model is that the child's concepts are constructed through his actions upon the environment (Turiel, 1975); the source of conceptual change is the individual's active ordering of experienced events (Turiel, 1974, 1977). A corollary hypothesis is that the types of conceptual frameworks constructed by the child would be, in part, influenced by the nature of the environment. That is, if the child interacts with fundamentally different types of objects and events, then we would expect that child to form different conceptual frameworks. Different domains of social concepts therefore reflect different types of constructions on the part of the individual.

Our approach derives from several fundamental assumptions. The first is that an individual's thinking within a domain is characterized by a unity of organization. In delineating distinct conceptual domains, it is proposed that each conceptual domain has a unity of organization analytically distinguishable from each of the other conceptual domains. Second, it is assumed that developmental change entails a process of reorganization of one form of thinking into another. Within a domain, development is characterized by sequential changes in the organization of concepts, which are constructed by the individual out of his interactions with the environment.

In our approach to development, therefore, the child acts to construct conceptual frameworks in social domains. In this sense, our constructivist assumption is consistent with the structural-developmental theories of Piaget (1947, 1954, 1970), Werner (1957), and others (Flavell et al, 1968; Flavell and Wohlwill, 1969; Inhelder and Piaget, 1958, 1964; Kohlberg, 1969, 1971). However, we also assume that there are distinctly different forms of individual-environment interaction which result in distinct conceptual frameworks. In this way our model differs from most other structural-developmental theories. In postulating that there are different conceptual frameworks, each forming a unity of organization, we are not assuming that all aspects of the individual's thinking are structurally interrelated. Nor do we assume that development is directed toward the achievement of such interrelatedness. Rather, our hypothesis is that thinking is organized (and changes sequentially) within a domain, but not necessarily across domains.

In contrast, others (see especially, Keasey, 1975; Kohlberg, 1969; Kuhn, 1977; Rest, 1975; Selman, 1971, 1976) have interpreted the idea of structural development to mean that all forms of thought are interrelated. From their perspective, the concept of structure is defined in terms of a total unity of mental processes. Structural development is seen as involving certain common elements that are applicable across what we propose are distinct and separable domains.

Clear examples of the holistic approach are evident in theories that postulate that logical, physical, and social concepts are all interrelated. In these formulations the stages of cognitive development (including logical and physical concepts) described by Piaget (1947, 1970) are taken to define a core or central cognitive structure. The development of social concepts is seen as partially dependent on, and related to, this presumed central cognitive structure. For instance, it has been proposed (Kohlberg, 1969, 1971, 1976; Kuhn et al, 1977; Tomlinson-Keasey and Keasey, 1974) that development within stages of logical and physical concepts is necessary but not sufficient for the development of corresponding levels of moral judgments. The hypothesis of interrelatedness between the logical, physical, and social domains has been tested only through assessments of correlational levels between the different measures (the correlational levels have varied widely from study to study). The correlational method, however, is an inadequate way of dealing with the proposed structural relations between the different domains of conceptual development. Correlations show only that there is (or is not) a systematic relationship in the rates of development of the two measures being used. They do not indicate the nature of the relation between two measures, nor do they provide evidence for their interdependence. In fact, the presence of systematic correlations between the developmental rates of different structural systems is not at all inconsistent with our hypothesis of independent, parallel structural systems. It is quite likely that the influences on an individual's rate of change will be similar in a variety of domains. It is our view, then, that the existing data cannot be used as evidence for the holistic model.

To understand the conceptual products of the child's interactions it is necessary to distinguish between different types of environmental events. Environmental events, however, do not determine the forms of thought developed by the individual. Contrariwise, the form of the environment, in itself, does not direct development. The primary source of structural development is in the activities of the subject in dealing with objects and events. Nevertheless, we would expect the individual-environment interactive process to result in the construction of distinct conceptual frameworks, given fundamentally different properties in different aspects of the environment.

The environment with which the child interacts includes objects in the physical world, social objects, social relationships, and social systems. As one example of how the nature of the child's interactions may vary, we may contrast experiences with the physical and the social environments. There are differences in (a) the ways in which the child manipulates and experiments with physical and social objects, and (b) the child's methods of verifying or validating his knowledge about each domain (Turiel, 1975). Of more direct relevance for our present purposes is the question of differentiating those categories of social experience that serve as the source for developing moral and social-conventional concepts. Our proposition is that social-conventional concepts originate from experiences that are distinguishable from experiences that produce moral concepts. Examples of the types of social interactions likely to generate moral concepts would include events that involve inflicting physical or psychological harm on another person, actions that serve to benefit others, the sharing of goods (Damon, 1971; De Mersseman, 1976; Piaget, 1932), or events entailing retribution (Irwin and Moore, 1971; Piaget, 1932). In contrast, events likely to generate concepts of social convention would include those that serve to coordinate social interactions and define or maintain social order and regularity (e.g., forms of address, modes of greeting, modes of dress). In the case of events that would stimulate moral concepts, social regulation is not necessary for the child to respond to them as transgressions or to begin formulating prescriptions. In those cases (for example, one child hitting another), the individual's view of the events as transgressions and his formulation of prescriptions can originate from the events themselves (e.g., from a perception of the intrinsic consequences of an act). This would not be the case for events revolving around social conventions. Such events are arbitrary in that alternative courses of action could serve the same functions. It is regulations and uniformities in behavior forming part of social organization that are likely to stimulate concepts of social convention.

A recently completed study (Nucci and Turiel, 1978) provides support for these developmental hypotheses and suggests some of the ways in which young children's social interactions revolving around social-conventional events differ from their interactions revolving around moral events. In this study, observations of social behaviors were made in ten different preschools that varied in the children's social-class backgrounds and in the teachers' instructional and socialization practices. At each school an observer (a) recorded narrative descriptions of a series of naturally occurring events that entailed social transgressions and (b) on a standard checklist rated the responses made by both children and adults (teachers) to each transgression. The checklist used by the observer contained a listing of categories of potential responses (statements pertaining to injury or loss, emotional reactions, rationales; statements about feelings of others, physical reactions; statements about disorder, rules and sanctions, commands).

The descriptions of the spontaneously occurring events were reliably classified as social-conventional or moral according to the definitions we have provided. On the basis of the frequencies of responses on the category checklist it was determined that responses to moral events did, indeed, differ from those made to social-conventional events. In the first place, children rarely initiated responses to transgressions of social conventions. Most of the responses to such transgressions were made by adults. In contrast, children and adults responded at about equal frequencies to moral transgressions. Generally, the observed moral transgressions involved actions among the children. Moral transgressions frequently produced communications (regarding injury or loss and emotional reactions) by the victim to the transgressor. The children's responses revolved around the intrinsic consequences of actions and often resulted in direct feedback regarding the effects of the acts upon the victim. Adult responses to moral transgressions complemented the responses initiated by children. Adults often responded either by pointing out to the transgressor the effects of his actions upon the victim or by encouraging the victim to do so.

Adults responded to children's social-conventional transgressions differently from the way they responded to moral transgressions. Their responses to social-conventional events were primarily related to the social order of the school. Adults responded with statements about rules and sanctions and with commands to refrain from norm-violating behavior. They also responded with statements specifying school rules.

Another set of findings from this same study demonstrates that the preschool children discriminated between the two types of events. While the observed events were actually occurring, another experimenter interviewed the preschool children who were witnessing the events. The child was asked whether or not the act would be wrong if there were no rule in the school pertaining to the act. The child's interpretation of the event was classified as moral if he stated that the action was wrong regardless of the presence or absence of a rule and as social-conventional if he stated that the action was wrong only if a rule pertaining to the act existed in the school. There was agreement in 83% (60 of 72) of the cases between our classifications and the children's classifications of the events. In most cases, therefore, the children's view of the events corresponded with the identified domain of the event.

The findings from the Nucci and Turiel study provide support for the developmental hypothesis that different conceptual domains stem from different forms of social interaction. Findings from this study provide only partial support for the hypothesis that social-conventional and moral concepts form distinct developmental systems since only preschool children were involved. However, in another study (Turiel, 1978) in which we examined concepts of social rules, it was found that older children and adolescents (ages 6 to 17 years) also distinguished between these two domains. One of the procedures used was to question subjects about rules with which they were familiar and which they had generated. The questions dealt with (1) rules pertaining to conventional issues that existed in the subject's home and school, (2) rules pertaining to moral issues that existed in the subject's home and school, and (3) game rules (the relevance of game rules is considered in a later section). Subjects were also questioned about rules we presented that pertained to the prohibition of stealing within the legal system (moral rule), mode of dress in a business office (conventional rule), use of titles in school (conventional rule), and dress code in school (conventional rule).

As part of a more general inquiry, subjects were asked to rate the importance attributed to the rules and questioned about their view of the relativity of the rules (e.g., *Suppose there is another country in which the rule does not exist. Is that all right?*) First, we found that the moral rules consistently were given higher ratings of importance than the conventional rules. On the average, the rule pertaining to stealing was attributed the most importance; moral rules in the school and in the home were given somewhat lower ratings than the stealing rule. The rules pertaining to conventional issues were given lower ratings than the moral rules. This pattern applied to the school and home rules generated by the subjects, as well as the rules we presented to the subjects. Game rules were also given lower ratings of importance than the moral rules; game rules were given about the same rating as the conventional rules. Of particular relevance to the hypothesis that social convention and morality form distinct conceptual frameworks is the finding that there were virtually no differences in the ratings of subjects in the different age groups. Subjects of different ages rated a given rule in very similar ways.

Corresponding results were obtained from responses to questions dealing with the relativity of rules. Most subjects *at all ages* viewed the conventional rules in relativistic terms. That is, they regarded those rules as legitimately changeable from one setting to another. This finding was also obtained for the game rules. In contrast, moral rules were viewed as nonrelative (not legitimately changeable) by subjects *at all ages*. At all the ages, therefore, an individual's understanding of a given rule is related to his concept of the act to which the rule pertains. Rules pertaining to moral events are not viewed as relative to social settings because the regulated acts are evaluated on the basis of intrinsic factors. In contrast, rules pertaining to conventional events are viewed as relative to a given social setting because the regulated acts, in themselves, are seen as part of social organization.

In sum, we interpret these findings, along with the Nucci and Turiel findings, to mean that different types of social experiences produce qualitatively different individual-environment interactions, which result in distinct conceptual frameworks. In addition, we are saying that the same individual conceptualizes different types of social events in different ways. In the Nucci and Turiel study it was found that spontaneously occurring events could be reliably classified for domain and that children conceptualized events identified as social-conventional differently from the way they conceptualized events identified as moral. This finding has an important methodological implication—namely, that in studying the development of social concepts it is necessary to ensure that the stimuli used fall within the domain studied. Using stimuli that are, for instance, in the conventional domain to study moral concepts or behaviors would produce inaccurate results. Earlier we stated that most theories of moral development have failed to distinguish between social convention and morality. It would follow, then, that most research methods have failed to make the corresponding distinction in the events or stimuli used to elicit subjects' responses. It becomes important, therefore, to take a detailed look at: (a) the class of events theorized to constitute moral judgment or behavior and (b) the types of stimuli included in experiments, interviews, and questionnaires used to study moral development. We do this in the following section.

Social Stimulus Situations in Research and Theory

An implication of the domain perspective we have presented is that the types of events considered to be part of the moral domain bear upon the validity of a theory of moral development. If it is the case that the individual's conceptual frameworks guide his ways of structuring events, then the appropriateness of stimuli used in research to elicit responses from subjects is also of central importance to the validity of theoretical formulations. Such responses, of course, provide the data for the formulation and verification of theory. The importance of ascertaining the appropriateness of the domain of stimuli can be illustrated through the following example. Suppose that in order to investigate moral reasoning a researcher used a series of mathematical problems with subjects of different ages. Such a procedure would be questionable because we could not be confident that subjects in the study had engaged in moral reasoning at all. Clearly, it is necessary to formulate criteria for determining the appropriateness of the stimuli used to study a particular class of concepts or behaviors. The inadequacy of using mathematical problems in research presumably designed to study moral development is quite apparent. In this respect our example simplifies the issue. Generally, moral-development researchers have not used anything so blatant as mathematical problems. Rather, they have focused on a variety of social situations. The adequacy or inadequacy of the different types of social situations used is not as clear as it is in our hypothetical example.

The ambiguities and difficulties faced in attempting to classify different kinds of social situations are also manifest in the ways in which some researchers have defined morality. For example, morality has been defined as the evaluation of (Berkowitz, 1964; Mischel and Mischel, 1976) or standards for (Aronfreed, 1976) good and bad or right and wrong. The problem with this type of definition is that it leaves entirely open the referent for the evaluative process. Judgments of good and bad can be made about a range of actions that may or may not be in the moral domain: esthetic, prudential, economic, social, and moral judgments may all entail evaluations of good and bad. Consequently, such a definition is inadequate because it does not discriminate moral standards from many other kinds. Similar shortcomings exist in the definition of morality as respect for rules (Havighurst and Neugarten, 1955; Piaget, 1932). In this formulation the type of rule to be respected is left unspecified. One may respect rules of a game, of etiquette, of traffic, of religion, of government, etc. Is respect for any kind of rule to be defined as morality?

We can see, then, that two commonly used definitions of morality are inadequate; they do not provide a basis for discriminating between a wide variety of social situations which entail different ways of judging the good or the right. Such attempts as have been made to distinguish between one type of evaluation of good and another have not been entirely satisfactory. We shall detail one illustrative example. It has been proposed by Campbell (1964) that moral standards are a subset of the more general category of standards. He has pointed out that while standards of "efficiency and performance" may be involved in learning to shift gears in an automobile, such standards are nonmoral. Having made this distinction, Campbell then chose to study high school students' attitudes toward "drinking alcohol and getting high" as an example of a moral standard. Attitudes toward drinking were taken as representing a moral norm because the culture is one in which "strong adult-based socialization practices encourage abstinence" (p. 399). This justification, however, does not avoid the problem Campbell himself raises regarding gear-shifting standards. Suppose that a society had strong adult-based socialization practices that emphasized the importance of properly shifting gears in an automobile. In that case, would the standards of proper gear shifting be moral ones?

Another example of this kind can be seen in a definition of morality used by A. Stein (1967) in an experiment on imitative activities in children. In that study children were assigned to do a boring job while a very attractive movie was being shown in the same room. Children who left their assigned task to look at the film were considered to have violated a moral standard. Stein classified "duty and responsibility in performing a job" in this way on the grounds that such behavior reflects a moral value of the society. As with Campbell's example of abstinence from alcohol, it is not clear that a sense of duty in the performance of a job is one of society's moral standards, nor that children and adolescents construe it as such. For instance, it may be that such standards are nonmoral and relate instead to social and economic organization.

These considerations underscore our earlier point regarding the importance of evaluating the types of stimuli and events used in moral-development research. In this regard, our first task is to categorize the predominant theories and research studies on the basis of the kinds of situations considered moral. Information relevant to our own classification of the stimulus situations used in moral-development research can be found in Table 1. Included in this table are: (1) a list of studies, (2) a brief description of the event (or events) used to elicit responses from subjects, (3) a description of the type of responses obtained from subjects, and (4) our own classifications of the domain into which the stimulus events fall. It is not our intention to present a comprehensive list of moral-development studies and we have not done so in Table 1. Rather, Table 1 contains a sampling of studies that are representative of the types of events used and, insofar as possible, we have included those studies to which we refer in our discussion.

It should also be noted that studies using survey and questionnaire methods are presented separately in Table 2. Typically in such studies the subject is presented with a variety of items to rate or rank. Given the large number of items used (sometimes as many as 50 to 100), we have included in Table 2 only a random sampling.

It should be apparent from a perusal of Table 1 that a wide variety of stimuli have been used in this body of research. While every situation listed has been classified by the researchers as moral, alternative categorizations of many of the stimuli result from application of our model of distinct social-conceptual domains. Our identifications of the category of event used in each of the studies are listed in the last column of Table 1. We have classified the range of stimulus events into the following four categories: (1) social convention, (2) quasi-convention within the social structure of the experimental situation, (3) moral, (4) game. The criteria for each of these categories are presented in Table 3.

Three factors were taken into account in our classification of items. The most central factor was the type of action required of the subject. Second, consideration was given to the social-situational context for the act. The third factor was the explicit or implicit instructions given to the subject. Furthermore, in classifying stimulus events we made some assumptions which are not necessarily shared by those who conducted the studies. These assumptions are: (1) the subject cognizes about the overall situation encountered; (2) the subject's conceptualization of the stimulus event is related to domain;[1] (3) the subject attempts to determine what is expected of him by the experimenter; (4) the subject attends to explicit or implicit communica-

Table 1
Social Stimulus Events Used in Research

Reference	Event Used to Elicit Response	Type of Response	Classification
Hartshorne and May (1928–1930)	Academic tests in classroom situations, with possibility of cheating	Behavior in classroom experimental situation	Testing situation (see text)
	Academic tests done at home, with possibility of cheating	Behavior in home experimental situation	Testing situation (see text)
	Athletic contests, with possibility of cheating	Behavior in school experimental situation	Testing situation (see text)
	Party games, with possibility of cheating	Behavior in party experimental situation	Game
	Party game, with possibility of stealing money	Behavior in party experimental situation	Moral
	Classroom situations, with possibility of stealing money	Behavior in classroom experimental situation	Moral
	Questionnaire about previous classroom cheating, with possibility of lying on questionnaire	Questionaire responses	Moral
	General questionnaire about conduct, with possibility of lying	Questionnaire responses	Moral
Allinsmith (1960)	Imagined aggression (wishing someone else's death)	Reactions to transgression in story: projective story completion (guilt)	Moral
	Theft (stealing a baseball glove)	Reactions to transgression in story: projective story completion (guilt)	Moral
	Disobedience of parental instructions (not to take boxes down from closet)	Reactions to transgression in story: projective story completion (guilt)	Social convention

Study	Description	Measure	Classification
Aronfreed (1960)	Verbal aggression resulting in other's death	Reactions to transgression in story: projective story completion (guilt)	Unclassified
	Negligence resulting in other's death	Reactions to transgression in story: projective story completion (guilt)	Moral
	Causing loss of someone else's money	Reactions to transgressions in story: projective story completion (guilt)	Moral
	Cheating in a race	Reactions to transgression in story: projective story completion (guilt)	Moral
	Withholding important information as form of retaliation in conjunction with	Reactions to transgression in story: projective story completion (guilt) plus	Moral
	Material damage: machine breaks in course of experimental manipulation	Reactions to own presumed transgressions in experimental situation (guilt)	Material damage (see text)
Aronfreed (1963)	Material damage: doll breaks in course of experimental manipulation	Reactions to own presumed transgression in experimental situation (self-criticism, reparation)	Material damage (see text)
Aronfreed, Cutick, and Fagen (1963)	Material damage: doll breaks in course of experimental manipulation	Reactions to own presumed transgression in experimental situation (self-criticism, reparation)	Material damage (see text)
Aronfreed and Reber (1965)	Prohibition against touching desirable toy	Behavior in experimental situation	Quasi-convention within experimental situation
Burton, Maccoby, and Allinsmith (1961)	Bean-bag game, with possibility of cheating	Behavior in experimental situation	Game
Burton, Allinsmith, and Maccoby (1966)	Bean-bag game, with possibility of cheating	Behavior in experimental situation	Game
Cheyne (1971)	Prohibition against touching desirable toy	Behavior in experimental situation	Quasi-convention within experimental situation

Table 1
Social Stimulus Events Used in Research
(continued)

Reference	Event Used to Elicit Response	Type of Response	Classification
Cheyne and Walters (1969)	Prohibition against touching desirable toy	Behavior in experimental situation	Quasi-convention within experimental situation
Cheyne, Goyeche, and Walters (1969)	Prohibition against touching desirable toy	Behavior in experimental situation	Quasi-convention within experimental situation
Grinder (1961, 1962)	Ray-gun game, with possibility of cheating	Behavior in experimental situation	Game
La Voie (1974)	Prohibition against touching desirable toy	Behavior in experimental situation	Quasi-convention within experimental situation
Parke (1967)	Prohibition against touching desirable toy	Behavior in experimental situation	Quasi-convention within experimental situation
Parke and Walters (1967)	Prohibition against touching desirable toy	Behavior in experimental situation	Quasi-convention within experimental situation
Sears, Rau, and Alpert (1965)	Prohibition against touching desirable toy	Behavior in experimental situation	Quasi-convention within experimental situation
	Ring-toss game, with possibility of cheating	Behavior in experimental situation	Game
	Rule of bowling game—violations imposed by situation	Behavior in experimental situation	Game
	Live hamster disappears when subject leaves caretaking to play with toys	Behavior in experimental situation	Unclassified
	Prohibition against taking someone else's candy	Behavior in experimental situation	Moral

Study	Situation	Method	Classification
Slaby and Parke (1971)	Prohibition against touching desirable toy	Behavior in experimental situation	Quasi-convention within experimental situation
A. Stein (1967)	Prohibition against momentarily leaving assigned task to look at an attractive movie	Behavior in experimental situation	Social convention
Stouwie (1971)	Prohibition against touching desirable toy	Behavior in experimental situation	Quasi-convention within experimental situation
Walters, Parke, and Cane (1965)	Prohibition against touching desirable toy	Behavior in experimental situation	Quasi-convention within experimental situation
Wolf (1973)	Prohibition against touching desirable toy	Behavior in experimental situation	Quasi-convention within experimental situation
Piaget (1932)	Rules of marble game	Observations of naturalistic behavior/judgments about naturalistic behavior	Game
	Material damage: breaking cups, soiling tablecloth, cutting hole in dress	Judgments about hypothetical situation presented in story form	Material damage (see text)
	Lying	Judgments about hypothetical situation presented in story form	Moral
	Stealing	Judgments about hypothetical situation presented in story form	Moral
	Retributive justice: Child ignores father's request to buy bread	Judgments about hypothetical situation presented in story form	Social convention
	Lying	Judgments about hypothetical situation presented in story form	Moral
	Ignores request not to play ball and breaks window in process	Judgments about hypothetical situation presented in story form	Material damage (see text)

Table 1
Social Stimulus Events Used in Research
(*continued*)

Reference	Event Used to Elicit Response	Type of Response	Classification
	Breaks brother's toy	Judgments about hypothetical situation presented in story form	Material damage (see text)
	Breaks pot of flowers while playing ball	Judgments about hypothetical situation presented in story form	Material damage (see text)
	Spots picture book	Judgments about hypothetical situation presented in story form	Material damage (see text)
	Betrays fellow criminal	Judgments about hypothetical situation presented in story form	Moral
Kohlberg (1958, 1969)	Saving another person's life	Judgments about hypothetical situation presented in story form	Moral
	Stealing	Judgments about hypothetical situation presented in story form	Moral
	Mercy killing	Judgments about hypothetical situation presented in story form	Moral
	Breaking promise	Judgments about hypothetical situation presented in story form	Moral
	Reporting person who escaped from prison	Judgments about hypothetical situation presented in story form	Moral
Gilligan, Kohlberg, Belenky, and Lerner (1970)	Sexuality	Judgments about hypothetical situation presented in story form	Social convention (see text)
J. Stein (1973)	Sexuality	Judgments about hypothetical situation presented in story form	Social convention (see text)

Damon (1971)	Sharing of goods	Judgments about hypothetical situation presented in story form	Moral
De Mersseman (1976)	Sharing of goods	Judgments about hypothetical situation presented in story form/behavior in experimental situation/judgments about behavior in experimental situation	Moral
Irwin and Moore (1971)	Material damage	Choices about hypothetical situations presented in story form	Material damage (see text)
	Stealing	Choices about hypothetical situations presented in story form	Moral
Freud (1923, 1930)	Aggression	Clinical observations/historical reports	Moral
	Sexuality	Clinical observations	Social convention (see text)

Table 2
Survey Studies of Moral Values or Judgments

Reference	Sample Questionnaire Items
	Sample Questionnaire Items
Black and London (1966)	From Crissman (1942) and Rettig and Pasamanick (1959a):
Coombs (1967)	Kidnapping and holding a child for ransom.
Crissman (1942)	Habitually failing to keep promises.
London, Schulman, and Black (1964)	Girls smoking cigarettes.
Mann (1966)	A legislator, for a financial consideration, using his influence to secure the passage of a law known to be contrary to public interest.
Middleton and Putney (1962)	
Rettig and Lee (1963)	Betting on horse races.
Rettig and Pasamanick (1959, 1960a, 1960b, 1962)	Living beyond one's means in order to possess luxuries enjoyed by friends and associates.
Rossi, Waite, Bose, and Berk (1974)	Driving an automobile while drunk but without accident.
Tomeh (1968)	Holding up and robbing a person.
Thurstone (1927)	Not giving to charity when able.
Wright and Cox (1967)	Falsifying about a child's age to secure reduced fare.
	Keeping extra change given by a clerk in mistake.
	Charging interest above a fair rate when lending money.

Married persons using birth-control devices.

Using profane or blasphemous speech.

Seeking amusement on Sunday instead of going to church.

Misrepresenting the value of an investment in order to induce credulous persons to invest.

Nations at war using poison gas on the homes and cities of its enemy behind the lines.

A man deserting a girl whom he has got into trouble without himself taking responsibility.

From London, Schulman, and Black (1964):

Admitting your faults to yourself.

Working for high grades in school.

Getting drunk.

Falling in love with a married person.

Stealing.

Lying.

Disobeying one's parents.

Smoking.

Premarital intercourse.

Reporting to a teacher that someone else cheated on an exam.

Aggressively (but honestly) striving for personal success.

Questioning the validity of one's own religion.

Contraception or birth control.

Table 3

Criteria for Classifications of Social Stimulus Events Used in Research

Classification	Description
1. Social Convention	Stimulus events classified as social convention are shared or common modes of behavior that regulate social interactions and social organizations. These are events that are part of social order, but which do not prescribe behaviors related to welfare of others, protection of rights, or avoidance of physical or psychological harm to others. Convention defines shared or common modes of behavior that establish mutual (though not necessarily reciprocal) expectations of interacting individuals. Conventional regularity is based on mutual expectations, accepted usage, and uniform standards that have the aims of facilitating social interactions and coordinating systems of social organization with numbers of people.
2. Quasi-convention within the Social Structure of the Experimental Situation	Stimulus events classified as quasi-convention within the social structure of the experimental situation have two components. The first component is that the subject is confronted with an arbitrary restriction or request that is established by the experimenter. There is no intrinsic moral basis for designated action. The behavior is designated as such by the experimenter (usually for reasons intrinsic to the aims of the experiment). The second component is that the experimental situation has implicit or explicit rules and expectations established by the experimenter and communicated to the subject.
3. Moral	Stimulus events classified as moral are acts or situations that involve the welfare and rights of individuals or groups of people. These are events that entail infliction of physical or psychological harm to persons, including the deprivation of something to which the person is entitled. Conversely, these are also acts that serve to promote the welfare of individuals or groups of people, prevent physical or psychological harm, serve and promote rights and equal treatment of individuals and groups of people.
4. Game	Stimulus events classified as games are those in which there is observation of subjects playing games, or measures of adherence to or violations of rules of games, or assessments of concepts of games and game rules. Games are defined as activities performed for amusement, fun, or sport. Games usually, though not necessarily, involve organized play and competition in which there is an acknowledged winner according to certain criteria. The end point of such games is to determine a winner. Games usually have implicit or explicit rules that are particularistic—they pertain to that game and form part of the definition of the specific game.

tions regarding his own role and the experimenter's expectations. In what follows we elaborate on the classifications of stimulus events used in moral-development research. Earlier, we referred to the ongoing dialectic between those who define moral development in terms of internalization of values and those who maintain that it entails the construction of universal judgments of right and wrong. First, we consider the internalization approach, which is represented by social-learning theory. We then turn to the constructivist approach, which is represented by structural theory.

Internalization Approaches

Three types of experimental paradigms have been used most frequently in studies reflecting an internalization approach. Two of these paradigms—"forbidden toy" and "cheating"—were designed to measure degree of transgression. A third paradigm, "contrived damage," was designed to measure *reactions to* presumed transgressions. As can be seen in Table 1, we have classified each of these paradigms in categories other than the moral. In order to explain the basis for these classifications, we first examine the forbidden-toy paradigm in some detail and then briefly consider the other two.

Forbidden-toy paradigm. In the forbidden-toy paradigm the basic experimental event is one in which the experimenter prohibits the subject from touching or playing with some toys that are available in the room. The effects of a number of variables on the subject's "internalization" of the prohibition have been studied. These include nurturance (Parke, 1967; Parke and Walters, 1967), modeling (Parke and Walters, 1967; Slaby and Parke, 1971; Walters, Parke, and Cane, 1965), intensity of punishment (Parke and Walters, 1967), verbal instructions (Aronfreed, 1966; Cheyne, 1971; Cheyne, Goyeche, and Walters, 1969; Cheyne and Walters, 1969; Stouwie, 1971), and timing of punishment (Aronfreed, 1966; Aronfreed and Reber, 1965; Parke and Walters, 1967; Walters, Parke, and Cane, 1965).

Various techniques for presenting the forbidden-toy paradigm have been used. Since the basic paradigm is generally the same, we need only describe the most frequently used method. First, the subject is told he will be presented with a series of pairs of toys (one toy is always discernibly more attractive than the other) and that he is to choose one of the two to pick up and talk about. The subject is also told that some choices, which the experimenter does not specify, are not permitted. Then the subject is given a series of successive trials, in which different pairs of toys are presented. Each time the subject chooses the more attractive toy a punishment is administered (e.g., a verbal reprimand, a high-intensity tone, or deprivation of candy). In addition, the *timing* of the punishment is varied—e.g., the punishment may be administered just before the subject touches the toy (early punishment) or after he has picked up the toy (late punishment). Finally, the experimenter finds some pretext to leave the room. The subject is left with a pair of toys—one more attractive than the other—and with the experimenter's reassurance that he is free of surveillance. The experimenter then observes the subject's behavior (perhaps through a one-way mirror) and measures the amount of transgression—i.e., touching of the more attractive toy.

The amount and duration of toy touching engaged in while the subject is alone is considered to be an indication of the degree of learning or internalization of a *moral* response. However, on the basis of the criteria listed in Table 3, we have classified the toy-touching event not as moral, but as "quasi-convention within the social structure of the experimental situation." We have not classified this situation as moral because there is no basis on which the subject is likely to think that touching the forbidden toy will result in an injustice. In touching or playing with the prohibited toy there is no apparent harm inflicted and no violation of another's rights, freedom, or equality. The prohibition against playing with the more attractive toy is an arbitrary restriction established by the experimenter. That this is so is evidenced by the fact that, without altering the moral value of the act, an experimenter could just as well require the subject to engage in the opposite action: i.e., playing with the more attractive toy. Or for that matter, the experimenter could allow the subject to play with all the toys. The restrictions placed on the subject are related solely to the scientific aims of the experiment: how the subject responds to a prohibition when there is some temptation to violate it.

In fact, the stated aim of research using the prohibited-toy paradigm to study moral development is to determine how children learn to behave according to restrictions established in the laboratory setting (which presumably parallels children's learning of restrictions in naturalistic settings). Therefore, in this paradigm the implicit (and sometimes explicit) definition of "moral" is adherence to the experimenter's instructions. The subjects who followed instructions are considered to have behaved morally (i.e., resisted temptation), while those who did not are considered not to have behaved morally.

The problem with this definition—which relies on adherence to instructions and in which the nature of the event is not considered—is clearly illustrated by Milgram's (1963, 1974) experiments, which were explicitly designed to examine the subject's obedience to instructions from the experimenter. In those studies subjects were told to administer elctric shocks to another person. The forbidden-toy paradigm and the Milgram obedience experiment share a common feature: the experimenter provides the subject with instructions as to how to behave (not to touch a toy or to inflict pain). In contrast to the forbidden-toy paradigm, it is almost always assumed that in the Milgram situation the "moral" response would be disobedience to the experimenter's instructions (e.g., Brown, 1965; Brown and Herrnstein, 1975; Hoffman, 1970; Kohlberg, 1969; Milgram, 1974). Comparing these two situations illustrates the ambiguity involved in studies using the forbidden-toy paradigm, which entail an implicit definition of morality as adherence to the experimenter's instructions. Of course, the difference between the two experimental situations we are considering is in the nature of the action required of the subject. The reason that disobedience in the Milgram experiment is generally assumed to be the morally desirable response is not because of the value of disobedience per se, but because of the nature of the experimental event—that is, inflicting pain.

Our contention, therefore, is that in the forbidden-toy paradigm the question of adherence to, or internalization of, the experimenter's instructions is not a sufficient basis for classifying the stimulus event as falling within the moral domain. If we take into account the type of act involved, this situation does not appear to involve a moral issue. Instead, it is our contention that this experimental situation can best be understood as a social structure. That is, through his participation the subject constructs the rules and conventions of the social interactions relevant to the situation. Here the situation includes the experimental context as a whole as well as the particular experimental manipulations and instructions presented. In view of this analysis, we have classified the forbidden-toy experiment as falling within the category called "quasi-convention within the social structure of the experimental situation." We will attempt to show that findings from studies using this paradigm (including the observed effects of modeling and timing of punishment on "resistance to temptation") can best be accounted for in terms of the way the subject conceptualizes the social structure of the experimental situation.

The most consistent finding from these studies has been that subjects receiving early punishment transgress less than those receiving late punishment. The data have been interpreted to mean that moral behaviors are most strongly internalized through the conditioning that stems from the anxiety produced by the punishment and associated with the initiation of the "prohibited" responses (Aronfreed, 1968, 1969; Parke, 1969). Two features of the forbidden-toy experiments are central to our alternative explanation of these findings. The first feature, already discussed, is that the restriction placed on the subject's behavior is morally neutral and idiosyncratic to the experiment. In that the reason for the restriction is likely to be unclear to the subject, the prohibition itself presents a source of ambiguity.

Second, the instructions themselves are quite ambiguous. The subject is first told that his task will be to pick up and describe some of the toys. He is also told that there are some toys that he should not pick. However, he is *never told which toys* should not be chosen. The failure to provide that piece of information gives the task the quality of a guessing game or a testing situation. As a result, the subject has the problem of determining which toys have been (arbitrarily) designated for him and which toys he is not supposed to touch.

This is actually a simple discrimination problem which is solved fairly quickly during the training sessions. Subjects in all of the punishment conditions reported have figured out in two or three trials that they should not choose the more attractive toy. Having solved this problem, the subject is then presented with another ambiguous situation. When the experimenter leaves the room he does not say whether or not the subject should continue to avoid touching the more attractive toy. The subject's behavior should then depend, in part, on what he has determined about the experimenter's expectations and the rules and conventions of this "unusual situation"—a situation perhaps interpreted as a game. The subject then faces the following questions: (a) does the experimenter still want me not to touch the more attractive toy? and (b) should I go along with his expectations?

In this light, let us consider how the subject might be responding cognitively to various aspects of the overall situation and to the explicit communications from the experimenter. It is our hypothesis that, given the ambiguities of the situation, the experimenter's behaviors serve as cues for the subject in his attempt to understand the experimenter's intentions and his expectations. Thus, the subject's own interpretation of what the experimenter expects of him—or put another way, the subject's interpretation of the rules—is the critical factor in determining the subject's behavior.

We can illustrate this hypothesis more concretely through an examination of the experimental manipulations of the timing of punishment. As already stated, early punishment produces less transgression than does late punishment. However, timing of punishment is not the only way to characterize the differences between the two conditions. That is, in the *early* punishment condition the experimenter actively stops the subject from touching the more attractive toy each time he is about to reach for it. In the *late* punishment condition the experimenter *allows* the subject to touch the more attractive toy before stopping him. What differentiates the two conditions is not merely that the subject does or does not touch the more attractive toys, but that the subject is *allowed to* touch the toys in one case and *prevented from* doing so in the other.

The two experimental conditions can therefore be seen as constituting two different communications about the experimenter's expectations. When the subject in the early punishment condition is prevented from touching the attractive toys, it is likely that the situation will be perceived as revolving around the prohibition against touching those toys. In contrast, because the subject in the late punishment condition is allowed to touch the toys, it is likely that the experimental situation will be seen as revolving around only the task of identifying or guessing which toys are permitted. In short, subjects in the early punishment condition are likely to surmise that th experimenter expects them to refrain from touching certain toys, while such a communication is much less clearly conveyed to the subjects in the late punishment condition.

Our hypothesis is therefore that the early and late punishment conditions constitute two different sets of implicit instructions regarding the experimenter's expectations and the conventions of the experimental situation. An implication of this hypothesis is that a clearer communication of the experimenters expectations in the late punishment condition should produce a similar amount of touching of the attractive toys (transgression) to that shown by subjects in the early punishment conditions. This expectation has been clearly supported by findings in other studies using this paradigm (Aronfreed 1966; Cheyne, 1971; Cheyne, Goyeche, and Walters, 1969; Cheyne and Walters, 1969; Stouwie, 1971). In some experimental conditions subjects were presented with a verbal explanation regarding the reasons for not touching the attractive toys (e.g., ". . . some of these toys you should not touch or play with because I don't have any others like them, and if they were to get broken or worn out from boys playing with them, I wouldn't be able to use them anymore, so for that reason, I don't want you to touch or play with some of these toys" [Cheyne, 1971, p. 1253]). The verbal explanation communicates in an unambiguous way the expectations, the rules, and the reasons for them. As we would expect, subjects in early or late punishment conditions receiving the verbal explanation showed the same amount of transgression. Both these groups showed considerably *less* transgression than subjects in the condition of early punishment without the verbal explanation. This finding strongly suggests that it is the implicit instructions communicated by early and late punishment that results in less transgression with early punishment when no verbal explanation is given.[2]

Several studies using experimental conditions other than timing of punishment can also be interpreted as supporting our hypothesis that behavior in the experimental situation is guided by implicit communications. Studies in which filmed modeling (Slaby and Parke, 1971; A. Stein, 1967; Walters, Parke, and Cane, 1965) was presented are particularly relevant to our analysis of ambiguities in experimental situations because the usual procedure in those studies has been to interject the showing of a film in the midst of the subject's other activities. Although the aim of such studies has been to assess the effects of modeling on children's behavior, from our perspective such a procedure is likely to provide him with implicit instructions.

For instance, the procedure used by Slaby and Parke (1971) requires the subject to contend with three distinct phases. First, the subject is shown an array of toys and told that he is not supposed to play with them because they are for another child. Then the subject is shown a film. The film portrays a situation in which a child is first led by an adult into a room that has a table with an array of toys on it (identical to those in the experimental room) and then the child is told not to play with the toys (this replicates what has actually just occurred). The adult in the film then leaves the room and the child proceeds to play with each of the toys. The next sequence in the film depends on the experimental condition to which the subject has been assigned. In one condition the film continues with the adult's returning to the room and *rewarding* the child playing with the toys, while in the other condition the adult returns and *punishes* the child. In the third phase of the experiment the film ends and the experimenter, on some pretext, leaves the subject alone in the room (as has occurred in the film). This situation allows a measurement of the effects of the film on the amount of toy touching of the subjects.

Slaby and Parke found that subjects who viewed the "reward" film played with the toys more than did subjects who viewed the "punishment" film. These results were interpreted as reflecting the influence of modeling on children's social behavior. Alternatively, the same results can be explained from the point of view of the subject's inferences about expectations and conventions in the experimental situation. The similarities between the film viewed and the experimental situation must be apparent to the subject. Given that the subject's experience is exactly recapitulated in the film, it is likely that the film serves as an implicit communication to the subject as to what is expected of him. The film depicting the rewarded model conveys the instruction that it is all right to touch the toys, while the film depicting the punished model conveys the opposite message.

Another study (Walters, Parke, and Cane, 1965) combined the filmed modeling procedure with early and late timing of punishment. Subjects in early and late punishment conditions transgressed equal amounts when they also viewed a film of a model being punished; the amount of transgression was about the same as for subjects in the early punishment condition. Similarly, subjects in the *early* punishment condition who viewed a film of a model being rewarded transgressed as much as the subjects in the *late* punishment condition who saw no film. It appears, therefore, that the film presentations serve the same function as verbal explanations insofar as these results parallel those obtained from studies in which verbal explanations were added to the timing of punishment conditions (Aronfreed, 1966; Cheyne, 1971; Cheyne and Walters, 1969).

From our point of view, therefore, the usefulness of the forbidden-toy experimental paradigm lies in its demonstration of how implicit rules and conventions can be derived from social interactions in nonmoral situations. Our analysis of this experimental paradigm has both methodological and theoretical implications. On the methodological side, we have pointed out that the experimenter's behavior and the experimental manipulations may serve as implicit instructions to the subject.[3] On the theoretical side, our claim is that these experiments can best be used to study the child's learning of conventions in the (limited) social structure that is inherent in the interactions of the experimental situation.

In this scheme, the conceptual domain of the stimulus event is central to the subject's conceptualization of, and behavior in, the experimental situation. The analysis we have proposed *applies to morally neutral* stimulus events. In the case of experiments using events within the moral domain, we would expect the subject's evaluation of the prohibited or required act to be more salient in guiding behavior. Support for this proposition can be seen in what appeared to be anomolous findings in studies done by Sears, Rau, and Alpert (1965). In addition to the forbidden-toy paradigm, Sears et al. used a situation they labeled "candy temptation," which we have classified as moral. In this situation the subject was informed by the experimenter that candies in the experimental room should not be touched because they belonged to someone else. Then the subject was left alone and the amount of candy he took was measured. The relevant finding from this study is that the candy-temptation measure did not correlate with the other resistance-to-temptation measures (Sears et al., 1965, pp. 214–215), although they showed moderate levels of correlation (around .40) with each other. Recently we have reanalyzed the Sears et al. data pertaining to the forbidden-toy–candy-temptation comparison.[4] Our analysis shows that subjects transgressed less in the candy-temptation situation (35% of the subjects transgressed) than in the forbidden-toy situation (55% of the subjects transgressed).

These findings lend further support to our basic claim that different social-conceptual domains exist. The subject's responses in an experimental situation are based on at least two factors: the nature of the event and the social structure of the situation. We maintain that from the subject's point of view the restriction upon touching the attractive toy is an arbitrary one, while the restriction upon taking another's candy has a moral base to it. Consequently, in the candy-temptation situation the experimenter's expectations are likely to be in greater synchrony with the subject's orientation than is the case in the forbidden-toy situation. We suggest, moreover, that a generally useful way to approach experimental situations of the sort we have been considering is in terms of the synchrony or conflict between the subject's classification of the stimulus event and the social structure of the situation. For instance, in the Milgram (1963) obedience experiments described above most subjects' evaluation of the moral event (hurting another person) was in conflict with their perception of the expectations, rules, and conventions in the experiment (as established by the experimental instructions).

Cheating paradigms. Another experimental paradigm often used by internalization theorists in the study of moral development entails measurement of cheating behavior. In this case, too, we have not classified all the cheating situations as moral ones. Several types of situations have been used. The usual experimental procedure has been to provide the subject with an opportunity to change a test or game score (presumably without detection) in order to obtain a higher score and, in some cases, a prize. The initial and most extensive research on this type of deceit was done by Hartshorne and May (1928–1930), who used 28 different tests of cheating in classroom or game situations. More recently, a number of studies have measured cheating in game situations (e.g., the bean-bag and ray-gun games devised by Grinder [1961]).

Two types of findings have emerged from these studies. First, it has been shown (Hartshorne and May, 1928–1930) that there is relatively little generality in cheating behavior within individuals. That is, for the same person, cheating scores across different tests are not highly correlated. While there is some debate regarding the actual degree of consistency of behavior (Burton, 1963, 1976), it is accepted that consistency is moderate, at best. The relatively low correlations have generally been interpreted to mean that "honesty" does not constitute a stable character or personality trait (Hartshorne and May, 1928–1930; Kohlberg, 1963a; Mischel, 1969).

The second and related finding that has emerged from studies of classroom or game situations is that the large majority of subjects did show some cheating behavior. Burton, Maccoby, and Allinsmith (1961) found that 66% of the 4-year-old subjects cheated on the bean-bag game. In studies by Grinder (1961, 1964), with 7- to 12-year-olds, it was found that 70% of the subjects cheated on the ray-gun game. Hartshorne and May found that on most tests over 50% of their subjects cheated, while on some of the tests over 75% cheated. This was true regardless of age.

These striking findings of rather widespread cheating have been taken to mean that "moral" behavior is largely determined by external situational factors. We propose an alternative interpretation which is based on some unattended-to results from the original Hartshorne and May study. Hartshorne and May included in their battery of tests two situations that provided subjects with opportunities to steal money (again, presumably without detection). Behavior in these stealing situations was radically different from that observed in the classroom and game cheating situations. In contrast to the findings of over 50% and over 75% of subjects cheating on the classroom and game tests, respectively, *less than 15%* of the same subjects stole money (see Hartshorne and May, 1928–1930 Book II, p. 83).

This large discrepancy between deception on tests or games, and deception in stealing someone else's money suggests that children discriminate between the two types of events. An understanding of the nature of such a discrimination requires further investigation. However, the observed discrepancy between "cheating" and "stealing" behaviors indicates that cheating on academic-type tests should not be considered *solely* in terms of the dimensions of honesty-dishonesty or high-low resistance to temptation. Our hypothesis is that behavior in classroom-test or experimental-game settings is related to the individual's conceptualization of the social context of the tests. Cheating behavior on tests needs to be analyzed from the perspective of the child's view of the schooling and testing enterprise, academic achievement, and conflicting or alternative aims of the teacher (i.e., tester) and student. Clearly, there is deception involved in cheating behavior. However, the interplay of moral and nonmoral social factors in test situations has not been examined. The need to examine this interplay is clearly suggested by the findings that cheating on tests (rather than noncheating) is the norm, while in the Hartshorne and May "stealing" situations honesty was the norm.

Contrived-damage paradigm. Finally, we turn to a consideration of the contrived-damage paradigm, as used by Aronfeed (1963) and Aronfreed, Cutick, and Fagen (1963). In this case, the basic experimental procedure was as follows. The subject was presented with a board containing a cluster of toy soldiers, behind which stood a doll dressed as a nurse. Using a miniature hoe, the subject's task was to push the nurse doll off the table into a box behind the board. The toy soldiers were clustered in such a way that in order to do this, some of them would inevitably be knocked over. The toppling of the toy soldiers was considered an "act of aggression" (Aronfreed, 1963, p. 439) by the researchers. The subject was first given a series of training tasks that involved pushing the doll off the table. On a subsequent trial, however, the experimenter surreptitiously unscrewed a leg from the nurse doll and, with a surprised expression, informed the subject that the doll was "broken."

The purpose of these experiments was to measure the self-critical responses subjects make under various experimental conditions. Because subjects ostensibly believe they have caused the damage, it was assumed that the "breaking" of the doll by the subject constituted a moral transgression. Like the forbidden-toy experiments, these contrived-damage situations raise questions about whether or not the transgression should be categorized as moral. Although the researchers labeled the relevant act as "aggressive," there is not a very convincing case for this. Moreover, while the subject may very well evaluate the material damage as undesirable, it is not at all clear whether material damage is regarded as *morally* undesirable by children—or by adults, for that matter. Furthermore, in this specific case the damage (a) was not intentionally caused, (b) was minor and reparable, and (c) occurred in the context of a game of skill or test of achievement. Taken together, these factors make it even less likely that the subject would view the damage as a moral transgression.

The findings from studies using this paradigm also support our contention that experimental manipulation provide cues for the subjects interpretation of the experimental events. One of the experimental conditions involved variations in the explicitness of statements regarding the need to be "careful and gentle" in order to avoid toppling the toy soldiers. In one case, the need for care was stated explicitly, while in the other case no such statements were made. The explicit statements produced more self-critical responses than the non-explicit conditions. These findings show that the experimenter's explicit communication regarding the subjects' control (via the rough-gentle dimension) over events in the experimental situation resulted in their taking greater responsibility for consequences. As a result, these subjects attributed the cause of the damage to their own activities.

Questions regarding the status of material damage as a stimulus event, as well as the importance of intentionality in such instances, are considered in more detail in the discussion below of Piaget's (1932) research on moral judgments. As we shall see, it appears that children do not consider causing material damage, in itself, as a moral transgression. As far as the continued-damage paradigm is concerned, it is our hypothesis that children would not view unintended and reparable damage to a toy doll in a gamelike situation as a moral transgression. More generally, our conclusions regarding the internalization approaches have been twofold. First, we have claimed that morality and convention are not distinguished, in that morality is viewed as a form of convention. Second, we have claimed that many of the social stimulus events used in experiments guided by an internalization model are nonmoral and best suited for the study of convention. Further, we maintain that these two considerations also apply to the structural approaches to moral development. Thus, we now turn to a discussion of (a) the ways in which structural theories deal with the distinction between morality and convention, and (b) the stimulus events that they have used in the study of moral development.

Structural Approaches

In distinguishing between the societal and moral domains we have proposed that morality (which we define as justice) constitutes a domain that is distinct from convention (which we define as part of an underlying conceptualization of social organization). This view implies that there are distinct developmental sequences for each of these domains. The structural explanations of moral development previously put forth (i.e., Piaget, 1932; Kohlberg, 1963b, 1969, 1971) have also defined morality as justice. However, these structural approaches have not adequately kept to this definition of morality in their descriptions of the course of moral development. That is, the

'societal has not been identified as a distinct domain, and morality
and convention have been treated as part of the same sequence of
development.

Correspondingly, in research stemming from the structural approach a variety of stimulus events have been used—not all of which
fall within our moral classifications. Before discussing those stimulus
events, we will consider the ways in which convention and morality
have been treated as part of the same domain in the structural explanations of the developmental sequence of moral judgment.

Theoretical orientations. Piaget (1932) first proposed a sequence of
stages in the development of moral judgment, which has more recently been extended and modified by Kohlberg (1936b, 1969, 1971).
Although there are differences in the specific stage descriptions, a
central feature of both the Piaget and Kohlberg explanations is the
view that moral development is a process of differentiating convention from morality. That is, both formulations are based on the assumption that moral development progresses from (1) conceptions in
which morality and convention are undifferentiated, to (2) conceptions in which the two are differentiated, but convention is subordinated to morality. Thus, in both devlopmental sequences the most
advanced forms of morality are stages in which concepts of justice are
differentiated from and replace concepts of convention. Consequently, both Piaget and Kohlberg make the following implicit or
explicit assumptions that diverge from our own model: (1) that convention and morality are closely intertwined as part of one conceptual
domain; (2) that convention is a conceptually less adequate form of
morality; (3) that development is, at least in part, a process of differentiating the moral from the conventional; and (4) that at the developmental end point convention becomes transformed into
morality.

First consider the moral-judgment stages formulated by Piaget.
Piaget maintains that two types of morality exist:

> It shows finally that if . . . we wish to distinguish between opinion and
> reason, between the observance of custom and that of moral norms, we
> must at the same time make a vigorous distinction between a social pro-
> cess such as constraint, which simply consecrates the existing order of
> things, and a social process such as cooperation, which essentially imposes
> a method and thus allows for the emancipation of what ought to be from
> what is [1932, p. 350].

Piaget views these two moralities as forming a hierarchical organization. He proposes that after a nonmoral or premoral phase development proceeds from a heteronomous stage to an autonomous stage.

That is, the child's moral orientation develops from a heteronomous level of unilateral respect for adult authority (generally corresponding to ages 3 to 8) to an autonomous level involving relationships of mutual respect among equals. At the heteronomous level, therefore, morality is based on constraint: the right or good is seen by the child as adherence to externally determined, but fixed, commands and rules. In turn, the social order and its adult authorities are regarded as sacred.

Developmentally, the young child's morality of constraint and unilateral respect becomes transformed into a morality of cooperation and mutual respect. The basis for this second, autonomous stage is the emergence of concepts of reciprocity and equality. At this level, rules are viewed as products of mutual agreement, serving the aims of cooperation, and are thus regarded as changeable. The autonomous level, in contrast with the heteronomous level, is one in which cooperation and equality are based on a sense of justice.

Piaget's stages describe a developmental shift from convention to justice. Thus, for Piaget the heteronomous morality of constraint and unilateral respect is a morality of custom, convention, and tradition. With development, the autonomous morality of mutual respect and cooperation prevails over custom and convention. In this scheme, therefore, prior to the development of concepts of justice, the child must progress through the "simpler," conformity-based conventional orientation. This is stated clearly by Piaget in the way he contrasts the heteronomous and autonomous orientations:

> In short, law now (autonomous stage) emanates from the sovereign people and no longer from the tradition laid down by the Elders. And correlatively with this change, the respective values attaching to custom and the rights of reason come to be practically reversed. In the past (heteronomous stage), custom had always prevailed over rights. . . . But from now on, by the mere fact of tying himself down to certain rules of discussion and collaboration, and thus cooperating with his neighbors in full reciprocity the child will be enabled to dissociate custom from the rational ideal [1932, p. 64].

Piaget goes on to discuss the relation between the two forms of morality he proposes:

> In a word, as soon as we have cooperation, the rational notions of the just and the unjust become regulative of custom, because they are implied in the actual functioning of social life among equals. . . . During the preceding stages, on the contrary, custom overbore the issue of right, precisely insorfar as it was deified and remained external to the minds of individuals [1932, p. 66].

There are two reductionistic consequences to Piaget's propositions that convention and justice are part of the same domain, and that convention is prior to (less equilibrated) justice.[5] First, for the younger child concepts of justice are equivalent to convention or custom. Second, convention is reduced to an inadequate form of morality. Furthermore, in Piaget's scheme morality is regarded as involving reasoning processes, while convention does not. It follows, then, that convention loses its function (i.e., is displaced) once morality is differentiated from it. Moral development is defined as a process of freeing constraint, or convention, in favor of moral reasoning.

It should also be noted that in the process of reducing the young child's morality to convention, Piaget's formulation also serves to place constraints on the development of concepts of culture. Indeed, a developed view of social convention is attributed to the 6- or 7-year-old. From that age on, the conventional orientation undergoes no further change but merely becomes subordinated to the emerging morality of the next stage.

We have indicated that in Kohlberg's (1969, 1971, 1976) extensions of Piaget's stage formulations the assumption that morality and convention are part of one domain is maintained. In fact, the stage descriptions proposed by Kohlberg are considerably influenced by Piaget's notions that morality and convention are part of one domain and that at the highest developmental levels justice displaces convention.

In contrast to the Piagetian two-stage system outlined above, Kohlberg presents a six-stage system. The differences between Piaget's and Kohlberg's formulations may be characterized as follows. While Piaget maintains that there are two kinds of morality—a morality of constraint and a morality of cooperation, Kohlberg states that there are three kinds of morality—a morality of restraint, a morality of conformity, and a morality of principle. Kohlberg views these three moralities as forming a hierarchical organization. The three moralities are represented by three levels into which the six stages are grouped. The first level includes the first two stages and is labeled preconventional morality. At these stages morality is external to the self and the moral orientation is toward power, punishment, individual instrumentalism, and physical consequences. The right or good is defined as obedience to concrete rules whose violation would result in punishment. The bases for moral decisions at this level are self-interest, deference to power, and avoidance of physical harm to self and others (see Kohlberg, 1975). The second level includes the third and fourth stages and is labeled conventional morality. At these stages, morality is defined as an orientation toward conforming to and maintaining the rules of social groups and society. The right or good at this level is seen as adherence to the social system. The third level encompasses the last two stages and is labeled postconventional or principled morality. These last two stages are so labeled because morality is differentiated from conformity to rules or maintenance of social order.

The major modifications of Piaget's moral-stage scheme in Kohlberg's formulation are (a) that at the earliest levels moral judgments are based not on respect for authority and rules, but on an orientation to power and punishment, and (b) that the preconventional level is followed in adolescence by the conventional level so that autonomous morality is seen as developing during late adolescence or early adulthood. In spite of these differences, Kohlberg's formulation is similar to Piaget's in that stage development is defined as a process of differentiating the moral from the nonmoral and in that the most advanced level represents a differentiation of morality from convention. That Kohlberg views moral development as entailing such differentiations is demonstrated in the following:

> This increasingly prescriptive nature of more mature moral judgments is reflected in the series of differentiations we have described, which is a series of increased differentiations of "is" and "ought" (or of morality as internal principles from external events and expectations). As we shall elaborate later, this series of differentiations of the morally autonomous or categorical "ought" from the morally heteronomous "is" also represents a differentiation of the moral from the general sphere of value judgments [Kohlberg, 1971, p. 184].

Thus Kohlberg has, in part, explained moral-judgment development as a differentiation process. In such a differentiation model there is a failure to distinguish the societal domain from the moral domain. Much like Piaget, Kohlberg has treated convention as an inadequate form of morality. In Piaget's heteronomous stage morality is equivalent to convention, while in Kohlberg's level of "conventional morality" (stages 3 and 4) the two are equivalent. Furthermore, like Piaget, Kohlberg has equated convention with conformity: "The term 'conventional' means conforming to and upholding the rules and expectations and conventions of society or authority just because they are society's rules, expectations or conventions" (Kohlberg, 1976, p. 33). In this view convention is conformity and it is stage-specific (rather than developmental).

From our perspective, it is incorrect to relegate convention to a position of nonreasoning or conformity. We are claiming (with some support from our research to date) that (a) conventional thinking represents part of the individual's *conceptualization* of nonmoral aspects of social interaction and social structure, and that (b) out of interactions with the social environment the child constructs both concepts of justice and of convention. Neither of these domains fits the model of heteronomy or conformity in that conceptual development occurs within each domain. Earlier we presented research findings showing that social convention and morality form distinct conceptual domains. Furthermore, the age-related sequence presented in Table 1 (and to be discussed in a later section) shows that concepts of convention form a developmental system. There is also evidence supporting the proposition of distinctively moral concepts in early childhood; (Damon, 1971, 1975; De Mersseman, 1976, Irwin and Moore, 1971). Damon, for example, has found that children as young as 5 or 6 years have developed concepts of fairness, equality, and reciprocity that are distinct from their nonmoral concepts. These findings do not support the view that in development there is a differentiation of moral and nonmoral values.

Our conclusion, therefore, is that through the failure to distinguish between different social domains, the structural approaches have not described the development of moral concepts in a sufficiently precise way. However, our own approach is consistent with other structural approaches in some major ways. We are in agreement with their stated aim of attempting to describe the development of distinctive concepts of justice, but there is still need for a more precise specification of the development of justice concepts than presently exists (Damon, 1975). We are proposing that in order to accomplish this, it is necessary to distinguish the development of concepts of justice from other types of social concepts.

Stimulus events. The failure to distinguish domains in the structural explanations of moral development is reflected in the types of stimulus events that have been used in research paradigms. As shown in Table 1, a variety of stimulus events were used in Piaget's research, including the rules of games, material damage, lying, stealing, and sharing. According to our criteria, the game rules and material-damage stimulus events do not fall under the "moral" category. In Kohlberg's initial research (1958) the stimulus events used were within the moral domain (Table 1). In more recent studies (Gilligan et al., 1970; J. Stein, 1973), however, nonmoral stimulus events have been used.

First consider the use of game rules in Piaget's research. The study of game rules constituted the initial phase of his research and the findings heavily influenced subsequent analyses. That phase of the research dealt with (a) children's rule-following behavior when playing marble games, and (b) the judgments they make about rules of marble games. Piaget chose to study games because they generally involve clear and simply specified rules that children deal with directly. Piaget has justified the use of games to study morality in the following way: "as psychologists we must ourselves adopt the point of view, not of the adult conscience, but of child morality. Now, the rules of the game of marbles are handed down, just like so-called moral realities, from one generation to another, and are preserved solely by the respect that is felt for them by individuals" (1932, p. 2).

The use of game rules as a stimulus event for study of moral judgment is thus consistent with Piaget's assumption that children do not distinguish different social domains, but rather have an undifferentiated conception of morality. An additional, and more general, theoretical assumption implicit in the study of game rules is that the individual at a given developmental level has a unitary concept of social rules. On that basis, Piaget has reasoned that findings from the study of the child's concepts of game rules, or any type of social rule, may legitimately be generalized to moral rules. A similar approach has been used in a more recent study of the development of concepts of rules or laws (Tapp and Kohlberg, 1971). Tapp and Kohlberg also assume that individuals have a unitary concept of rule. On that basis they have questioned subjects about rules and laws in general; responses were scored for moral-judgment stage, with no independent analyses made of concepts of different types of rules.

As discussed earlier, on the basis of the distinct-domain hypothesis we were led (Turiel, 1978) to a different hypothesis from that of Piaget regarding the individual's conceptions of social rules. Namely, the child does not possess a unitary concept of rules, but rather different meanings are attributed to different types of social rules. We further postulate, therefore, that the meaning attributed to rules will vary according to (a) the type of action to which the rule pertains— e.g., moral or conventional, and (b) the social context in which the rule occurs—e.g., game, family, school, or legal system. We have already discussed the findings from a recent study (Turiel, 1978) in which we examined subjects' concepts of rules pertaining to conventional and moral issues. Those findings support our hypothesis. It was found that children and adolescents interpreted conventional rules differently from the ways they interpreted moral rules.

In that same study results were obtained that bear upon the validity of the use of game rules as a stimulus event for the study of moral judgments. The majority of subjects from 6 to 17 years of age viewed game rules as alterable by those playing the game. The majority of subjects of all ages also accepted the possibility and legitimacy of the rules of a game being different when played by people in other social contexts (e.g., in a different country). In contrast, rules pertaining to moral issues were not viewed as relative to social settings. These findings indicate that children do conceptualize the game context and its rules differently from moral events. That is, children do not attribute the same meaning to game rules that they attribute to rules pertaining to moral issues. Consequently, the use of game rules is not an appropriate stimulus event for obtaining data on moral judgments and behaviors (see the category descriptions in Table 3).

In addition to game rules, another stimulus event used by Piaget (as well as subsequent researchers) involves acts that result in material damage to objects. In Piaget's research, material damage was used to study the ways in which children weigh intentions and consequences in attributions of moral blame. Specifically, subjects were presented with contrasting hypothetical stories. In one story a (presumably) well-intended act results in a great deal of material damage (for example, a boy is called to dinner and accidentally causes 15 cups to break while opening a door). In the other story a (presumably) negatively intended act results in a small amount of material damage (for example, in his parents' absence, a boy attempting to take jam from a high cupboard causes one cup to break). After hearing such story pairs subjects were asked to judge which of the two boys (or acts) is worse.

On the basis of responses to these stories, Piaget theorizes that younger children attribute moral blame according to the magnitude of consequences (breaking 15 cups is worse) while older children do so according to "motive" (taking the jam is worse). This is seen as part of a more general shift from judging moral wrongness by consequences (objective responsibility) to judging by intentions (subjective responsibility). The validity of intentions-consequences as a developmental dimension has been questioned by several researchers (see Keasey [in press] for a comprehensive review). For the present purposes, though, our concern is with the validity of Piaget's assumption that children (as opposed to adults) view material damage as a moral transgression. In our earlier discussion of the contrived-damage paradigm we pointed out that the relevance of material damage to moral reasoning or behavior is quite unclear. That is, although children may evaluate acts causing material damage as undesirable, it is not clear that they consider material damage, in itself, to be morally undesirable. In addition to the questionable status of material damage as a moral issue, a number of the items used by Piaget also pose a problem concerning the element of intentionality. Consider as an example the story pair just described (others can be found in Piaget, 1932, p. 118) in which (a) one boy is called to dinner and accidentally causes 15 cups to break, and (b) another boy attempts to take jam from a high cupboard and causes one cup to break. Clearly, in neither of these stories is the material damage intentional. The boy who broke one cup did not intend to do so, although the implication is that he disobeyed his parents in attempting to obtain the jam.

Some data do show that children's responses to material-damage items differ from their responses to other types of items. These findings indicate that young children do differentiate material consequences from moral ones. In one study (Lickona, 1971) first-grade subjects were tested on material-damage items and on items that varied the intentionality and plausibility of deceptions. The results showed that the majority of deception items were judged on the basis of intention, while the majority of material-damage items were judged on the basis of consequences. In two other studies subjects were administered material-damage items and similarly constructed items that varied intention and physical harm to human beings. In one study (Berg-Cross, 1975), first-graders judged the human-harm items (high or low consequences) as worse than the material-damage items (high or low consequences). In the other study (Imamoglu, 1975) children as young as 5 years judged on the basis of intentions on the human-harm items, but not on the material-damage items. Finally, Piaget (1932) has also reported obtaining more clear-cut age trends on intention-consequence items dealing with theft than on material-damage items.

If it is true that children do not view causing material damage as a moral transgression, then the types of story pairs used by Piaget would present them with an ambiguous problem. In effect, the child is being asked to compare (a) the undesirability of some degree of material damage (e.g., breaking cups), with (b) an act of disobedience (e.g., taking jam). This is likely to be a more confusing question for younger children than for older children because it requires a comparison across domains. It is possible that older children more consistently respond on the basis of intention because they give priority to a social transgression over material damage. Such interpretations require further study of the ways in which children conceptualize the undesirability and culpability of causing material damage.

A final example of a stimulus event we classified as nonmoral (but ostensibly used to study moral judgment) comes from studies (Gilligan et al., 1971; J. Stein, 1973) of adolescents' responses to hypothetical stories dealing with sexuality (e.g., a high-school-age couple engaging in sexual intercourse). In these studies high-school-age subjects were administered the interview about sexuality, as well as the interview used in Kohlberg's (1958) initial research (see Table 1 for a listing of the types of items used in that interview). The findings obtained, however, do not support the contention that judgments about sexuality are equivalent to moral judgments. First, Gilligan et al. found that the same subjects showed a greater frequency of seemingly instrumental responses (i.e., Stage 2) on the sexuality interview than on the moral-judgment interview (in which there were more higher-level responses). The discrepancy between the two interviews suggests that the judgments made on the sexuality interview were nonmoral: since nonmoral responses most closely resemble the Stage 2 classification, an attempt to fit nonmoral responses into moral-judgment categories should produce a greater frequency of Stage 2 scores. Furthermore, in a longitudinal follow-up study J. Stein (1973) found that (a) over a two-year interval stage changes were sequential on the moral-judgment interview, which is in accordance with theoretical expectation, while (b) the longitudinal stage scores on the sexuality interview did not follow the sequence, which suggests that it is inappropriate to score subjects' judgments about sexuality as moral judgments.

Conclusions

The classification of a wide range of stimulus events as moral reflects the fusion of moral and nonmoral domains made by theorists and researchers in this area. In neither the internalization nor the structural approaches we have examined has there been an explicit attempt to evaluate the validity or appropriateness of the stimulus events used. Just as internalization theorists have used the forbidden-toy and contrived-damage paradigms to study moral behavior, structural theorists have used game rules, material damage, and sexuality as stimulus events in the study of moral reasoning. It should be noted that there are parallels in the results obtained from studies based on both of these approaches. That is, we have seen that a consistent discrepancy exists between the findings obtained from stimulus events we classify as nonmoral and those obtained from stimulus events we classify as moral. There are four such examples. First, it was found in the Hartshorne and May studies that deception was much greater in game and classroom test situations than in situations providing an opportunity to steal money. Second, in the Sears, Rau, and Alpert studies greater transgression was found in the forbidden-toy situation than in a situation providing an opportunity to take someone else's candy. Third, in a number of items used by Piaget it has been shown that young children's judgments of intentions and consequences in situations involving material damage were different from their judgments in situations involving lying or physical harm to persons. Finally, in applying moral-judgment stage classifications to judgments about sexuality, the Gilligan et al. and Stein studies showed that adolescents' judgments about sexuality did not fit into a developmental sequence in the same way as their judgments about a variety of moral events. It is our conclusion that these findings support the hypothesis of distinct domains of social conceptualization. Furthermore, these results clearly illustrate the necessity of coordinating the domain of study with the type of stimulus event used.

As a final point, it should be mentioned that in focusing on stimulus events in experimental studies this review is incomplete. Naturalistic studies as well as a number of the more general theoretical discussions have been omitted. Indeed, there are several psychological and anthropological explications of social development, not touched upon here, in which morality and convention are treated as part of the same domain (e.g., Benedict, 1934; Edel and Edel, 1968; Hogan, 1973; Kardiner, 1954; Maccoby, 1968). A brief discussion of the psychoanalytic theory (Freud, 1923, 1930) of moral development is necessary, given its impact on research in this area. As Parsons (1960) has pointed out, Freud's explanation of the relationship between the individual and the social system dealt almost exclusively with moral regulation. That is, Freud focused primarily on superego formation, to the exclusion of nonmoral societal influences. However, Freud's theory of moral development does include both moral and conventional components. Simply stated, Freud defined individual morality as restraint or control of instinctual gratification. He assumed that the social system, for functional reasons, imposes restrictions upon the individual's gratification of his sexual and aggressive impulses (see especially Freud, 1930). In fact, he posited that it is the restriction or redirection of a combination of sexual and aggressive impulses that produces the superego (Freud, 1923). Freud thus defined individual morality in terms of the restraint or control of instinctual demands.

We suggest that this definition is inadequate in the same way that other definitions we have discussed are inadequate: i.e., the type of restriction is left unspecified. Thus, in psychoanalytic theory any form of instinctual inhibition is considered to be within the moral domain. In our model, however, we have not classified restrictions on sexuality and aggression as within the same domain. Freud's explanation does not include (a) discriminations between different types of restrictions, or (b) classification of different aspects of the individual's conceptualization of the social system (Parsons, 1960).

Finally, although naturalistic studies of the relationship between child-rearing practices and children's moral development are too numerous to discuss in detail here (for extensive reviews see Becker, 1964; Hoffman, 1970; Kohlberg, 1963a), we should briefly consider them in the light of our hypotheses. First, as with experimental research, it should be pointed out that in naturalistic studies both moral and nonmoral events have been used interchangeably. For example, in studies by Sears, Maccoby, and Levin (1957) the effects of maternal training practices on a variety of child behaviors were examined. Findings pertaining to several areas of child rearing were reported: these included aggression, dependency, sex, and the development of "conscience." The features of parental training or children's behavior that the authors associated with conscience development (see Sears, Maccoby, and Levin, 1957, Chapter 10) are not distinguishable from the features of parental training or children's behavior they associated with other areas, which were not classified as part of conscience development (e.g., see Chapter 6 on "Sex" or Chapter 8 on "Restrictions and Demands"). Conscience was defined as inner control in the face of temptation, coupled with self-punishment in the face of deviation. The examples provided of parental training practices supposedly influencing conscience development (such as telling the child not to touch a toy or a medicine cabinet) were not different from the examples provided for the nonmoral areas (such as neatness, orderliness, safety or bedtime restrictions). In other words, defining conscience as inner control did not discriminate between behaviors that were classified as part of conscience development and behaviors in several other categories.

In addition, many studies have examined the effects of discipline techniques, such as power assertion, love withdrawal, or "reasoning" (called induction) on the child's socialization. It would seem that our reinterpretation of the role of punishment techniques in experimental studies (as used in the prohibited-toy experiments) would also be applicable to understanding the effects of different forms of parental discipline practices. As in the experimental work discussed earlier, in the naturalistic studies it has been assumed that punishment causes the internalization of moral behaviors. In contrast, we assume that children cognize the social situations in which they participate. This means that parental discipline techniques must be seen as forms of communication that provide the child with information about both the other's expectations as well as the rules and conventions of the social situation. This hypothesis clearly parallels that put forth earlier in connection with the experimental findings. That our hypothesis has validity for naturalistic situations, as well, comes from the finding that parental use of reasoning (or verbal explanations) has consistently been related to the development of social judgments and behaviors, while parental use of physical punishment or love withdrawal has not shown this relationship (Aronfreed, 1968; Hoffman and Saltzstein, 1967; Kohlberg, 1969).

Related Research Findings on Social Convention

In the course of examining the shortcomings of previous research in moral development, we have hypothesized that children's moral concepts follow a developmental course distinct from that of social conventional concepts. The next two sections are devoted to an elaboration of the analyses of social-conventional concepts. The research discussed in this section, which was conducted primarily with adults, demonstrates the general validity of convention as a dimension of social interaction as well as the relevance of convention in adult behavior. In the following section we elaborate on research on the developmental levels of social-conventional concepts.

As mentioned briefly earlier, survey studies (some of which are listed in Table 2) have typically included items dealing with convention. Although most of these studies initially classified all of the questionnaire items under the moral rubric, their results show that either (a) the convention items form a cluster or factor, or that (b) subjects do not consider the violation of conventions to be as serious as the violation of moral prohibitions. In addition, survey studies have shown that ratings of (or attitudes toward) convention items are more variable both over time and across social contexts than ratings of moral items.

To illustrate, let us consider several survey studies which provide evidence that convention items form a distinct dimension. In both the Rettig and Pasamanick (1959) and Middleton and Putney (1962) studies, subjects were asked to rate a number of items (taken from Crissman, 1942) on their degree of "rightness" or "wrongness." Using a factor analytic approach, Rettig and Pasamanick identified a factor they labeled "puritanical" and a factor they labeled "general morality," while Middleton and Putney distinguished between "ascetic" standards and "social" standards (moral in our terms). Support for our claim that there is a distinct conventional domain comes from the fact that the items associated with the Rettig and Pasamanick "puritanical" factor and the Middleton and Putney "ascetic" category are generally consistent with the criteria for convention we have presented.

Additional corroborative findings were obtained in surveys by Rossi, et al., (1974) and by Wright and Cox (1967). Subjects in the Rossi et al. study rated the seriousness of 140 criminal offenses. Again, items used in this survey corresponded to the conventional and moral domains. It was found that subjects of different ages, sex, educational levels, and social groups consistently gave high ratings of seriousness to offenses pertaining to moral issues and low ratings to offenses pertaining to conventional issues (see also Sellin and Wolfgang [1964] and Velez-Diaz and Megargee [1970] for similar results). From the point of view of criminal culpability, then, convention violations were not regarded as serious. These results also clearly relate to our hypothesis that an individual's conception of social rules is not unitary. That is, the Rossi et al. findings demonstrate that evaluations of rule violations vary on the basis of the domain to which the rule pertains.

A survey conducted in England by Wright and Cox (1967) produced the same general findings as the surveys already mentioned. Wright and Cox have summarized the questionnaire items they used into eight categories: Gambling, Drunkenness, Smoking, Lying, Stealing, Premarital Sexual Intercourse, Suicide, and Colour Bar. In subjects' (ages 17 and 18) ratings of the items, behaviors falling into the categories of stealing, racial discrimination, and lying were most consistently considered wrong. Actions falling under the convention categories were not rated as wrong with the same consistency.

This survey was conducted in 1963; in 1970 Wright and Cox administered a second survey (reported in Wright, 1971) that yielded results of interest. Using the same items with a sample of subjects comparable to that of the earlier survey, they found that attitudes toward stealing, lying, and racial discrimination were much the same. However, there were noticeable differences in attitudes toward the convention items, which were considered less wrong in the second survey than in the first. Such changes were most pronounced for attitudes toward premarital sexual intercourse (particularly among

females). Many more of the adolescents viewed premarital intercourse as wrong in the 1963 sample than in the 1970 sample.

The patterns of change in the two Wright and Cox surveys are
consistent with our expectation that attitudes toward conventional
issues are likely to be more variable than attitudes toward moral issues. Several other studies, in which the types of survey items discussed here were used, have also shown variability in ratings of
social-conventional issues. In another Rettig and Pasamanick study
(1960b), they administered their scale to students and alumni from
the same university. While these two groups displayed similar rating
scores on the general morality factor, there were differences on the
puritanical factor: students judged those items as more wrong than
did the alumni. Rettig and Pasamanick (1962) also compared American and Korean university students. Again, the two groups were quite
similar on the general morality factor but different on the puritanical
factor. In addition, the Middleton and Putney (1962) scale, which
distinguished between social and ascetic standards, was administered
to religious and nonreligious groups. Two measures were obtained:
an assessment of the degree to which an act was considered ethically
wrong and a self-report of recent engagement in the act. In connection with social standards, there were no differences between the
religious and nonreligious groups for either measure. However, the
religious group expressed a greater belief in the ascetic standards and
reported less engagement in those acts than did the nonreligious
group.

The observed variations regarding convention in all these studies
do not mean that conventions reflect specific habits of behavior that
are independent of a more general conceptual framework. If convention is an aspect of social organization, as proposed here, then it may
well vary with shifts in social organization. Nevertheless, in this view
convention serves an integrative role in social organization.

This point is supported by research on usage of forms of address
(Befu and Norbeck, 1958; Brown and Ford, 1961; Brown and Gilman, 1960; Foster, 1964; Lambert, 1967; Slobin, 1963; Slobin, Miller,
and Porter, 1968) and modes of greeting (Foster, 1964; Goody, 1972).
On the basis of extensive psycholinguistic studies, Brown and his associates (Brown and Ford, 1961; Brown and Gilman, 1960) have maintained that form of address is regulated by the social relations between the speaker and the addressee, which in turn is (at least in part)
regulated by the social structure. These conclusions are based on
analyses of the use of pronouns of address (e.g., *tu* or *vous* in French)
in a number of languages in different historical contexts (Brown and

Gilman, 1960), as well as the use of first names or titles (Brown and Ford, 1961) in a variety of contexts (e.g., usage in modern American plays and in a business firm).

These investigations have shown that there are consistent patterns of use of forms of address which are based on either (a) the relative social status of the individuals involved in the interaction or (b) the social distance between them. Generally, titles are used to refer to individuals of higher status by those in positions of lower status. For example, nonreciprocal patterns of address (e.g., one individual refers to the other by his title, while the other uses the first name) exist when there are differences in age and social, political, or occupational status. The same holds true for the use of personal pronouns. Such patterns were found to apply in a large variety of settings and in a number of languages. The researchers concluded that they reflect universal features of social interactions.

This view has been confirmed by several other investigators. Slobin et al. (1968) found that forms of address used in a business firm were largely determined by the organizational structure of the firm. First names were used for those of equal or lower status, while titles were used in addressing those of higher status. Patterns of forms of address reflected the organization's social structure. Foster's (1964) study of forms of address and modes of greeting in a Spanish-speaking Mexican village produced findings that are quite consistent with those of Brown and Slobin: forms of address reflect status differences (age, occupation, authority). In addition, modes of greeting serve to maintain different levels of social distance between individuals. Thus, the shared or common understandings that regulate social interactions are manifested in forms of address and modes of greeting which reflect the social structure of the village. Studies of Japanese (Befu and Norbeck, 1958), Canadian French (Lambert, 1967) and Yiddish (Slobin, 1963) speech forms have all shown that titles are generally used nonreciprocally between individuals of unequal status. In addition, Goody's (1972) studies in Northern Ghana indicate that modes of greeting serve the function of acknowledging status rankings within the social system.

In addition, a series of social psychological studies (Bickman, 1971; Keasey and Tomlinson-Keasey, 1973; Lefkowitz, Blake, and Mouton, 1955; Raymond and Unger, 1972) provide evidence consistent with our basic hypothesis. The basic design in these studies involves a natural situation in which a request is made of the subject (e.g., presentation of an anti-Vietnam War petition, a request for change of two nickels for a dime). The individuals making the request are confederates of the experimenter who are dressed either in a formal way (coat and tie) or in an informal way (work clothes, "hippie" style, or disheveled). These studies have consistently shown that a variety of the individual's behaviors are influenced by the style of dress worn by others. Generally, the formally dressed confederates obtained greater compliance with the request. Thus, these studies have shown that adults respond in consistent ways to another stimulus event fitting our criteria for convention—style of dress.

The Development of Concepts of Social Convention

We have proposed that children's social-conventional concepts follow a course of development distinct from other forms of social concepts. In that context, we have criticized other theories for assuming a dichotomy between the nonreasoning or conformist states of individuals at earlier developmental levels and the reasoning or principled states of individuals at advanced developmental levels. It is noteworthy that this kind of dichotomy has a parallel in some anthropological explanations of "primitive" and "advanced" societies. This proposition has been challenged by Lévi-Strauss (1962, p. 3):

> This thirst for knowledge is one of the most neglected aspects of the thought of people we call "primitive." Even if it is rarely directed towards facts of the same level as those with which modern sciences is concerned, it implies comparable intellectual application and methods of observation. In both cases the universe is an object of thought at least as much as it is a means of satisfying needs.

Malinowski (1926) has also criticized the assumption that individuals in primitive societies merely conform to the social system. He has maintained that individuals from primitive societies reason about custom and law in ways not dissimilar to those found in other types of societies.

We are making an analogous point in regard to the social concepts of children. The paradigm we have presented is not based on a dichotomy between conformity (heteronomy) and reasoning (autonomy). Our hypothesis is that young children form social concepts out of their social interactions. Furthermore, we have maintained that it is incorrect to view convention as merely the conformity side of morality or to associate convention with developmentally lower forms of thinking. Individuals do not merely conform to norms of conventionally shared behavior. Rather, convention is part of the conceptual construction of social systems.

The evidence presented thus far has not consisted of descriptions of the development of social-conventional concepts, but has been based on (a) inferences from children's behavior in experimental situations, (b) subjects' ratings on questionnaires, (c) common usages (e.g., forms of address), and (d) subjects' discriminations between conventional and moral rules. In the present section we discuss the developmental course of concepts of social convention.

Methods and General Findings

The age-related changes to be described here are based on analyses of responses to an interview about social-conventional issues. One hundred ten subjects ranging in age from 6 to 25 years were administered an interview that revolved around a series of hypothetical stories. Each of these stories dealt with a form of conventional usage, about which subjects were extensively probed. Two of the interview stories dealt with social-conventional issues we have already discussed: (a) forms of address and (b) styles of formal and informal attire. Other stories dealt with (c) sex-appropriate occupations (a boy who wants to become an infant nurse when he grows up), (d) patterns of living arrangements in different cultures (fathers living apart from the rest of the family), and (e) modes of eating (knife and fork vs. hands).

The analyses of responses to the interview showed a progression in social-conventional concepts from childhood to early adulthood. We have identified changes in social-conventional thinking, which are summarized by the seven levels presented in Table 4. The levels represent age-related changes (the correlation of the levels with age was found to be .90) in social-conventional concepts that can be reliably assessed (Turiel, 1978).

As we describe each level, three general characteristics of the levels should be kept in mind. The first is that the development of social-conventional concepts progresses toward (a) viewing conventions as shared knowledge of uniformities in interactions within social systems, and (b) viewing such uniformities as functional to the coordination of social interactions. Second, at all levels conventions are understood to be social constructions. Thus, throughout the sequence, two factors are salient. One is the conceived arbitrariness of social-conventional acts, and the other is the conceptual connections made

Table 4
Major Changes in Social-Conventional Concepts

	Approximate Ages
1. *Convention as descriptive social uniformity.* Convention viewed as descriptive of uniformities in behavior. Convention is not conceived as part of structure or function of social interaction. Conventional uniformities are descriptive of what is assumed to exist. Convention maintained to avoid violation of empirical uniformities.	6–7
2. *Negation of convention as descriptive social uniformity.* Empirical uniformity not a sufficient basis for maintaining conventions. Conventional acts regarded as arbitrary. Convention is not conceived as part of structure or function of social interaction.	8–9
3. *Convention as affirmation of rule system; early concrete conception of social system.* Convention seen as arbitrary and changeable. Adherence to convention based on concrete rules and authoritative expectations. Conception of conventional acts not coordinated with conception of rule.	10–11
4. *Negation of convention as part of rule system.* Convention now seen as arbitrary and changeable regardless of rule. Evaluation of rule pertaining to conventional act is coordinated with evaluation of the act. Conventions are "nothing but" social expectations.	12–13
5. *Convention as mediated by social system.* The emergence of systematic concepts of social structure. Convention as normative regulation in system with uniformity, fixed roles, and static hierarchical organization.	14–16
6. *Negation of convention as societal standards.* Convention regarded as codified societal standards. Uniformity in convention is not considered to serve the function of maintaining social system. Conventions are "nothing but" societal standards that exist through habitual use.	17–18
7. *Convention as coordination of social interactions.* Conventions as uniformities that are functional in coordinating social interactions. Shared knowledge, in the form of conventions, among members of social groups facilitate interaction and operation of the system.	18–25

between such acts and the societal context. At each level conventional acts are viewed, in some sense, as arbitrary. At each level conventional acts are related to a conception of social structure. Each level, then, reflects a change in conceptualization of social systems on the one hand, and in the understanding of the connections between convention and social structure, on the other.

The third and most striking characteristic of social-conventional concepts is that the pattern of development involves oscillation between the affirmation and negation of convention and social structure. This pattern of oscillations reflects the developmental process within the social-conventional domain. In each affirmation phase there is a construction of concepts of conventions and social structure. Each phase of affirmation is followed by a negation of the validity of that construction. The negation phases entail a re-evaluation of the social-structure conception of the previous level and, thereby, provide the basis for the construction of concepts at the next level. Consequently, each phase of negation leads to a new construction of concepts of convention and social structure. Social-conventional development does not follow a simple linear course. Development is a dialectical process in which the re-evaluation of existing concepts of social structure prepares the way for the construction of new concepts.

The different forms that the affirmation and negation phases take are described in what follows.

First Level: Convention as Descriptive Social Uniformity

It is necessary to begin the description of the first level (and the second) with a cautionary statement. The data available for an explanation of the social-conventional concepts of 6- or 7-year-olds are still limited. The younger children in the sample were administered an interview that included only two hypothetical stories because a highly verbal procedure can be used in only limited ways with such young children. (We are, however, currently investigating the thinking of young children using methods less dependent on verbal explanations.) This first level is the earliest level we have thus far identified, but it does not necessarily represent the earliest level in ontogenesis. Research with younger subjects may indicate still earlier levels.

One of the stories used with these young subjects dealt with forms of address. In this story a boy who has been brought up to call people by their first names is expected to address the teachers in his new school by their formal titles. He comes into conflict with the teachers and principal who insist that he use titles and last names rather than first names. The other story dealt with a young boy who wants to become a nurse caring for infants when he grows up, but his father thinks that he should not do so. We begin the description of this level with presentation of some responses made by two 6-year-olds. The basis of conventional thinking at this level is in the assumption and interpretation of the existence of descriptive social uniformities.

First we present responses to the story dealing with forms of address (ages in years and months are presented in the parentheses following the name):

Joan (6:5)

Should Peter call his teachers by their first names?
He is wrong because if like if everyone called her Mrs. Loomis, and he called her by her first name, she expects to be called Mrs. Loomis instead.
Why is that better than by her first name?
Because it sounds a little bit better and everyone else calls her Mrs. Loomis.
What if he wants to do something different than everyone else does? Do you think he would be right or wrong in calling her Carol instead of Mrs. Loomis?
No, wrong. Because if everyone else calls her Loomis, she would want him to call her Loomis and like when he says hey Carol, and not Mrs. Loomis, it would sound different.
Do you think it matters if you call people by first names or Mr. or Mrs. or Doctor? Do you think it makes a difference?
Yes. If you were Mrs. and they called you Miss, it would be wrong because you would be married.
What if they called me Helen instead of Mrs.? What would you think of that? Does it make a difference?
Yes. Helen is a girl's name.

The following responses were made to the story dealing with the boy who wants to become a nurse.

Joan

Should he become a nurse?
Well, no because he could easily be a doctor and he could take care of babies in the hospital.
Why shouldn't he be a nurse?
Well, because a nurse is a lady and the boys, the other men would just laugh at them.
Why shouldn't a man be a nurse?
Well, because it would be sort of silly because ladies wear those kind of dresses and those kind of shoes and hats.
What is the difference between doctors and nurses?
Doctors take care of them most and nurses just hand them things.
Do you think his father was right?

Yes. Because well, a nurse, she typewrites and stuff and all that.
The man should not do that?
No. Because he would look silly in a dress.

Betty (6:4)

Do you think he should become a nurse?
No. He would just look funny. Like most boys aren't nurses because that
is not a very big job and most boys like to do things, like doctors.
What do you mean, girls like nursing better?
Girls probably don't like to operate or something. Because like they
probably don't know enough to do it.
How come girls don't know as much as the boys do?
Because men are smarter than women because they have jobs; and they
learn more, because nurses are like giving shots and things.
So why shouldn't he do it, do you think?
Because he just wouldn't look right. He would just look funny.

In these subjects' thinking social convention is related to the meaning attributed to what are perceived to be uniformities in behavior.
Uniformities in social behavior are not understood to be regulations
or coordinations of social interactions or part of a social system. Uniformities in behavior are descriptive of what is assumed to exist. In
turn, what is assumed to exist uniformly is interpreted as necessary
and requires conservation. For instance, these subjects stated that
titles are necessarily associated with certain classes of people and that
occupations (nurse, doctor) are necessarily associated with the class of
male or female. Thus, for these subjects, titles are not signs of role or
status, nor are they seen as serving communicative functions. Rather,
titles are descriptive of the person.

Similarly, observed behaviors or physical traits of classes of persons are interpreted as fixed and necessary of individuals within the
classification. This notion was clearly apparent in subjects' consideration of whether or not a male could become a nurse. It was maintained
that two types of (nondesirable) violations of empirical uniformity
would result if a male became a nurse: type of activity and type of
dress. Activities and physical characteristics (e.g., dress) serve to
classify roles and persons for these subjects. The role of a nurse is
defined by (a) activities like taking care of babies, giving injections,
typewriting, etc., and (b) wearing a particular kind of dress. In turn,
females are defined by similar activities and types of dress. According
to subjects at this level, if a male were to become a nurse the necessary
associations of activities or dress to the classes male and female would
be violated because a male would be engaging in female activities and
wearing female dress. Insofar as there is a conception of social struc-

ture at this level, it is based on the perceived status distinctions that stem from empirical uniformities.

It should be noted that even at this level it appears that conventional uniformities are conceptualized as social in nature. Uniformities in conventional behavior are presumed to be regulated primarily by social sanctions. The only sanction for violation of uniformities mentioned by these subjects was that of ridicule by others.

At the next level—one of negation of social convention—it is asserted that empirical uniformity is not sufficient for judging behaviors as necessary, fixed, or requiring conservation.

Second Level: Negation of Convention as Descriptive Social Uniformity

While at the first level perceived empirical regularities are regarded as requiring specified behavior of individual actors, at the second level children cease to see empirical uniformities as implying fixed or necessary behaviors. Furthermore, children at the second level have yet to construct an understanding of the functions of convention as a means of coordinating social interactions. Consequently, at this level there is a negation of the necessity for adherence to convention.

Susan (8:6)

Right, because it doesn't matter. There are men nurses in the hospitals.
What if there were not any in Joe's time? Do you still think he should have done it?
Yes. It doesn't matter if it is a man or woman, it is just your job taking care of little children.
Why do you think his parents think he should not take care of little kids?
Because his father might be old-fashioned and he would think that men could not take care of babies.
Why do you think he thinks that?
Because it is a lady's job, because ladies know what babies are because they have them.
You don't think that is true?
No. Because ladies are the same and men might know a lot about babies too.

Emily (8:11)

Well, it hard to say, because you should obey your parents, but he has all the rights to be what he wants. And even if people did laugh, he should just ignore them because they don't know and why should they laugh. A lot of ladies are doctors and some men are nurses.
Is that all right?

Yes, sure. Because everyone has a right to do what they want. If they want
to be a nurse or a doctor or a fireman or something like that, then they
can, if they agree the job is okay.
What do you mean if they agree that the job is okay?
If he checks with his father and if he really wants it. Maybe his father will
change his mind.
Do you think it would be okay if a girl wanted to be a fireman?
Well, usually they don't let them I don't think.
Do you think that is right that they don't?
Well, if a woman really wants to and feels she can handle the job, yah. It is
okay.
Why, even though it is kind of a big, heavy job?
Yah, if she really wants to, she can do it.
Why do you think his parents see that job as for women only?
Being a nurse—because not many men are nurses so they get used to the
routine. I know a lot of ladies who are doctors, but I don't know a man
who is a nurse, but it is okay if they want to.

It can be seen from these responses that empirical uniformities in
behavior no longer have the meaning that they did at the previous
level. These subjects understand that there may exist (or at one time
there may have existed) uniformities in these behaviors. Uniformity
does not imply necessity. The empirical associations of activities, roles,
or labels (e.g., titles) with classes of persons are no longer seen as
necessary associations. Viewing uniformities as implying social necessity is attributed to others, but it is not accepted by these subjects. One
8-year-old boy stated the following:

Why do you think his parents see that job as for women only?
Because most women do it. But on my baseball team there is a girl. So you
can't say he can't. She is a good player in fact.

Furthermore, variations in behavior are taken into account and
used as evidence for the nonnecessity of the usual associations of acts
to classes of persons. One boy argued that the use of first names on
the part of adults in referring to teachers implied that children, too,
can use teachers' first names:

*Do you think it matters if teachers are called by their first names or titles of Mr. and
Mrs.?*
No. All the other teachers call teachers by their names, like Patty and
Dave, you know, and I think if the teachers can do that, why can't the
kids. There is really no reason, if they can do it, the kids can do it.

The most salient feature of social-conventional thinking at this
level is that the acts are regarded as arbitrary: it is assumed that there
is no intrinsic basis for acting one way or the other. It is on this basis
that subjects at the second level negate the necessity for convention.

Third Level: Convention as Affirmation of Rule System; Early, Concrete Conception of Social System

Subjects at the third level still regard social-conventional acts as arbitrary—in the sense that it is assumed that there is no intrinsic basis for the action. At this level, however, there is a concrete conception of social structure: social-conventional acts are evaluated in relation to rules and authoritative expectations which are part of a social system.

The following responses illustrate these changing conceptions. The first set of responses were to questions pertaining to the story dealing with forms of address. The second set of responses were to questions about a story dealing with formal and informal dress. In that story, one lawyer (Ken) decides to dress informally in the law office despite objection from his partner (Bob).

Bruce (11:5)

Do you think Peter was right or wrong to continue calling his teachers by their first names?
Wrong, because the principal told him not to. Because it was a rule. It was one of the rules of the school.
And why does that make it wrong to call a teacher by his first name?
Because you should follow the rules.
Do you think if there weren't a rule, that it would be wrong—or would it be right to call teachers by their first names?
Right. Because if there wasn't a rule, it wouldn't matter. . . . It wouldn't matter what they called her if there wasn't a rule.
What about the rule makes it wrong?
They made the rule because if there wasn't any rules, everybody would just be doing things they wanted to do. If they didn't have any rules everybody would, like, be running in the corridor and knocking over people!

Robert (11:0)
I think he was wrong because those were the rules of the school and they were different rules than at his house.
Do you think that rule was fair?
Yes, because it was just another rule that they have to call the teachers by Mr. and Mrs.
Do you think it matters what people are called? Whether they are called by their titles or their first names?
No, because as long as someone is understanding you and they know what you are talking about, I don't think it is wrong.
Why do you think Peter should follow that rule if he does not think it is wrong either?
Well, that is the rule in the school.

Mark (10:9)

Do you think Ken was right or wrong in his decision to continue wearing sports clothes to the office?

I think that you can wear whatever you want as long as you get the work done. . . . It doesn't matter what you look like, it's how the work is and what it's like, not how you dress, because no one's going to care, I don't think.
What if there was a rule in the office—Do you think he would be right or wrong in breaking that rule?
I think he would be wrong, because you shouldn't break any rule, really.
Why not?
Because if he made a rule, that means you should stick to it or else you don't even have to make the rule. There's no sense in making a rule if no one's going to pay any attention to it.
Why should you follow through if you don't believe in it?
Rules are rules, and you have to stick to the rules.

In one sense these subjects regard social-conventional acts as arbitrary and changeable. Apart from concrete rules or specific demands for compliance from authorities, conventional acts are not seen as necessary. In the absence of rules or authoritative expectations, conventions like forms of address, modes of dress, or manner of eating "do not matter."

Three aspects of social structure are related to convention at this level: authority, adherence to rules, and maintenance of social order. Social relationships are now seen as governed by a system in which individuals hold positions of authority, such as principals or teachers in a school or employers in a business firm. The authority is seen to come primarily from the power of individuals in such positions. Rules pertaining to conventions (i.e., acts otherwise regarded as arbitrary) are viewed as requiring adherence.[6] In addition, it is assumed that maintenance of an existing social order is based on conformity to rules and authoritative expectations.

At this level, therefore, conventions are contingent upon the social context: rules and authoritative expectations require adherence to the conventions. The demands of authority or existing rules may vary from one context to the next—as from one school to another. However, in each context conventions should be maintained if there are authoritative expectations or rules pertaining to them. As we have seen in the responses already presented, conventions must be followed if there is a rule pertaining to the act. Similarly, if the lawyer "owns" half of the business (i.e., is a partner) then, it is maintained by these subjects, he can decide whether or not to wear informal clothing. However, if he is not in a position of authority, then he must adhere to the conventions.

At this level the individual's conception of convention is not coordinated with his conception of rules or social context. The rule is treated as obligatory and invariable, though it pertains to an act which is otherwise treated as variable. At the next level, which takes the form of negation of convention, there is a coordination of rules and action.

Fourth Level: Negation of Convention as Part of Rule System

At the fourth level the conception of conventional acts as arbitrary is maintained, as was the case with subjects at the previous two levels. Unlike subjects at the third level, however, subjects at the fourth level coordinate their evaluation of an act with the evaluation of the rule or expectation to which the act pertains. Given that conventional acts are viewed as arbitrary, it is maintained by these subjects that rules or expectations about such acts are not valid. This level therefore represents another form of negation of convention.

Bill (12:11)

Do you think Peter was right or wrong to continue calling his teachers by their first names?
I think it is up to him what he calls them because a name is just like a symbol or something and it doesn't really matter, just as long as the teacher knows or everybody else knows who you are talking about.
What about the rule? Do you think it would be wrong to disobey it in the school?
No.
Is there a difference in doing it in a school where it is allowed and in a school where it is not allowed?
I don't think so. . . . I don't really think it makes that much difference. I think that kids should call teachers by their first names, so I don't see any difference in it.
Why do you think kids should call teachers by their first names?
They call everybody else by their first names, and it seems more friendly, too.
Some people might argue that it shows a lack of consideration and respect to call a teacher by their first name. What would you say to that?
I think that is stupid. There is nothing wrong with a name no matter which you say. It doesn't really matter.

Robert (12:11)

Well, all the teachers were strict, right, and felt that he should call them sir, or mister. Well if I were a teacher, I don't think it should bother a teacher that he be called by his first name and if I had anything to say about it, I would call a teacher by his first name, but the way it is now, you really can't. But Peter actually should not have done it, because he could get himself into trouble, but I guess he could because that was the way he had been brought up and that was the way he thought it should be done.
Why do you think he should not break the rule?
He shouldn't break the rule? Because he could get into trouble for it and

if you have to go to school you might as well not make it harder for
yourself.
*What if Peter really believed that the rule was wrong? Do you think then it would
be right or wrong for him to break a rule?*
Well, still, it is actually not wrong, because it is not going to make any
difference because like I said before, maybe it is right for him to do it, but
he would be getting himself into trouble if he did it.

Bill

*Do you think Ken was right or wrong in his decision to continue wearing sports
clothes to the office?*
I don't see any difference about wearing clothes, like it does not change
how he works or anything like that. It isn't very important.
*Do you think it would make any difference if it was the boss that told him it was the
office policy to get dressed up to go the office?*
It's up to him, what he wants to wear. Unless he signed a contract or
something saying that he would always wear a shirt and tie, then he
should have to, but it's really up to him what he wants to wear.
How come?
It is something, that it does not affect anybody else, what he wears, it is up
to him, what he prefers.

The distinguishing features of the fourth level are that: (a) social-
conventional acts are regarded as arbitrary, (b) rules and authoritative
expectations are evaluated on the basis of the acts involved, and therefore, (c) those rules pertaining to social-conventional acts are seen as
unnecessary and unduly constraining. The changes from the third to
the fourth level result in the view that conventions are *nothing but* the
expectations of others. This "nothing but the expectations of others"
orientation stems from an awareness that, indeed, expectations do
exist regarding what appear to these subjects as arbitrary acts. Consequently, social expectations are rejected as an insufficient basis for
prescriptions of behavior.

The recognition that social expectations exist regarding conventional acts is illustrated in the responses already presented, and more
explicitly in the following response made by a subject who was asked
to compare the violation of customs of formal dress with dishonest
actions.

That is not the same as doing something dishonest. It is doing something
people really don't take to, like eating with your hands at the dinner
table. It's not wrong—like other people might not like it that much.

In this case, the issue of table manners was raised spontaneously.
Other children responded similarly to a story about a boy who wanted
to eat with his hands in public. The following subject's response also

reflected a lack of concern with social expectation as a guide to behavior:

Do you think he was right or wrong to continue to use his hands to eat?
It's up to him if he wants to. If it created anything bad I think he ought to change it. If there was something actually wrong with it, not socially but healthwise. I think he should keep on doing this if this is what he wants, if there's no health hazard.
Do you think it is right for people to expect others to eat in certain ways?
Well, I think most people do, but I think it doesn't really . . . they expect everyone to but I don't think it really matters. Everyone does so they expect him to, but if someone else came along and did it differently and it didn't harm anyone or anything I think it doesn't matter.

At this level, therefore, the expectations of authorities regarding conventional acts are not regarded as sufficient justification for their validity. At the previous level such expectations or rules were regarded as sufficient justification for adherence to convention. Now, this is not the case because such rules or expectations are regarded as arbitrary labels or designations of expected and unexpected behavior. In addition, the necessity for adherence to a rule is evaluated pragmatically.

Fifth Level: Convention as Mediated by Social System

The previous two levels can be viewed as forming the foundations for concepts of convention as mediated by social structure. At the third level conventions form part of uncoordinated concepts about concrete rules and authoritative expectations. The fourth level constitutes a negation of convention through the coordination of conventional acts and regulations. In this negation phase the adolescent still does not have a systematic understanding of the organization of social interactions. It is at the fifth level that we see the formation of systematic concepts of social organization. Subjects at the fifth level have formed notions about the role of individuals within social units or collective systems. Social units are defined by these subjects as systems of individuals interconnected in an organization with a hierarchical order.

At this level convention is defined as shared behavior mediated by common concepts of society. Therefore, one of the defining characteristics of a social system is uniformity. Conventionally shared behavior is necessary because of the functions served by uniformity in the social system.

There are two phases in the fifth level. During the first phase, uniformity is a defining characteristic of a collectivity and adherence to conventional uniformities is necessary for participation in the social system. In the second phase, uniformity represents a general consensus that is codified and functions to maintain the social order. First, we consider examples reflective of the first phase.

Richard (17:1)
Do you think Peter was right or wrong to continue calling his teachers by their first names?
I think he was wrong, because you have to realize that you should have respect for your elders and that respect is shown by addressing them by their last names.
Why do you think that shows respect?
Informally, you just call any of your friends by their first names, but you really don't have that relation with a teacher. Whereas with parents too, you call them Mom and Dad and it's a different relation than the other two.
What if Peter thought it didn't make any difference what you called people, that you could still respect them no matter what you called them?
I think he'd have to realize that you have to go along with the ways of other people in your society.
Do you think Ken was right or wrong in his decision to continue wearing sports clothes to the office?
I think he was wrong, because you have to sacrifice some things if it would be better for the company. But if he really felt that strongly about it, I guess it's his prerogative to do it.
Do you think he'd be right in doing it, sticking to his beliefs?
I don't know, I think he should go along with what is set up, really, by the office to begin with, because when he first worked there he did dress up. So he's working on the understanding that you should dress up because it's a professional service.

Ben (16:0)
Do you think it was right or wrong to continue using his hands to eat?
He was wrong because, well, every place he goes, nobody else likes it, and he should have respect for other people's feelings. Just because he did it from when he was a child doesn't make it right.
What makes it wrong?
Society says it's wrong. It's just not something you're supposed to do. It's impolite; society says it's impolite. You're not supposed to. Well, I've been brought up by society and I say it looks disgusting.

In a general sense, these responses illustrate the new concepts of this level. Social acts are now judged in relation to a group or social system to which the individual is subordinate. Social systems are viewed as providing a context for rules and expectations. More specifically, these subjects made clear distinctions between different social units and defined social units by the specified uniform behavior. The individual's adherence to uniformities is a necessary accommodation to the group in order to be a participant. Participation in group or collective life is not considered obligatory for the individual. However, if an individual is part of the group, then adherence to its uniformities is necessary. Deviance from the conventions is a violation of the legitimate expectations of others who are part of the group.

That these subjects view conventions as constructions of social systems is suggested by the fact that they maintain that sanctions for deviations should take the form of exclusion from the group. The following responses illustrate this point.

Frank (14:11)

Do you think it was right or wrong to continue using his hands to eat?
That's like the guy with the suit, if he is with other people who object to it, and the majority object to the way he is eating, then he should eat their way, with a knife and fork. And if he wants to eat like that he can go off and eat at home like that.
Why should he go along with the majority?
Because if he doesn't, he will be looked down upon and he will be considered a lower class and maybe an animal or something like that.

Mike (14:6)

I don't think he should be punished just because it's an accepted custom. If there's some reason that this custom is terribly bad there's a law against it, so that you won't be doing it. But if there's no law, I think that the punishment itself comes from society, and that's why you don't find a lot of people eating with their hands, because society has taught them not to. And those that have learned to, which are very few, you know, from their families or something, learn not to because society itself punished you by regarding you as an outcast.

In the second phase of this level the conception of social systems is extended. While in the first phase uniformity in conventions is related to group participation, in the second phase it is also assumed that conventional uniformities in a social group, particularly at the societal level, are necessary for its maintenance. During the first phase variance in an individual's behavior results in group exclusion for that person; at the second-phase variance or diversity may also imply a breakdown of the social unit.

James (15:11)

I think he's wrong, because in his family he can call his mother and father by their first names. But when he's in public he's got to respect the rules of the school.
Why does he have to respect the rules of the school?

How can you be one individual? If everyone else—he's one individual and his family is brought up with first names. In school, it's a rule to call people by their last names, and if it's a rule he can't be the only one who's not going to do it. He's just going to have to live with it. Even if his family taught him like that, he doesn't have to tell them . . . he cannot do it. It's just the principle of the thing. Because it's different if a lot of families did it, but I think he probably is just one exception. And he should obey the rules of the school.

Michael (15:6)

I think it was wrong. His parents said it was all right for him to do it, and I think that was fine in his house, but I don't think that he should—what he's able to do at home, I don't think he should be able to think what he's able to do there he can do anywhere else. He should follow the rules of where he is and act accordingly.
Why should he follow the rules of where he is?
I don't know, I guess if nobody ever followed the rules of what they were supposed to do, we'd have chaos. Nobody would do anything that anybody else would want to do, everybody would do everything that they wanted to do. You'd just have chaos.
Do you think it matters what you call people, whether you call them by their title or by their first name?
I guess this is a little thing, but it sort of hits on what you're able to do, and it's kind of important because it's kind of a little thing but it concerns what a person has a right to do. Whether he should—has to follow rules or not.

At this level conventions are seen as representing common or shared knowledge on the part of the members of a social system. Conventions are determined by general acceptance and are thereby binding on all members. Furthermore, the nature of relations between members of a social group is determined by social organization. For instance, the relation between student and teacher is determined by the social context of the school. Within the school context, the use of titles represents a uniform means for signifying the student-teacher relation. This orientation is evident in the following response.

Brian (18:8)

I think he was wrong because when he finds himself in school and everybody else calls the teacher Mr. or Mrs. or Miss, or whatever else it might be, he places himself in a position which is unfair to the other students; he establishes sort of personal relationships with the teachers by calling them by their first names and the other students might take it as an offense.
Would that make it wrong?
I think it would make him superior in the other students' eyes, or he would think he was superior and it would upset the balance that the class had.

What do you mean by that?
It would upset the balance of the class in the sense that his role would not be the same as the other students. He would not have the role of a student, he would have the role maybe of a personal friend.

Having formed systematic concepts of social organization, subjects at the fifth level now define society as hierarchically ordered. Individuals are thereby classified on the basis of their role and status within the system. Conventions symbolize both roles and status. An example of the way in which conventions serve to symbolize roles can be seen in Brian's response.

Actually my answer would depend on what kind of firm it was, and actually I am not sure, but if it was an old established law firm and he had several law partners who dressed like lawyers do and then he came in wearing very casual clothes, I think he would be jeopardizing the people he worked with, comprising their willingness to wear clothes as part of their occupation. It would be unfair to them in the sense that since they are lawyers and dealing with people this guy would have certain responsibilities towards the company he worked for and by wearing casual clothes, he would create a bad impression that others would want to avoid; if he were a clerk and nobody ever saw him, then it wouldn't really matter.

The following responses provide an example of the ways in which these subjects use conventions to symbolize status designations.

George (16:0)

Do you think it matters if people are called by their titles?
Well, it makes some difference. At least to the person. If he worked through college for his title, he would probably like people to use it.
Do you think it makes any difference?
Yeah, it makes you aware of what the person is. If he is above you, older, smarter.
Is that important to know?
Yeah, you've got to respect that. . . . They have had a lot more experience and they know a lot more than you do.
Why is calling a teacher by his title a sign of respect or acknowledgment of that fact?
Well, he is smarter than you if he is teaching and you should be somewhat thankful and call him what he wants to be called by.
But the fact that you call him a doctor, why is that a sign of respect?
Just Mr. or Dr. you recognize that he is a doctor and got his doctorate in something.

At this level hierarchical distinctions are made between people of differing roles and status. Status distinctions are based on the roles and functions within the social system. Status distinctions place constraints upon relationships, and interactions between individuals of unequal status require conventional forms of address. In this sense, conventions regulate those relations between individuals that are determined by the social context and the relative status of the actors.

Sixth Level: Negation of Convention as Societal Standards

The sixth level represents another oscillation to the negation of convention. The previous form of negation (fourth level) entailed the assertion that conventions are "nothing but" social expectations. This negation was followed (fifth level) by the formation of social-system concepts, and conventions were interpreted as societal standards providing necessary uniformity. The sixth level is, once again, a phase of negation—in this case conventions are regarded as "nothing but" societal expectations. Conventional uniformities are no longer considered to serve the function of maintaining the social system. The following responses provide examples.

Kevin (17:10)

Do you think Peter was right or wrong to continue calling his teachers by their first names?
Well, obviously he was right. Just the fact that teachers in schools have to be called Mr. and Mrs. is no valid reason for that. And also they simply refuse to acknowledge the fact that he's used to calling people by their first names, which is a natural thing to do.
Why is there no valid reason for calling teachers by . . .
Well, there is no good reason for it, the reason is to give the teacher in the classroom respect and give him a feeling of power and authority over the kids in the class.
And why don't you think that's a good reason?
Well because classroom situations don't turn into learning situations, they turn into situations where there is one person in the class who has all the knowledge and has all the controlling force over the class. And you have a bunch of students who are supposed to play a role which is subservient to him. And it's a different situation when one person obviously has more knowledge than the other people but he doesn't require them to be subservient to him.

Jim (18:2)

I think it's a silly rule first of all. You know, the formal thing for the teachers so I don't think he would be wrong. Because the rule doesn't seem to be much of a rule. It seems to be sort of a rule you don't need.
Why do you think it's a silly rule?
Well, it's putting the teacher on a different level than the student. I don't think saying Sir and Mister and all that really shows anything for the teacher. It's just sort of a rule they throw in to make everything uniform.

Why do you think people are called by their titles?
Because that's what has been . . . they've made that into something, like you call somebody Mr. or Mrs. when you're showing respect. And by calling them that you're supposedly showing that you are acknowledging they are better than you . . . well, maybe not better, but you're giving them something, you're giving them a title.

The negation of convention at this level represents a rejection of the premises made at the previous level. Conventions are still defined as codified societal standards that serve the purpose of providing uniformity of behavior within the group. However, uniformity per se is no longer regarded as a necessary condition for the adequate functioning of social systems. Changes in conventions are interpreted to mean that uniformity within a social system is not necessary. Diversity in individual behavior is not seen as incompatible with social organization. Without the uniformity requirement, conventions are regarded as arbitrary dictates.

Bob (17:8)

Calling someone Professor or something isn't wrong because you are not doing physical harm. It is just a social rule, the way you have been brought up. Society says you call people Mr. and Mrs. That is not going to do anything to actual relationships, it is just something someone says— now you call him Mr. or Mrs.

Harry (18:0)

Well, I think the other lawyer is being arbitrary, probably without any real logic behind it. Society is doing the same thing, probably, but society is of such a size that it may not make sense to fight it.

Furthermore, it is assumed by subjects at this level that conventions exist, not to serve societal functions, but because they have become habitual. Convention is perpetrated by tradition. At this level tradition means the existence of conventions that have become unquestioned standard procedures. As a consequence of the habitual but arbitrary quality of conventions, they may also serve nonsocietal functions. For instance, some of these subjects maintained that the only function served by the use of titles is to enhance the status of the titled individuals.

Gerald (18:6)

I don't find anything of meaning in a title. I don't think the title serves any function except perhaps an ego boost to the person addressed, and I would think they would be so used to it, it wouldn't matter to them anyway.

Steve (19:9)

Yah, he was right. The fault is with society in general because people like kind of hierarchies for their own egos and part of that is having the old title, whatever it is. I think it is kind of unnecessary.

In sum, for subjects at this level conventions are societal standards. Conventions are arbitrary but habitual forms of behavior that in some instances serve nonsocietal functions. Perceived changes in conventions over time are taken to support the idea that conventions are arbitrary and maintained through habitual use.

Seventh Level: Convention as Coordination of Social Interactions

We have seen that by the fifth level conceptual connections are made between convention and uniformities in social organization. At that level, it is assumed that uniformities are societal standards necessary of all members of the collectivity. The negation of convention at the sixth level is based on the premise that conventional uniformities are not necessary for maintenance of a social system. At the seventh level conceptual connections are maintained between convention and the social system. The social system is seen as mediating convention, which is defined as uniformity that is functional in coordinating social interactions.

At this seventh level conventions are conceptualized as integral elements of the interactions of groups of people in stable relationships (e.g., school, business firm, society) forming an organizational system. The basic function of convention is to coordinate interactions between individuals and to integrate different parts of the system. Conventional acts are regarded as arbitrary in that alternative (and perhaps opposing) courses of action may be equally valid. However, uniform or specified courses of action on the part of members of the social system are necessary. These are generally agreed-upon and known modes of behavior. The purpose of these uniformities is to coordinate interactions and thereby facilitate the operation of the social system.

At this level the premise is that conventions are based on general knowledge (shared norms) within the social system. Conventions are seen as constituting uniformities in behavior, which are based on the mutual expectations, held by members of the social system, that each individual will act in specified ways in order to achieve coordination. It is assumed that individuals adhere to convention on the basis of (a) the expectation that others do so, and (b) the view that conventional acts are arbitrary (no intrinsic consequences to the act). In part, conventionally shared knowledge is based on the past behavior (traditional and customary) of members of the social system. We now consider some examples of responses reflective of this seventh level.

Joseph (26:8)

Well to the extent that conformity to these social norms is necessary probably even from the standpoint of his best interests, he has to get used to using the modes of address. They are social customs that are acceptable.

You said to the extent that social conformity is necessary; to what extent is it necessary?

Looking at it strictly from his point of view, he is going to be measurably better off if he learns to accept these things.

Better off in what way?

Well, from the standpoint of being able to get a job, just getting along with people. If he has some strong feeling about this in this matter, that would weigh in the balance on the other side. But it would probably be a mistake in our society today to allow a child to continue to deviate from the norms that he is going to be expected to follow, that are necessary in his success in anything that he would want to do.

Why do you think these norms are necessary?

I didn't say they were necessary. I said his conforming to them is necessary.

Why do you think his conforming is necessary?

Well, it doesn't matter to me, but probably every society has had some sorts of distinctions about what to call people under titles that are given, possibly meaningless or possibly they have some meaning. It goes back to the old sociology that people have to have some method of determining how they are expected to act, and they have to have some way of knowing how other people are going to act to them in order to carry on day-to-day interpersonal relations. They can't be carried on completely in the dark as to what other people are going to do.

Tom (19:0)

Do you think Peter was right or wrong to continue calling his teachers by their first names?

He was wrong. Because the teacher didn't like to be called by his first name, and I think this was right, if that was how he wanted to be addressed. . . .

Why shouldn't the teacher just change for him, why should he change for the teacher?

Well, I'd say the teacher has to make a general—rules have to be accepted between teacher and student. If it was tutorial then the student would probably be able to convince the teacher that it would be all right to do that, as long as the student is not showing any lack of respect by addressing the teacher by his first name. The thing is, in a class that has several kids assuming the rest of the kids have been brought up the same way we have, and they address the teacher formally, it would be breaking the generality of all the students addressing the teacher in the same manner if she lets this one student address her by her first name.

What do you mean showing respect for the teacher calling him by his first name?
I can see she would only be offended by the student calling her by her first name if she connected that with the students possibly thinking of her as a peer instead of someone with authority and a higher status.
Would that be wrong?
Would it be wrong for the student to think of the teacher as a peer? It wouldn't be wrong. It would only be inconvenient if the student thought he was just as authoritative on anything that comes up between the teacher and the student. Because in that case he would argue with the teacher who in the vast majority of the cases is bound to be right or would show better judgment because she is experienced a lot more. So it would be all right for the student to consider the teacher a peer as long as—the thing is it entails a definition of considering a peer, if you feel you have just as much authority when you say something as the other person. You can't, it isn't true. It would be wrong if the student considered himself just as authoritative as the teacher.

For subjects at this level convention is based on common or shared knowledge that facilitates social interactions. Violations of conventions produce the "inconveniences" stemming from the failure to coordinate interactions or to maintain a social organization. It is thought that to facilitate interactions the individual within social organizations needs to have ways of knowing how others will act in a given situation.

Tom

What would you prefer to be called or to call a teacher?
I don't really care, it is not what you call them, but what you think calling them a certain thing means. I would just address the teacher by what I thought was conventional and be thinking all the time or have established in my mind what my relationship with the teacher is. The name doesn't really matter.
Why would you do what was conventional?
Because it is the easiest thing to do. If I did something unconventional then I would have to stop and explain to the teacher why I am doing things that are unconventional and it is really trivial, the reason for it.
What are the reasons for conventions?
Well, conventions make things move along smoothly and also—are most consistently understandable communication. If something involved in the communication of two people involves a certain way, if you communicate with somebody about something, you probably have some conventional way of talking about the thing you want to communicate and the person you are trying to communicate to is also familiar with the general way of communicating this convention. Therefore he is able to follow you more quickly because he automatically is familiar with the way you start to do something, if it is the conventional way of doing something. So he doesn't have to stop and think how is that working, how is this thing said, because he has already been familiar with it. It shortens the process in many cases.

Do you think it is ever wrong to go against conventions?
It is wrong if quickness of communication is of great importance. Then obviously doing things that are unconventional or communicating things in an unconventional manner slows up the thing which is communicated. Or whatever you are doing, if you are not communicating, if you are going about a way of building up a building or you have a conventional way of doing it you might think of another way which is no quicker, but is just a different way to do it. And if everyone was unfamiliar with it, the building might be built in just as quick a time because you have to spend time communicating to everybody else just everything about it. You have to explain it to them and if they haven't been exposed to it, it slows up the time of the thing that you are trying to accomplish.

Richard (17:11)

Do you think they are important in any way?
Yah, sure they are important. They are important because they are a very real way in which societies act. Societies develop customs because through living together they find that certain patterns of meeting other people, of going out and working with other people are—work better, or they find more desirable than others and they develop into customs. So just the very fact that they are present and undisputably the way in which society always acts makes them important.

From the viewpoint of this level, conventions are no longer defined as codified standards, but rather as signs of elements of social organization.

Steve (24:3)

Do you think that Peter was right in calling his teachers by their first names?
No, I don't. I think it is important for a child not to be subservient to adults, but to certainly recognize the authority that adults have over children. I think that in calling a person by a more formal name, a teacher whose last name is either prefaced by Mr. or Mrs., or Miss, or Ms, that formal title illustrates the authority that the teacher has over the child. It also symbolizes a greater body of knowledge which he has or she has over the child—it symbolizes the experience that the adult has over the child. It should be recognized and I think formal names is one way of recognizing the differences between children and adults and because it is important for a child to recognize this authority, I think he should be made to call a teacher by their title.

According to these subjects, therefore, titles are signs of the role or position of the teacher in the classroom situation. In this case, the convention is an accepted form that signifies role and status and helps maintain the organization of the classroom. The purpose of maintaining the social organization is to accomplish the stated goal: the teaching and learning process.

Conclusion: Domains of Social Concepts

Through the seven levels just described it can be seen that the individual's concepts of social convention undergo a developmental progression. The age-related changes identified indicate that social convention is structured by underlying conceptualizations of social organization. A plausible developmental hypothesis that emerges from the observed pattern of oscillations between affirmations and negations is that changes within this domain involve a process of re-evaluating existing concepts of social structure that leads to the construction of new concepts. Furthermore, our analyses of social convention have been based on the hypothesis that such concepts are an aspect of the individual's descriptive understanding of social interactions and distinct from the domain of moral prescriptions. This hypothesis has received considerable support from the studies reviewed here (Nucci and Turiel, 1978; Turiel, 1978).

The more general thesis in our analyses of domains is that different forms of individual-environment interactions result in the construction of different conceptual frameworks (see pp. 29-35). In this developmental perspective, thought does not form a unitary structure, but is structured within domains. A potential problem raised by this proposition is that an unwieldy number of different structural domains may be put forth. The result may be, as a reviewer of this author's work put it, ". . . a possible proliferation of stages—a new sequence for each realm of thought to which cognitive-developmentalists turn their structuralist eye" (Lickona, 1976b, p. 420).

Regardless of this potential problem, it cannot just be assumed that individuals develop a unitary structure. Alternative hypotheses need to be tested. In our research we have examined the proposed distinction between social convention and morality. The findings point to the validity of the proposition that individuals develop different structural systems. More fundamentally, the task is to identify the basic categories of thought. To accomplish this it is necessary to explore categories of conceptual frameworks, domains of environmental events, and interactive processes.

Toward these aims, we have formulated a model of the development of social cognition, through which the attempt is made to delineate social domains (Turiel, in press a). In our model a distinction is made between the individual's conceptual frameworks, on the one hand, and the individual's *methods* of obtaining information about the social environment, on the other hand. Through this distinction we have proposed that different cognitive activities serve different functions. While the conceptual frameworks refer to ways of structuring or organizing the social environment, the methods represent the activities by which information about persons and social interactions is extracted and reproduced.

The methods of social information gathering include such activities as observation, communication, imitation, and role-taking. Since these methods serve the function of representing or extracting extrinsic information, they do not form organized systems. The methods constitute a class of activities that serve to represent social information without producing conceptual transformations.[7] In contrast, the conceptual frameworks are the basis for the individual's construction of intrinsic knowledge and they form organized and sequentially ordered systems. We have identified three basic domains of social concepts. Two of these domains have already been discussed: the moral and the societal (the societal refers to concepts about social systems and of which social convention forms a part). The third domain we have labeled the *psychological*; it refers to concepts about attributes of the person and causes of behavior. While a large body of social psychological research has dealt with psychological attribution (Heider, 1958; Jones and Davis, 1965; Kelley, 1967; Ross, 1977), it is only recently that some research has been initiated on the development of psychological concepts (e.g., Lemke [1973] and Wolfson [1972] on personal identity; Pratt [1975] on person description; and Josephson [1977] on predictions of behavior).

The distinction between social convention and morality, therefore, is part of a broader model of the development of social cognition (see Turiel [in press a] for further discussion). In this model premises regarding conceptual frameworks and developmental processes are interrelated. An understanding of developmental outcomes of individual-environment interactions requires delineation of the basic domains of social conceptualization. Consequently, there is need for further specification of developmental processes within the moral, societal, and psychological domains.

Notes

1. We are not proposing that *all* subjects would conceptualize stimulus events according to our classifications. It is possible that any given subject may relate to any given event in an idiosyncratic way. The assumption is the probabilistic one that there is a high likelihood that the subject's conceptual structuring would correspond to the domain

classification of the event. Furthermore, it is possible that a social situation may have components from more than one domain. In such a case, the task would be to determine how individuals coordinate (or fail to coordinate) the different components.

2. A different interpretaton from the one we put forth has been proposed by Aronfreed (1968, 1969). Aronfreed assumes that internalization occurs through both conditioning and the acquisition of what he calls "cognitive structure." Thus, Aronfreed maintains (a) that in the early punishment condition internalization results from conditioning through punishment, while (b) in the late punishment condition the verbal explanation produces internalization through acquisition of cognitive structure. This interpretation rests on the assumption that the subject cognizes only the information provided by verbal communication. In contrast, we assume that the subject cognizes about the entire experimental situation in which he participates. That the child's cognitive activities are not limited to events, presented verbally is a thoroughly documented finding in problem-solving and concept-formation research (Bruner, Goodnow, and Austin, 1965; Bruner, Olver, and Greenfield, 1966; Flavell, 1970; Inhelder and Piaget, 1958, 1964; Piaget, 1952, 1970; Sigel, 1964; Wallach, 1963; Werner, 1957; Werner and Kaplan, 1963). Consequently, there *is* reason to suppose that the subject also cognizes about the nonverbal aspects of the experimental situation.

3. The position we have presented on the forbidden-toy paradigm was supported by a recent experiment (Ross, Bierbrauer, and Hoffman, 1976) directly concerned with subjects' responses to ambiguous experimental tasks. The Ross et al. experiment dealt not with the forbidden-toy situation, but with the "social conformity" paradigm originated by Asch (1955, 1956). Subjects in the Asch experiments were required to judge the relative length of pairs of lines in a group setting. Unbeknownst to the subject, all the other members of the group were confederates of the experimenter who made incorrect judgments on certain trials. Asch found that a large number of subjects conformed to the (incorrect) response made by the group.

The feature of the conformity experiment relevant to our analysis is that the confederates' behavior resulted in ambiguity for the subject. Because the correct response regarding the length of the two lines was quite clear, the subject had no basis for explaining the judgments made by the confederates. In turn (according to Ross et al.), the subject had little basis for anticipating the other participants' (i.e., the confederates) expectations of his own behavior. Ross et al. hypothesized that the inability of the subjects to account for the others' judgments was a central factor in their conformity. This hypothesis was tested by providing some subjects with an explicit basis for explaining the confederates' judgments. These subjects showed significantly less conformity. In this way, Ross et al. demonstrated that subjects participating in social psychological experiments do attempt to explain the behavior of other participants and do infer others' expectations from their behavior.

4. We wish to thank Robert Sears for making the data available to us.

5. It should be noted that Piaget does not present a consistent position regarding the sequentiality of the two stages. While he generally views

the autonomous stage as representing a transformation of the heteronomous stage, at times he maintains that heteronomy and autonomy coexist at both levels; the first stage is characterized by a predominance of heteronomy and the second stage by a predominance of autonomy. Nevertheless, Piaget maintains that convention and morality are part of the same domain.

6. It should be noted that subjects at this third level do not reason in this way regarding moral issues. These subjects were also presented with a hypothetical situation in which stealing from others was not considered wrong in a given societal context and no rules or laws prohibited stealing. In response to the question of whether stealing would be right or wrong in such a case, subjects maintained that stealing would be wrong regardless of the existence or nonexistence of rules or laws.

7. In our model we have drawn a distinction between role-taking *activities* and the conceptual domains (e.g., psychological, spatial) to which they are applied. In our formulation role-taking is a method of information gathering and not a conceptual domain. That is, role-taking activities, which involve the attempt to symbolically put oneself in the place of another, serve to represent the states (thoughts, perceptions, feelings) of others without producing conceptual transformations. Thus, role-taking serves the function of obtaining information about others, which can then be put to varied conceptual uses. Our view is supported by the research findings (see Flavell [1974] and Shantz [1975] for reviews) which show that there is large age variation in children's production of the same type of role-taking across tasks and types of conceptual problems. To understand these observed age discrepancies in performance on role-taking tasks it is necessary to make a distinction, on any given task, between (a) the act of putting oneself in another's perspective (a method of information gathering), and (b) the concepts (e.g., moral, psychological, spatial, etc.) inherent in the problem posed. Most so-called role-taking tasks entail both role-taking activities and conceptual activities (e.g., a level of spatial conceptualization) on the part of the subject. When a task requires a level of conceptualization beyond that attained by the subject, role-taking is not manifested. However, the same subject may display role-taking ability when the task entails concepts not beyond his attained level. Thus, the manifestation of role-taking is dependent on the relation of the conceptual complexity of the task and the subject's conceptual level.

References

Allinsmith, W. The learning of moral standards. In D. Miller and E. Swanson (Eds.), *Inner Conflict and Defense*. New York: Holt, 1960.

Aronfreed, J. Moral standards, III. Moral behavior and sex identity. In D. R. Miller and G. Swanson (Eds.), *Inner Conflict and Defense*. New York: Holt, 1960.

Aronfreed, J. The effects of experimental socialization paradigms upon two moral responses to transgression. *Journal of Abnormal and Social Psychology*, 1963, *66*, 437–448.

Aronfreed, J. The internalization of social control through punishment: Experimental studies of the role of conditioning and the second signal system in the development of conscience. Proceedings of the XVIIIth International Congress of Psychology, Moscow, August, 1966.

Aronfreed, J. Conduct and Conscience: The Socialization of Internalized Control over Behavior. New York: Academic Press, 1968.

Aronfreed, J. The concept of internalization. In D. A. Goslin (Ed.), Handbook of Socialization Theory and Research. Chicago: Rand McNally, 1969.

Aronfreed, J. Moral Development from the Standpoint of a General Psychological Theory. In T. Lickona (Ed.), Moral Development and Behavior: Theory, Research and Social Issues. New York: Holt, Rinehart and Winston, 1976.

Aronfreed, J., Cutick, R., and Fagen, S. Cognitive structure, punishment, and nurturance in the experimental induction of self-criticism. Child Development, 1963, 34, 281-294.

Aronfreed, J., and Reber, A. Internalized behavioral suppression and the timing of social punishment. Journal of Personality and Social Psychology, 1965, 1, 3-16.

Asch, S. E. Opinions and social pressures. Scientific American, 1955, 193, 31-35.

Asch, S. E. Studies of independence and conformity: I. A minority of one against a unanimous majority. Psychological Monographs, 1956, 70, No. 9.

Bandura, A., and McDonald, F. J. The influence of social reinforcement and the behavior of models in shaping children's moral judgments. Journal of Abnormal and Social Psychology, 1963, 67, 274-281.

Becker, W. Consequences of different kinds of parental discipline. In M. L. Hoffman and L. W. Hoffman (Eds.), Review of Child Development Research, Vol. I. New York: Russell Sage Foundation, 1964.

Befu, H., and Norbeck, E. Japanese usage of terms of relationship. Southwestern Journal of Anthropology, 1958, 14, 66-86.

Benedict, R. Patterns of Culture. Boston: Houghton-Mifflin, 1934.

Berg-Cross, L. Intentionality, degree of damage, and moral judgments. Child Development, 1975, 46, 970-974.

Berkowitz, L. Development of Motives and Values in a Child. New York: Basic Books, 1964.

Bickman, L. The effect of social status on the honesty of others. Journal of Social Psychology, 1971, 85, 87-92.

Black, M. S., and London, P. The dimension of guilt, religion and personal ethics. Journal of Social Psychology, 1966, 69, 39-54.

Brown, R. Social Psychology. New York: Free Press, 1965.

Brown, R., and Ford, M. Address in American English. Journal of Abnormal and Social Psychology, 1961, 62, 375-385.

Brown, R., and Gilman, A. The pronouns of power and solidarity. In T. A. Sebeok (Eds.), Style in Language. New York: Wiley, 1960.

Brown, R., and Herrnstein, R. J. Psychology. Boston: Little, Brown, 1975.

Bruner, J. D., Goodnow, J. J., and Austin, G. A. A Study of Thinking. New York: Wiley, 1956.

Bruner, J. S., Olver, R. R., and Greenfield, P. M. Studies in Cognitive Growth. New York: Wiley, 1966.

Burton, R. The generality of honesty reconsidered. Psychological Review, 1963, 70, 481-499.

Burton, R. Honesty and dishonesty. In T. Lickona (Ed.), *Moral Development and Behavior: Theory and Research and Social Issues*. New York: Holt, Rinehart and Winston, 1976.

Burton, R., Allinsmith, W., and Maccoby, E. Resistance to temptation in relation to sex of child, sex of experimenter and withdrawal of attention. *Journal of Personality and Social Psychology*, 1966, *3*, 253–258.

Burton, R., Maccoby, E., and Allinsmith, W. Antecedents of resistance to temptation in four-year-old children. *Child Development*, 1961, 32, 689–710.

Campbell, E. Q. The internalization of moral norms. *Sociometry*, 1964, *27*, 391–412.

Cheyne, J. A. Some parameters of punishment affecting resistance to deviation and generalization of a prohibition. *Child Development*, 1971, *42*, 1249–1261.

Cheyne, J. A., Goyeche, J. R. M., and Walters, R. H. Attention, anxiety and rules in resistance to deviation in children. *Journal of Experimental Child Psychology*, 1969, *8*, 127–139.

Cheyne, J. A., and Walters, R. H. Intensity of punishment, timing of punishment and cognitive structure as determinants of response inhibition. *Journal of Experimental Child Psychology*, 1969, *7*, 231–244.

Coombs, C. Thurston's measurement of social values revisited forty years later. *Journal of Personality and Social Psychology*, 1967, *6*, 85–91.

Crissman, P. Temporal change and sexual difference in moral judgments. *Journal of Social Psychology*, 1942, *16*, 29–38.

Damon, W. The child's conception of justice as related to logical thought. Unpublished doctoral dissertation, University of California, Berkeley, 1971.

Damon, W. Early conceptions of positive justice as related to the development of logical operations. *Child Development*, 1975, *46*, 301–312.

De Mersseman, S. A developmental investigation of children's moral reasoning and behavior in hypothetical and practical situations. Unpublished doctoral dissertation, University of California, Berkeley, 1976.

Durkheim, E. *Sociology and Philosophy* (1924). New York: Free Press, 1974.

Durkheim, E. *Moral Education* (1925). Glencoe, Ill. Free Press, 1961.

Edel, M., and Edel, A. *Anthropology and Ethics*. Cleveland: Press of Case Western Reserve University, 1968.

Flavell, J. H. Concept development. In P. H. Mussen (Ed.), *Carmichael's Manual of Child Psychology*, Vol. I. New York: Wiley, 1970.

Flavell, J. H. The development of inferences about others. In T. Mischel (Ed.), *Understanding Other Persons*. Oxford: Basil Blackwell, 1974.

Flavell, J. H., Botkin, P., Fry, C., Wright, J., and Jarvis, P. *The Development of Role Taking and Communication Skills in Children*. New York: Wiley, 1968.

Flavell, J. H., and Wohlwill, J. Formal and functional aspects of cognitive development. In D. Elkind and J. Flavell (Eds.), *Studies in Cognitive Development*. New York: Oxford, 1969.

Foster, G. M. Speech forms and perceptions of social distance in a Spanish-speaking Mexican village. *Southwestern Journal of Anthropology*, 1964, *20*, 107–122.

Freud, S. *Group Psychology and the Analysis of the Ego* (1921). New York: Liveright, 1951.

Freud, S. *The Ego and the Id* (1923). New York: Norton, 1960.

Freud, S. *The Dissolution of the Oedipus Complex* (1924). *Collected Papers*, Vol. 2. New York: Basic Books, 1959.
Freud, S. *The Future of an Illusion* (1927). New York: Doubleday, 1953.
Freud, S. *Civilization and Its Discontents* (1930). New York: Norton, 1961.
Gilligan, C., Kohlberg, L., Lerner, J., and Belenky, M. Moral reasoning about sexual dilemmas: The development of an interview and scoring system. Unpublished paper, Harvard University, 1970.
Goody, E. "Greeting," "begging," and the presentation of respect. In J. S. La Fontaine (Ed.), *The Interpretation of Ritual*. London: Tavistock Publications, 1972.
Grinder, R. New techniques for research in children's temptation behavior. *Child Development*, 1961, *32*, 679–688.
Grinder, R. Parental child-rearing practices, conscience, and resistance to temptation of sixth-grade children. *Child Development*, 1962, *33*, 803–820.
Grinder, R. Relations between behavioral and cognitive dimensions of conscience in middle childhood. *Child Development*, 1964, *35*, 881–891.
Hartshorne, H., and May, M. S. *Studies in the Nature of Character*: Vol. I, *Studies in Deceit*; Vol. II, *Studies in Self-Control*; Vol. III, *Studies in the Organization of Character*. New York: Macmillan, 1928–1930.
Havighurst, R. J., and Neugarten, B. L. *American Indian and White Children: A Sociological Investigation*. Chicago: University of Chicago Press, 1955.
Heider, F. *The Psychology of Interpersonal Relations*. New York: Wiley, 1958.
Hoffman, M. L. Moral development. In P. H. Mussen (Eds.), *Carmichael's Manual of Child Psychology*, Vol. 2. New York: Wiley, 1970.
Hoffman, M. L., and Saltzstein, H. D. Parent discipline and the child's moral development. *Journal of Personality and Social Psychology*, 1967, *5*, 45–47.
Hogan, R. Moral conduct and moral character: A psychological perspective. *Psychological Bulletin*, 1973, *79*, 217–232.
Imamoglu, E. O. Children's awareness and usage of intention cues. *Child Development*, 1975, *46*, 39–45.
Inhelder, B., and Piaget, J. *The Growth of Logical Thinking from Childhood to Adolescence*. New York: Basic Books, 1958.
Inhelder, B., and Piaget, J. *The Early Growth of Logic in the Child (Classification and Seriation)*. New York: Harper, 1964.
Irwin, D. M., and Moore, S. G. The young child's understanding of social justice. *Developmental Psychology*, 1971, *5*, 406–410.
Jones, E. E., and Davis, K. E. From acts to dispositions. In L. Berkowitz (Ed.), *Advances in Experimental Social Psychology*, Vol. 2. New York: Academic Press, 1965, pp. 220–266.
Josephson, J. The child's use of situational and personal information in predicting the behavior of another. Unpublished doctoral dissertation, Stanford University, 1977.
Kardiner, A. *Sex and Morality*. New York: Bobbs-Merrill, 1954.
Keasey, C. B. Implicators of cognitive development. In D. J. De Palma and J. M. Foley (Eds.), *Moral Development: Current Theory and Research*. Hillsdale, N.J.: Erlbaum Associates, 1975.
Keasey, C. B. Children's developing awareness and usage of intentionality and motives. In C. B. Keasey (Ed.), *Nebraska Symposium on Motivation*, Vol. 25. Lincoln: University of Nebraska Press, in press.

Keasey, C. B., and Tomlinson-Keasy, C. Petition signing in a naturalistic setting. *Journal of Social Psychology*, 1973, *89*, 313–314.
Kelley, H. H. Attribution theory in social psychology. In D. Levine (Ed.), *Nebraska Symposium on Motivation*, Vol. 15. Lincoln: University of Nebraska Press, 1967.
Kohlberg, L. The development of modes of moral thinking and choice in the years 10 to 16. Unpublished doctoral dissertation, University of Chicago, 1958.
Kohlberg, L. Moral development and identification. In H. Stevenson (Ed.), *Child Psychology. 62nd Yearbook of the National Society for the Study of Education*. Chicago: University of Chicago Press, 1963(a).
Kohlberg, L. The development of children's orientations toward a moral order: 1. Sequence in the development of moral thought. *Vita Humana*, 1963, *6*, 11–33. (b)
Kohlberg, L. Stage and sequence: The cognitive-developmental approach to socialization. In D. A. Goslin (Ed.), *Handbook of Socialization Theory and Research*. Chicago: Rand McNally, 1969.
Kohlberg, L. From is to ought: How to commit the naturalistic fallacy and get away with it in the study of moral development. In T. Mischel (Ed.), *Psychology and Genetic Epistemology*. New York: Academic Press, 1971.
Kohlberg, L. Standard form scoring manual. Cambridge, Mass.: Moral Education Research Foundation, 1975.
Kohlberg, L. Moral stages and moralization: The cognitive-developmental approach. In T. Lickona (Ed.), *Moral Development and Behavior: Theory, Research and Social Issues*. New York: Holt, Rinehart and Winston, 1976.
Kuhn, D., Langer, J., Kohlberg, L., and Haan, N. The development of formal operations in logical and moral judgment. *Genetic Psychology Monographs*, 1977, *95*, 97–188.
Lambert, W. E. The use of Tu and Vous as forms of address in French Canada: A pilot study. *Journal of Verbal Learning and Verbal Behavior*, 1967, *6*, 614–617.
La Voie, J. Type of punishment as a determinant of resistance to deviation. *Developmental Psychology*, 1974, 10, 181–189.
Lefkowitz, M., Blake, R., and Mouton, J. Status factors in pedestrian violation of traffic signals. *Journal of Abnormal and Social Psychology*, 1955, *51*, 704–706.
Lemke, S. Identity and conservation: the child's developing conceptions of social and physical transformations. Unpublished doctoral dissertation, University of California, Berkeley, California, 1973.
Lévi-Strauss, C. *The Savage Mind* (1962). Chicago: University of Chicago Press, 1966.
Lickona, T. The acceleration of children's judgments about responsibility: An experimental test of Piaget's hypotheses about the causes of moral judgmental change. Unpublished doctoral dissertation, State University of New York at Albany, 1971.
Lickona, T. Research on Piaget's theory of moral development. In T. Lickona (Ed.), *Moral Development: Theory, Research and Social Issues*. New York: Holt, Rinehart and Winston, 1976 (a).
Lickona, T. What's new in moral development. *Contemporary Psychology*, 1976, *21*, 419–421. (b)

London, P., Schulman, R., and Black, M. Religion guilt and ethical standards. *Journal of Social Psychology*, 1964, *63*, 145–159.

Maccoby, E. The development of moral values and behavior in childhood. In J. A. Clausen (Ed.), *Socialization and Society*. Boston: Little, Brown, 1968.

Malinowski, B. (1926) *Crime and Custom in Savage Society*. Totowa, N. J.: Littlefield, Adams, 1962.

Mann, J. W. Family values in overlapping cultures. *Journal of Social Psychology*, 1966, *69*, 209–222.

Middleton, R., and Putney, S. Religion, normative standards, and behavior. *Sociometry*, 1962, *25*, 141–152.

Milgram, S. Behavioral study of obedience. *Journal of Abnormal and Social Psychology*, 1963, *67*, 371–378.

Milgram, S. *Obedience to Authority*. New York: Harper and Row, 1974.

Mischel, W. Continuity and change in personality. *American Psychologist*, 1969, *24*, 1012–1018.

Mischel, W., and Mischel, H. N. A cognitive social-learning approach to morality and self-regulation. In T. Lickona (Ed.), *Moral Development: Theory, Research and Social Issues*. New York: Holt, Rinehart and Winston, 1976.

Nucci, L., and Turiel, E. Social interactions and the development of social concepts in pre-school children. *Child Development*, 1978, *49*.

Parke, R. Nurturance, nurturance withdrawal and resistance to deviation. *Child Development*, 1967, *38*, 1101–1110.

Parke, R. D. (Ed.). *Readings in Social Development*. New York: Holt, Rinehart and Winston, 1969.

Parke, R., and Walters, R. Some factors influencing the efficacy of punishment training for inducing response inhibition. *Monographs of the Society for Research in Child Development*, 1967, *32*, 1.

Parsons, T. The superego and the theory of social systems. In N. Bell and E. Vogel (Eds.), *A Modern Introduction to the Family*. Glencoe, Ill.: Free Press, 1960.

Piaget, J. *The Moral Judgment of the Child* (1932). Glencoe, Ill.: Free Press, 1948.

Piaget, J. *The Psychology of Intelligence*. (1947) London: Lowe and Brydone, 1950.

Piaget, J. *The Child's Conception of Number*. New York: Norton, 1952.

Piaget, J. First Discussion (1954). In J. M. Tanner and B. Inhelder (Eds.), *Discussion on Child Development*. New York: Basic Books, 1958.

Piaget, J. Piaget's theory. In P. H. Mussen (Eds.), *Carmichael's Manual of Child Psychology*. Vol. I. New York: Wiley, 1970.

Pratt, M. A developmental study of person perception and attributions of social causality: Learning the what and why of others. Unpublished doctoral dissertation, Harvard University, 1975.

Raymond, B., and Unger, R. The apparel often proclaims the man: Cooperation with deviant, and conventional youth. *Journal of Social Psychology*, 1972, *87*, 75–82.

Rebelsky, F., Allinsmith, W., and Grinder, R. Resistance to temptation and sex differences in children's use of voluntary confession. *Child Development*, 1963, *34*, 955–962.

Rest, J. Recent research on an objective test of moral judgment: How the important issues of a moral dilemma are defined. In D. J. DePalma and J. M. Foley (Eds.), *Moral Development: Current Theory and Research*. Hillsdale, N.J.: Erlbaum Associates, 1975.

Rest, J. R. Recent research on an objective test of moral judgment: How the kona (Ed.), *Moral Development: Theory, Research and Social Issues*. New York: Holt, Rinehart and Winston, 1976.

Rettig, S., and Lee, J. Differences in moral judgments of South Korean students before and after the Korean revolution. *Journal of Social Psychology*, 1963, *59*, 3–9.

Rettig, S., and Pasamanick, B. Changes in moral values among college students: A factorial study. *American Sociological Review*, 1959, *24*, 856–863.

Rettig, S., and Pasamanick, B. Moral codes of American and foreign academic intellectuals in an American university. *Journal of Social Psychology*, 1960, *51*, 229–244. (a)

Rettig, S., and Pasamanick, B. Differences in the structure of moral values of students and alumni. *American Sociological Review*, 1960, *25*, 550–555. (b)

Rettig, S., and Pasamanick, B. Invariance in factor structure of moral value judgments from American and Korean college students. *Sociometry*, 1962, *25*, 73–84.

Ross, L. The intuitive psychologist and his shortcomings: Distortions in the attribution process. In L. Berkowitz (Ed.), *Advances in Experimental Social Psychology*, Vol. 10. New York: Academic Press, 1977.

Ross, L., Bierbrauer, G., and Hoffman, S. The role of attribution processes in conformity and dissent. *American Psychologist*, 1976, *31*, 148–157.

Rossi, P., Waite, E., Bose, C., and Berk, R. The seriousness of crimes: Normative structure and individual differences. *American Sociological Review*, 1974, *39*, 224–237.

Sears, R. R., Maccoby, E. E., and Levin, H. *Patterns of Child Rearing*. Evanston, Ill.: Row, Peterson, 1957.

Sears, R. R., Rau, L., and Alpert, R. *Identification and Child Rearing*. Stanford, Cal.: Stanford University Press, 1965.

Sellin, J. T., and Wolfgang, M. W. *The Measurement of Delinquency*. New York: Wiley, 1964.

Selman, R. L. The relation of role-taking to the development of moral judgment in children. *Child Development*, 1971, *42*, 79–91.

Selman, R. L. Social cognitive understanding: A guide to educational and clinical practice. In T. Lickona (Ed.), *Moral Development and Behavior: Theory, Research and Social Issues*. New York: Holt, Rinehart and Winston, 1976.

Shantz, C. U. The development of social cognition. In: E. M. Hetherington (Ed.), *Review of Child Development Research*, Vol. 5. Chicago: University of Chicago Press, 1975.

Sigel, I. E. The attainment of concepts. In: M. L. Hoffman and L. W. Hoffman (Eds.), *Review of Child Development Research*, Vol. 1. New York: Russell Sage Foundation, 1964.

Slaby, R. E., and Parke, R. D. Effect on resistance to deviation of observing a model's affective reactions to response consequences. *Developmental Psychology*, 1971, *5*, 40–47.

Slobin, D. I. Some aspects of the use of pronouns of address in Yiddish. *Word*, 1963, *19*, 193–202.

Slobin, D., Miller, S., and Porter, L. Forms of address and social organization in a business organization. *Journal of Personality and Social Psychology*, 1968, *8*, 289–293.

Stein, A. Imitation of resistance to temptation. *Child Development*, 1967, *38*, 157–169.

Stein, J. L. Adolescent's reasoning about moral and sexual dilemmas: A longitudinal study. Unpublished doctoral dissertation, Harvard University, 1973.

Stouwie, R. J. Inconsistent verbal instructions and children's resistance to temptation. *Child Development*, 1971, *42*, 1517–1531.

Tapp, J., and Kohlberg, L. Developing senses of law and legal justice. *Journal of Social Issues*, 1971, *27*, 65–92.

Thurstone, L. L. Method of paired comparisons for social values. *Journal of Abnormal and Social Psychology*, 1927, *21*, 384–400.

Tomeh, A. K. Moral values in a cross-cultural perspective. *Journal of Social Psychology*, 1968, *74*, 137–138.

Tomlinson-Keasey, C., and Keasey, C. B. The mediating role of cognitive development in moral judgment. *Child Development*, 1974, *45*, 291–298.

Turiel, E. Developmental processes in the child's moral thinking. In P. H. Mussen, J. Langer, and M. Covington (Eds.), *Trends and Issues in Developmental Psychology*. New York: Holt, 1969.

Turiel, E. Conflict and transition in adolescent moral development. *Child Development*, 1974, *45*, 14–29.

Turiel, E. The development of social concepts: Mores, customs and conventions. In D. J. DePalma and J. M. Foley. (Eds.), *Moral Development: Current Theory and Research*. Hillsdale, N. J.: Erlbaum Associates, 1975.

Turiel, E. Conflict and transition in adolescent moral development: II. The resolution of disequilibrium through structural reorganization. *Child Development*, 1977, *48*, 634–637.

Turiel, E. Social-convention and the development of societal concepts. In W. Damon (Ed.), *New Directions In Child Development. Vol. 1, Social Cognition*. San Francisco: Jossey-Bass, 1978, Forthcoming.

Turiel, E. Social-convention and the development of societal concepts. In W. Damon (Ed.), *New Directions In Child Development. Vol. 1, Social Cognition*. San Francisco: Jossey-Bass, 1978, Forthcoming.

Velez-Diaz, A., and Megargee, E. I. An investigation of differences in value judgments between youthful offenders and non-offenders in Puerto Rico. *Journal of Criminal Law, Criminology and Police Science*, 1970, *61*, 549–553.

Wallach, M. Research on children's thinking. In: H. Stevenson (Ed.), *The Sixty-Second Yearbook of the National Society for the Study of Education*, Part I: Vol. 62. Chicago: University of Chicago Press, 1963.

Walters, R., Parke, R., and Cane, V. Timing of punishmente and the observation of consequences to others as determinants of response inhibition. *Journal of Experimental Child Psychology*, 1965, *2*, 10–30.

Werner, H. *Comparative Psychology of Mental Development*. New York: International Universities Press, 1957.

Werner, H., and Kaplan, B. *Symbol Formation*. New York: Wiley, 1963.

Whiting, J. W. M. Resource mediation and learning by identification. In: I. Iscoe and H. W. Stevenson (Eds.), *Personality Development in Children.* Austin, Texas: University of Texas Press, 1960, pp. 112–126.

Wolf, T. Effects of Televised Modeled Verbalizations and Behavior in Resistance to Deviation. *Developmental Psychology,* 1973, *8,* 51–56.

Wolfson, A. Aspects of the development of identity concepts. Unpublished doctoral dissertation, University of California, Berkeley, 1972.

Wright, D. *The Psychology of Moral Behavior.* Baltimore: Penguin Books, 1971.

Wright, D., and Cox, E. A study of the relationship between moral judgment and religious belief in a sample of English adolescents. *Journal of Social Psychology,* 1967, *72,* 135–144.

4 Recasting the Lone Stranger

K. ALISON CLARKE-STEWART

Perhaps it was the intensity of terror displayed by some 8-month-olds when confronted by an unfamiliar adult, or the frequency with which distress occurred when young children were studied in the laboratory, or maybe it was the apparent suddenness of the shift in children's reactions from affability to fear, that riveted the attention of investigators on children's negative reactions to strangers. Perhaps it was not the observed occurrence of "stranger anxiety" itself that determined that focus, but the captivating implications the phenomenon had for psychological theory—as a demonstration of drive, the beginning of object relations (Spitz, 1950), the end of a sensitive period in the formation of attachment (Hess, 1970), or the disruption of phase sequences (Hebb, 1946) or expectancies (Bronson, 1972). Perhaps the high visibility of mother as the sole caregiving figure and the relative social isolation of the nuclear family blinded researchers to the possibility of children's significant and positive relations with adults outside the family. Perhaps the classic portrayal of 2-year-olds

The research described in this chapter was supported by a grant from the Office of Child Development (#OCD-CB-06) to William Kessen and Greta Fein and a Spencer Foundation grant to the author.

as socially inept, uninterested (Gesell, Ilg, and Ames, 1943), or bat-
tling (Maudry and Nekula, 1934) caused investigators to overlook the
beginnings of friendship with peers. At any rate, the study of young
children's social development, and particularly their interaction with
new and unfamiliar people, has been dominated by a simple in-
dependent-variable approach, where fear is seen as the main pro-
pellant of action, the mother is viewed as a necessary point of reference, and the social partner of interest is, inevitably, a strange adult.

It is now generally agreed (cf. Haith and Campos, 1977) that the
emphasis on children's negative reactions to strangers was a serious
and misleading oversimplification. Rheingold and Eckerman (1971,
1973) have even gone so far as to suggest that the phenomenon of
stranger anxiety may not exist. They sharply criticize previous research
for inadequate operationalization and measurement of fear and for
experimental designs that confound stranger, situation, and separation from mother, and they castigate investigators for theoretical explanations that do not completely account for the data. They emphasize empirical results from their own and others' research that are
inconsistent with the notion of fear of strangers as a developmental
milestone, pointing out that, at any age, the number of infants exhibiting fear by crying, fussing, whimpering, or avoiding the stranger is
generally low—never is it more than 50%—and that there is no consistency across situations, strangers, or kinds of behavior in children's
exhibition of distress, nor is there agreement between investigators as
to the age of onset of anxiety.

Other studies that have used more appropriate methods than
those reviewed by Rheingold and Eckerman, however, have confirmed the existence of a developmental shift in the first year toward
more wary reactions to strangers. Longitudinal studies show a de-
crease in positive responding and an increase in negative reactions to
strangers in nearly all infants tested (Fraiberg, 1975; Gaensbauer,
Emde, and Campos, 1976). More sophisticated measurement of children's behavior demonstrates physiological (cardiac acceleration) and
learning (punishment) effects of strangers as contrasted with mother
(Campos, 1975; Campos et al., 1975; Fouts and Atlas, 1974; Skarin,
1977; Waters, Matas, and Sroufe, 1975). And even when behavior to
the stranger is not confounded by effects of separation from mother
or stressful approach sequences, distress is still observed—though to a
lesser extent (Klein and Durfee, 1975; Ricciuti, 1974; Sroufe, Waters,
and Matas, 1974). Young children may not exhibit fear with "all of the
(unfamiliar) people all of the time," but as Morgan (1973) qualifiedly
concludes, "almost all infants show at least occasional instances of at
least avoidance at some point."

Nevertheless, fear of strangers is neither as predictable nor as universal at any one age as once was thought. It is not consistently manifested upon repeated testing even a few days apart (Shaffran and Décarie, 1973), and it is highly susceptible to differences in strangers' behavior (Rafman, 1974; Shaffran, 1974), familiarity (Bretherton, 1974; Ross, 1975),[1] and situational context (Skarin, 1977; Sroufe, Waters, and Matas, 1974; Waters, Matas, and Sroufe, 1975). Moreover, the display of negative behavior toward a stranger does not preclude the possibility of positive behavior to that same individual within the same encounter (Bretherton, 1974; Bretherton and Ainsworth, 1974; Clarke-Stewart, 1975). Complex findings like these are leading investigators to examine reactions to the stranger more carefully—for example, to distinguish between fear (emotion) and wariness (cognition) (Bronson, 1972)—and to treat them as the outcome of *multiple* processes like attachment, affiliation, fear, and exploration, the balance among which determines the child's response (Bretherton and Ainsworth, 1974; Bronson, 1972; Brooks and Lewis, 1976; Rand and Jennings, 1974).

Such examination and treatment represent a significant advance in the study of children's reactions to strangers, away from a single-variable approach and a single-minded focus on the strong emotions of attachment and fear. It is the purpose of the present chapter to explore issues of young children's behavior with strangers in order to expand thinking and research in the area even further. The problem of interest here is the child's social behavior when meeting a new person: How does the child behave? How does he or she know what to do or expect? How do the two people interact?

To address these questions, this chapter offers a perspective that expands the concept of "stranger" beyond its current reference to merely an unfamiliar person, and substitutes an approach that focuses on unfamiliar *individuals*, with specific characteristics, who behave toward the child in particular ways, and who engage the child in social interaction. The stranger is no longer considered an independent stimulus "out there," to which the child, motivated by fear or uncertainty, reacts, but in this view is recast as an interactive *partner*. The implications of this perspective—this recasting of "the lone stranger"—are explored here through presentation of a conceptual organizing framework for children's encounters with strangers, discussion of empirical data from a study that examined stranger encounters in 2-year-old children, and consideration of various theories that have been or could be used to explain the phenomena observed.

The conceptual framework, which is presented first (in Figure 1), sets out some of the parameters involved when a child meets and interacts with a stranger. Delineating the variables that constitute the apparently simple situation of a child confronted by a stranger, thus, clearly expands the traditional and myopic view of this social phenomenon, a view that has led researchers to try to account for children's behavior in terms of solitary independent variables. The fact that the enormous complexity of children's reactions to strangers illustrated by the framework has generally gone unrecognized or been ignored by researchers is no doubt responsible for the irregularities in reported observations of children's behavior with strangers. Researchers, moreover, have not been substantially helped by the few previous attempts that have been made to identify the relevant dimensions of the stranger situation (e.g., Lally in Gordon et al., 1973), since these attempts have been incomplete or oversimplified. Further research will undoubtedly demonstrate that the present framework, too, is incomplete, but for now it represents the most comprehensive attempt that has been made to go beyond unitary conceptualizations of children's reactions to strangers. Taken in toto it offers a research program of "life span" proportions for the investigator, but also, it is hoped, a framework with "life span" implications for the study of social development. That is, by translating "child" into "adult" and "mother" into other "attachment figure," the framework could be used for studying adult social interaction as well as that of children and strangers.

The complexity revealed by the conceptual framework makes it abundantly clear that a single chapter can explore only a limited aspect of the subject of children's encounters with strangers. In the past, when researchers have looked for more than the effect of stranger per se, they have directed their attention primarily to the first column of the framework, investigating so-called "characteristics" of the stranger, particularly the stranger's sex, age, and relative familiarity. Recently, some systematization of the influence on children's behavior of the immediate context or situation—the third column of the framework—has begun (e.g., Sroufe, Waters, and Matas, 1974). As yet, however, little attention has been given to studying the effects of variations in strangers' *behavior* (column 2). Our purpose here is to redress that imbalance by making this parameter the main focus of discussion. Not only has the stranger's behavior been ignored by researchers, but it seems to be an especially important dimension for the study of the stranger as an interactive social partner, which we have suggested is our primary interest in this chapter. The following section, therefore, presents and discusses data from a study of children's reactions to variations in strangers' behavior.

Stranger Characteristics	Stranger Behavior	Situation	Child Behavior	Child Characteristics	Child Background
Age*	Indirect Direct	Other people	Direct Indirect	Age	Amount and quality
Size	to M to C	present	to S to M		of contact with:
		proximal			mother
Physical appearance*	Tone*	interacting	Tone*	Physical appearance	father
	positive	with child	positive		other caregiver
Sex*	negative	interacting with	negative	Sex	other adults
		stranger			siblings
State	Mode*		Mode*	State	other children
emotional	visual	Distance	visual	emotional	
physical	verbal	between strang-	verbal	physical	
	physical	er and child	physical		
Culture	with object		with object	Temperament	Culture
		Timing		Capability	
		of stranger's		cognitive	
		approach		physical	
History*	Style*		Style*		
experience with people	intrusive	Place	initiatory	History	
experience with	responsive	familiar	responsive	experience with people	
children	playful	unfamiliar		experience with family	
experience with par-	programmed	pleasant		experience with	
ticular child	natural	unpleasant		strangers	
experience in experi-				experience with parti-	
mental situation		Physical conditions		cular stranger	
		light		experience with other	
		heat		people with stranger	
		objects		experience in experi-	
				mental situation	
		Preceding events			
		separation from			
		mother			
		people			
		sequence of			
		strangers			
		M's activity			

Arrows represent direction of influence.
*Categories discussed in this chapter.

Method

The data were collected in an intensive longitudinal study of the social development of 14 children from 1 to 2½ years of age. Families studied were all white, two-parent families, with one or two children, and represented a range of income levels and educational backgrounds; their names had been randomly selected from hospital birth records. The families were visited repeatedly over the 18-month investigation. Of the four visits reported here, three occurred in the home and one in the laboratory playroom; they occurred when the children were 17, 18, and 30 months old. Each visit included a variety of semistructured procedures for assessing children's reactions to adult strangers. The general format for each of these stranger "probes" was as follows.

Sometime after the observer had arrived at the home or after the mother and child were settled in the laboratory playroom, usually while the child was playing with a toy, a stranger entered the room. The mother had been instructed to stay in the room and play a receptive but noninitiatory role toward the child and the stranger. First, the stranger engaged in a "biased interaction" with mother or child; that is, she behaved with them in a certain specified way for a short period of time (3 to 7 minutes). Then she went through a standardized procedure, the "approach sequence," which consisted of the following activities: she sat down at a moderate distance (8 to 12 feet) from the child and ignored him or her for 1 minute, then she looked at him or her for 1 minute, smiled and gave a friendly greeting (½ minute), played for 1 minute with a toy that the child liked, talked to the child in a friendly way, including in her conversation a number of specified requests such as "come over here" (if not already there), "come and play with me," "look at the jack-in-the-box," "put the book on the table," "give me the toy," etc. (2 minutes), then she put her arm around the child and played a physical game (1 minute), waited quietly and receptively for 1 minute, and finally, left the room.

An observer (who had observed the child many times before) recorded the child's social behavior during both the biased interaction and the approach sequence on a 10-second-interval form, including the following kinds of behavior to both stranger and mother: (1) looks, (2) vocalizes, (3) expresses positive affect (smiles, laughs), (4) expresses negative affect (frets, cries, avoids, frowns, hits), (5) plays socially with a toy, (6) goes to, (7) contacts physically (touches, holds, clings to), and (8) imitates. Behaviors were also qualified as "responsive" when they were clearly in response to the stranger's behavior (e.g., compliance with a request). The substance of children's speech was recorded in an abbreviated form, and in the laboratory the child's proximity to stranger and mother was recorded according to his or her location in squares marked on the floor.

Since the sample for this study was small, the results should be viewed as highly tentative. Our purpose here is not to establish the "facts" of social development, but to suggest and explore some more elaborate conceptualizations and assessments than have been applied to the study of children's reactions to strangers heretofore.

Variations in Strangers' Behavior

Affective Tone

Indirect affect: stranger's affective behavior to mother. The first experimental manipulation of stranger behavior, which occurred in the laboratory at 30 months, was the most indirect in terms of the stranger's actual behavior toward the child. It involved variation in the *tone* of the stranger's affective behavior to the mother and consisted of prescribed verbal exchanges between the two, during which the child was ignored as far as possible. We labeled the variation in this manipulation "stranger's mood." In each interaction condition, the stranger entered the room and sat in a chair next to the mother. There ensued one of three distinctly different interactions (order counterbalanced): (1) the silent "neutral stranger" ignored and was ignored by the mother as each looked out the window, at magazines, etc., for a 5-minute period—a typical waiting-room scene; (2) the "hostile stranger" stomped into the room and launched into an angry and insulting dialogue with the mother (both guided by a previously prepared and individually rehearsed script) about who had just stolen whose parking space—not a trivial issue in New Haven!—and about to whom the magazine the mother was reading belonged; (3) the "happy stranger" bounced into the room, delighted to have just won a trip to Bermuda and full of joy, compliments, and animated conversation; she and the mother shared the magazine. This biased mother-stranger interaction was followed by the approach sequence described.

The manipulation of stranger's "mood" was designed to explore children's sensitivity to the emotional tone of adult interaction and their reactions to the individuals who participated in such interchanges. As it turned out, only one kind of child behavior was significantly affected by the happy or hostile tone of the mother-stranger interaction (Table 1). There were no differences in any kinds of social behavior to the stranger (looking at, going to, smiling, playing, vocalizing) during either the biased interaction or the approach sequence which followed.[2] Children were equally interested in the happy and hostile interaction, equally willing to approach and play afterwards with the happy or hostile stranger. If anything, they were *more* willing to play with the hostile stranger. The only kind of behavior that was clearly different for happy and hostile mother-stranger interactions was the child's physical contact with the mother (touching, going to, staying close to the mother). Contrary to what one might predict on the basis of differential stranger anxiety, however, the child was in

Table 1
Differences in Children's Social Behavior Related to Stranger's Affective Behavior to Mother ("Mood")[a]

Child's Social Behavior	Mean Scores			F[e]
	To Neutral (Silent) Stranger	To Happy Stranger	To Hostile Stranger	
Looks at stranger[b]	9.57	15.66	15.43	10.18**
Looks at stranger[c]	19.29	18.20	17.86	0.83
Social interaction with stranger[b,f]	2.29	3.29	2.00	0.61
Social interaction with stranger[c]	17.15	13.93	18.29	1.54
Close proximity to stranger[d]	4.79	7.93	5.29	1.65
Negative affect[d]	2.36	2.86	2.93	0.07
Looks at, vocalizes to mother[b]	23.93	19.29	22.00	1.93
Looks at, vocalizes to mother[c]	18.50	18.50	14.86	0.75
Physical attachment to mother[b,g]	18.36	29.07	20.79	3.71*
Physical attachment to mother[c]	24.22	24.29	13.93	4.37*

Note: Physical contact with stranger did not occur sufficiently often in this situation to warrant analysis.
[a]Assessed in laboratory at 30 months.
[b]During biased stranger-mother interaction.
[c]During approach sequence with stranger.
[d]During entire visit.
[e]Analysis of variance for repeated measures; df 2, 26.
[f]Social interaction = sum (goes, positive affect, plays, vocalizes, responsive to stranger).
[g]Physical attachment to mother = sum (goes, physical contact, close proximity to mother).
*$p < .05$ **$p < .001$

physical contact with the mother *less* during and following her interaction with the hostile stranger and *more* during and following the happy interaction.

Since only the child's behavior toward the mother and not to the stranger was affected, a plausible interpretation of this finding might be that children were affected by the mother's mood rather than by the stranger's; our manipulation had, of course, created not just a happy or hostile stranger, but also a correspondingly happy or hostile mother. Informal observation suggested that what was happening in the situation was that when something pleasant, fun, and exciting was going on—in this case, between mother and stranger—the child wanted to be in on it. He or she came over to the mother and attempted to participate in the interaction or to get the mother's attention by staying close and holding on to the mother. When the mother was acting hostile, on the other hand, even though that hostility was directed at someone else, the child was more likely to stay away from her. Only one precociously articulate little girl stood up for her mother against the diatribe of the angry stranger—and that was from the discreet distance of the other side of the room, while she pretended to be playing with a toy. It may well be, as clinicians have suggested, that the emotional tone of interaction between parents affects children's behavior, or even that children are sensitive to adults' mood, but apparently they are not as likely to react to the mood of a transient stranger as they are to that of their mother.[3] If there was a reaction to the tone of the interaction, moreover, it had no apparent longlasting effect on preferential social behavior to the strangers, assessed immediately after the interaction or at the end of the visit some 20 minutes later, when the child was asked to play with, give a cookie to, and react to pictures of the three strangers.

Research on children's reactions to adults' affective behavior has generally focused on subjects who were either younger or older than the 2-year-olds in the present study. Research on infants demonstrates that by 6 months, or possibly as early as 3 months, infants can perceptually discriminate facial and vocal expressions of emotion (Kreutzer and Charlesworth, 1973; LaBarbera et al., 1976; Young-Browne, Rosenfeld, and Horowitz, 1977). But although this suggests that children are capable of discriminating the tone of adults' emotional behavior, mere perceptual discrimination is not the issue here. In fact, our gross behavioral measures did not reveal a difference in children's relative visual attention to happy and hostile strangers or to a happy or hostile mother (the basis for ascribing discrimination in the studies of infants). The same research on infants also claims that by 10 months, infants not only discriminate between different emotional expressions but respond with affect that parallels that of the stimulus (Kreutzer and Charlesworth, 1973). Our results also are not explainable in terms of reflection of affect; no difference in children's expression of positive or negative emotion was observed when they watched or interacted with happy or hostile strangers.

Research with older children (3 to 9 years) also demonstrates that children can discriminate and label emotional cues, at that age, in more complex tasks involving filtered speech (McCluskey et al., 1975), animated cartoons (Girgus and Wolf, 1975), photographs (Odom and Lemond, 1972), and films (Deutsch, 1974)—although their accuracy is not infallible. Accuracy is enhanced when more than one dimension (e.g., face, voice, and movement) varies (Girgus and Wolf, 1975) and when action and facial expression are congruent (Deutsch, 1974). These conditions of redundancy and congruency were met in the present manipulation, but, as we have mentioned, the issue of concern here is not accuracy of perception or labeling. The question is what determined the observed difference associated with happy or hostile emotional tone—the difference in proximity to mother.

Research assessing the social abilities of these older children has most often been concerned with the development of the skills of perspective-taking, role-taking, or empathy (Deutsch and Madle, 1975; Shantz 1975; Urberg and Docherty, 1976). This work suggests that children as young as 3 years old have some rudimentary form of perspective-taking (closely related to identification of appropriate emotions in various situations) (Borke, 1971; Urberg and Docherty, 1976). Perhaps the difference in children's behavior in the present manipulation of the adult's "mood" was related to this perspective-taking skill. It is not clear, however, that this is the case. These 2-year-old children did not express sympathy to mother in the face of hostile attack by a stranger, reject the hostile stranger on the mother's behalf, or retaliate with angry aggression toward her—responses which might be considered to show empathy for the mother. Nor is it likely that their responses were empathic to the stranger. What they seemed to be doing was reacting as if the mother's anger were directed *at them*, and avoiding her. Apparently they were aware of, perhaps even recognized, differences in the mood or emotional tone of adult interaction. But experience living with the mother and observing her angry expressions—directed at the child, his siblings, or his father—may have made the mother's emotional signals more recognizable than the stranger's, and, moreover, have led the child to expect a negative outcome *for him* from the mother's outburst. This explanation seems more reasonable than one that the child was "re-jecting" and avoiding the mother because he was taking the perspec-tive of the stranger.

Emotional mood cues are probably an important aspect of mother-child interaction; they do not, however, seem to be a central feature determining children's reactions to strangers. This conclusion is consistent with Lévy-Schoen's (1964) finding that although children under 8 years old could *recognize* emotional facial expressions, they did not *use* these cues to form impressions about people.

Direct affect: stranger's affective behavior to child. Our next attempt to examine effects of the affective tone of adults' behavior was one which involved direct interaction with the child. One to two weeks after the "mood" visit to the laboratory, two strangers came to visit the child at home. The positive stranger was "nice" to the child—she played with the child in a positive, pleasant, cooperative, and friendly way, with toys the child liked, for 7 minutes. The tone of the other [4] stranger's interaction with the child was negative—for several minutes the stranger played cooperatively, but then she accused the child of break-ing an already-broken toy, reprimanded the child no matter what he or she did, took the toys away, and acted unpleasant, unfriendly, in-sulting, selfish, and demanding for 3 minutes. This stranger was re-ferred to as the "nasty" stranger, and the dimension of affective tone to the child was labeled "stranger's manner." After her biased interac-tion, each stranger went through the standard approach sequence described.

This second variation in strangers' affective behavior was related to children's social behavior (Table 2). For no type of social behavior was the "nasty" stranger ever reacted to more positively than the "nice" stranger. Moreover, when 10-second observational intervals were classified according to the child's recorded behavior as being either predominantly positive: the child's behavior included only approach-ing, smiling, vocalizing responsively or positively (according to the content), playing, imitating, touching affectionately, or cooperating with the stranger; or predominantly negative; the child's behavior consisted of avoiding, aggressing, frowning, fretting, crying, or saying "no" or some other negative thing to the stranger, the difference was statistically significant. The nice stranger was responded to more posi-tively, the nasty stranger, more negatively. The difference in positive behavior occurred, moreover, not only during the interaction—which might be expected—but also, to a less significant extent, during the subsequènt approach sequence in which both "nice" and "nasty" strangers behaved identically. It appears that a stranger's affective tone during direct interaction with the child can have a marked effect on the child's positive or negative social behavior toward that person.

In contrast to the indirect "mood" manipulation, no effect of the stranger's direct affective "manner" was apparent in the child's behavior with the mother during or after the interaction with the stranger. Children behaved relatively more positively (to the nice stranger) or negatively (to the nasty stranger), but they did not involve their mothers differentially. The picture, once again, is not one of children frightened by the nasty stranger and running to mother. Behaviors directed to the mother were, in fact, quite infrequent during the stranger's visit in this home situation.

One other study with children has explicitly manipulated this variable of stranger "manner"; that one, in the context of examining the relative effectiveness of positive versus negative reinforcement.[5] Morris and Redd (1975) exposed 4-year-old children to adults who systematically praised them (like our "nice" stranger) or reprimanded them (like our "nasty" stranger) for their performance on a task. The results of that study were comparable to ours: after the experimental session children always preferred to play with the nice adult rather

Table 2
Differences in Children's Social Behavior Related to
Stranger's Affective Behavior to Child ("Manner")[a]

| Child's Social Behavior | Mean Scores | | F^b |
	To Nice Stranger	To Nasty Stranger	
Looks at stranger	31.14	31.00	0.00
Vocalizes to stranger	20.07	15.00	1.24
Positive affect to stranger	11.79	8.65	2.79
Plays with stranger	8.64	6.57	0.50
Goes to stranger	1.36	0.43	4.49†
Physical contact with stranger	3.93	4.36	0.01
Imitates stranger	0.86	0.57	0.67
Responsive to stranger	6.50	4.21	2.39
Positive social intervals	14.86	8.29	11.10**
Negative social intervals	1.36	3.93	7.78*
Positive social intervals only during biased interaction	12.86	8.08	3.24†
Looks at, vocalizes to mother	10.93	8.57	0.44
Physical attachment to mother[c]	6.93	5.43	0.25

[a]Assessed at home at 30 months.
[b]Analysis of variance for repeated measures; df 1, 13.
[c]Physical attachment to mother = sum (goes, physical contact with mother).
†$p < .10$
*$p < .05$
**$p < .01$

than the nasty one (although we found that measures of social behavior in a subsequent "approach sequence" were more sensitive indicators of children's preference than merely asking with whom they would most like to play). The results of both studies, moreover, are compatible with research on adults which demonstrates that subjects consistently like and prefer to interact with those whom they perceive as liking them (Jones, Gergen, and Davis, 1962; Raven and Rubin, 1976; Tagiuri, Blake, and Bruner, 1953). Clearly young children are sensitive to the affective behavior adults direct toward them, and their reactions when meeting and interacting with strangers are tempered by some of the same dimensions that affect adult interactions. Direct affective "manner" is one such dimension.

"Mode" of Behavior

The second dimension of strangers' behavior that was examined in the present study, in both the home and laboratory visits at 30 months, was the communicative "mode" of the stranger's behavior— that is, whether the stranger ignored, looked at, talked to, played with, or physically contacted the child. In previous research, strangers have tended to use some combination of behavioral modes in interacting with the children, and, unfortunately, analysis of data in these studies has seldom separated the effects of different modes (see Table 3). Even when modal comparisons have been made, the results are not as helpful as they might be because they are often given in terms of percentages of children rather than relative frequencies of children's behaviors (e.g., Rheingold and Eckerman, 1971, 1973). In the present study, different modes of stranger behavior were separated in the experimental manipulation and the statistical analysis[6] (Tables 4, 5). Of all the behavioral manipulations attempted in the study, this one most clearly, consistently, and significantly affected children's behavior.

Ignoring versus looking at the child. When the stranger ignored the child—that is, did not look at him or her—children, although they watched her, uniformly initiated little or no interaction with her (Table 4). Only one insensitive child vocalized to her. (This child, who seemed oblivious to the stranger's deliberate ignoring and unresponsiveness and persisted in vocalizing to her, was accustomed to such interaction. His mother spent most of her time at home watching TV, and only occasionally directed a comment to the child, while she continued to watch her programs.) When the stranger merely *looked* at the children, however, this behavior opened the lines of communica-

Table 3
Investigations of Various "Modes" of Stranger's Behavior

Investigation	Modes Assessed					Modes Compared
	Passive, silent, noninterventive stranger	Look, talk, and smile	Approach or close proximity	Pick up, touch, hold	Play or invite to play	
Belkin and Routh (1975)					X	
Bretherton (1974)	X	X	X		X	Ignore/Play
Brody and Axelrad (1971)	X					
Bronson (1972)			X	X		Approach/Pick up
Brookhart and Hock (1976)	X	X	X		X	
Brooks and Lewis (1976)	X	X	X	X		
Campos et al. (1975)			X			
Connolly and Smith (1972)	X	X				Ignore/Look-smile/Talk
Corter (1973)	X					
Eckerman (1973)	X	X				
Eckerman and Rheingold (1974)		X				
Eckerman and Whatley (1975)	X	X				
Fein (1975)	X					
Feldman (1975)	X	X	X		X	
Gordon et al. (1973)	X	X	X	X	X	Approach/Pick up Play
Goulet (1974)	X	X	X	X		
Klein and Durfee (1975)		X		X	X	
Lewis and Brooks (1974)	X		X	X		Approach/Touch
Lewis et al. (1975)	X					

Table 3
Investigations of Various "Modes" of Stranger's Behavior
(continued)

Investigation	Modes Assessed					Modes Compared
	Passive, silent, noninterventive stranger	Look, talk, and smile	Approach or close proximity	Pick up, touch, hold	Play or invite to play	
Maccoby and Feldman (1972)	X	X	X		X	
Main (1975)		X			X	
Marvin and Abramovitch (1973)	X	X	X		X	
Morgan (1973)	X	X	X	X	X	Hold/Play
Paradise and Curcio (1974)	X	X	X	X	X	
Rand and Jennings (1974)	X	X	X	X		Smile-talk/Pick up/Put down
Rheingold (1956)	X	X	X	X		
Rheingold and Eckerman (1971, 1973)	X			X	X	Ignore/Look/Pick up/Play
Ricciuti (1974)	X	X	X	X		
Roedell and Slaby (1977)	X	X		X	X	Ignore/Talk-Play/Hold-Rock
Ross (1975)	X	X				
Ross and Goldman (1977)	X	X			X	Look-smile/Smile-Talk-Play
Shaffran and Décarie (1973)	X	X	X	X		
Stevens (1971)	X	X	X		X	
Tautermannová (1973)	X	X				Look/Smile-talk
Tizard and Tizard (1971)	X	X		X	X	
Waters, Matas, and Sroufe (1975)	X	X	X	X		Talk/Approach/Pick up

tion between them. Then, children not only looked at the stranger, but also vocalized, smiled, and approached. The "eyes," it seems have it!

The most comparable examples of other research on this dimension of stranger behavior are provided by Connolly and Smith (1972) and Roedell and Slaby (1977). The first investigators found that 3½-year-old children in a nursery school setting were significantly more likely to approach, smile, and talk to an observer when he looked and smiled at them responsively than when he ignored them. The second investigators found that 3-month-old infants in the laboratory were significantly less likely to fuss and cry (to the point of terminating the session) when they encountered a stranger who interacted with them responsively rather than facing them but not making eye contact.

Table 4
Differences in Children's Social Behavior
Related to Stranger's Mode of Behavior

	Mean Scores				
	Stranger Behavior				
Child's Social Behavior	Ignores	Looks	Talks/Plays	Touches	F^d
Looks at stranger[a]	58.72	66.57	135.00		54.99***
Looks at stranger[b]		1.59	3.33	4.06	41.48***
Vocalizes to stranger[b]		0.67	2.36	2.08	49.19***
Positive affect to stranger[b]		0.34	1.29	3.26	55.59***
Plays with stranger[b]		0.40	1.44	0.29	20.45***
Goes to stranger[b]		0.09	0.06	0.12	0.88
Physical contact with stranger[b]		0.30	2.48	3.45	5.11*
Imitates stranger[b]		0.03	0.12	0.17	4.29*
Responsive to stranger[b]		0.10	2.08	3.36	26.53***
Social approach to stranger[a,c]	10.93	76.93	163.93		6.40**
Social approach to stranger[b,c]		1.49	4.64	5.73	66.39***
Negative affect[b]		0.02	0.03	0.34	2.87†
Looks at, vocalizes to mother[a]	246.14	100.93	56.07		19.67***
Looks at, vocalizes to mother[b]		1.08	0.68	0.58	1.37
Physical attachment to mother[a,e]	56.29	51.36	63.22		0.33
Physical attachment to mother[b,f]		0.93	1.00	0.43	1.37

[a]Assessed in laboratory at 30 months.
[b]Assessed in home at 30 months.
[c]Social approach = sum (goes, positive affect, plays, vocalizes to stranger).
[d]Analysis of variance for repeated measures; df 2, 26.
[e]Physical attachment = sum (physical contact with, goes to, close proximity to mother).
[f]Physical attachment = sum (physical contact with, goes to mother).
†$p < .10$
*$p < .05$
**$p < .01$
***$p < .001$

Connolly and Smith attributed their finding to the relative responsiveness of the observer in the two conditions; Roedell and Slaby might have concluded the same for their strangers. In the present study, however, in *both* conditions being compared (ignoring and looking) the stranger was unresponsive, yet the same social behaviors of the children that Connolly and Smith observed (approach, smile, vocalize) increased significantly when the stranger merely looked at the child and did not smile responsively. This suggests the importance of eye contact or visual attention as a key to social overtures and social interaction. It is not simply that visual attention leads to greater eye-to-eye contact (there was no increase in the amount of time the child looked at the stranger), but that it seems to signify that a person is "open" to social interaction, that he or she can be approached and talked to.

A study of 18-month-olds by Fein (1975) provides another instance of a stranger ignoring a child, this time by chatting with the mother. This situation is comparable to the first manipulation of stranger behavior described in the present study: the happy and hostile strangers ignored the child while chatting with the mother. Fein found that children did not talk to or go close to mother or stranger while the two were chatting, but instead played with their own toys. We also found (Table 1) that the child's interaction with the stranger was minimal during the biased stranger-mother interaction and, moreover, that there was no significant difference when the stranger chatted with mother and ignored the child (the happy and hostile interactions) as opposed to ignoring the child by reading a magazine or looking out the window (the silent, neutral stranger). These findings, too, support the contention that visual attention is a vital cue to potential social interaction.

Research on infants provides a useful background for understanding the significance of visual attention for social interaction. The importance of the distance receptors in establishing reciprocal mother-infant interaction was first pointed out by Walters and Parke (1965). Since then a number of studies have explored the specific details of that process. They, too, demonstrate that even in the early months of life the orientation of the mother's eyes and face is a critical aspect of social interaction. In one such study, Brazelton and his associates (1975; Adamson et al., 1975) observed the normal infant of blind parents. The mother, who had been blind only for the last few years and still oriented his face to the infant *even though he was not responsive to the baby's facial expressions*. A somewhat similar situation to the blind parents. The mother, who had been blind from birth, did not face or look at the baby during interaction; consequently, the infant came to avert her gaze from the mother. The baby did, however, look at the father, who had been blind only for the last few years and still oriented his face to the infant *even though he was not responsive to the baby's facial expressions.* A somewhat similar situation to the blind parents was artificially created in further work by this group (Tronick et al., 1975). Infants' mothers were instructed to look at their babies but to remain still-faced and unresponsive. By 7 weeks of age, when the mother *looked* at the infant, he or she "greeted her expectantly" and "made repeated attempts to get the interaction into its reciprocal pattern."

That typical or normal or expected reciprocal pattern has been analyzed in naturalistic observation of mother-infant interaction by Stern (1974). These observations suggest a *reason* that infants are likely to respond to their mother's looking with further social behavior. First, mothers themselves never vocalized or made faces at the infant without looking at him or her—and found it impossible to do so when asked—and second, the predictable consequence of the infant's gazing at mother was a rewarding and social response of exaggerated facial and vocal behaviors.

Research with infants has also explored infants' reactions to social stimuli outside of the mother-infant relationship. Of particular relevance for illustrating the importance of adults' looking are Watson's observation that infants smile more to a face stimulus when it is oriented at the same angle as the infant's face (1965), presumably because that is the position of the face associated with playful and responsive social interaction (1972); Bloom's (1975) finding that social stimulation by an adult—whether contingent on the infant's response or not—increases the infant's rate of vocalization only when the infant can see the adult's eyes; and Haith, Bergman, and Moore's (in press) observation that by 7 weeks infants presented with the image of a face fixate on the eyes (earlier, they look at the edges of the stimulus), *especially when the face is talking.* The latter investigators explicitly suggest that their finding is because "eyes have become meaningful signals of social interaction."

Taken as a whole these studies of infants provide strong support for the position that *looking* at the infant suggests to him or her that social interaction will follow. As Tronick et al. (1975) put it, entering the room and looking at the infant says "hello." The obverse might also be inferred: leaving or not looking says "goodbye," or at least, "I vant to be alone."

The study of the social psychology of adult interaction provides further corroboration for the view that looking is a significant cue in social interaction. Microanalysis of interaction between college students, for example, confirms empirically the importance of visual regard by demonstrating that the most common conversational states are "*A* looks and *B* talks" or "*B* looks and *A* talks." "*A* not looking" does not elicit conversation from *B* (Stokes and Dabbs, 1976). Similarly, in an experimental waiting-room situation, mutual eye contact upon entry was highly predictive of whether or not a pair of unacquainted college students would converse during the time they were waiting together (Cary, 1976). Tiryakian (1968) makes a parallel point about the phenomenological meaning of interaction signals:

> . . . facial gestures are of major importance in regulating the psychological distance between persons. Thus turning your back on someone or looking the other way symbolizes your wish not to face him, that is, your wish not to interact with him. . . . The very quality of social interaction, a gauge of intimacy, is indicated by the term face to face contact [p. 83].

Data from the present study suggest that children, too, operate according to these "rules" of social exchange, while research on infants provides a preliminary account of the acquisition of such understanding of reciprocal social participation in terms of infants' early reciprocal interactions with their mothers.

Active versus passive behavior toward the child. The second dimension implicit in investigations of the mode of strangers' behavior is that of relative "inter*activity*," that is, the difference between passively looking at the child and actively interacting with him. In the present study, with the stranger's active social overtures—smiling, talking, playing—the child's social behavior increased dramatically in all ways (Table 4). Children looked, smiled, vocalized, played, touched, imitated, and responded to the active stranger significantly more than they did to the stranger who merely looked at them. Looking at and vocalizing to the mother correspondingly decreased, particularly in the laboratory playroom. These differences in children's reactions to active and passive strangers were robust and highly significant: they occurred in two settings and were of a substantial order of magnitude (e.g., 16× for difference in social approach) and a high level of significance ($p < .001$).

Unfortunately, reports of other studies that have separated and examined modes of strangers' behavior do not always make clear whether their silent, noninterventive, "passive" strangers looked at the child or ignored him or her, thus confounding the dimension of activity with visual attention. Consequently, it is difficult to fit these studies into the present context contrasting passive visual regard with active talking and playing, and to get unequivocal corroboration for our findings. As far as can be determined from those studies, however, support for our results does exist. Tautermannová (1973) observed that infants as young as 2 or 3 months of age smiled longer at an active stranger who smiled and talked than at a passive one who merely looked. In the 8- to 12-month age range, three studies have compared the effects of the stranger's interactiveness. Rheingold and Eckerman (1971, 1973) observed that more children smiled at a stranger who played than at one who merely looked, but they observed no difference in the number of children who looked at or vocalized to each. It is difficult to use their results for confirmation or disconfirmation of ours, since they report only numbers of children not numbers of smiles—and nearly all their subjects did look at and vocalize to the strangers. Ross and Goldman's (1977) strangers' behavior and assessment procedures seem most similar to ours. They found that 1-year-olds spent more time near the active stranger, touched her and played with her more, and were less likely to fret or stay near the mother. These results are similar to ours, but 2-year-olds' reactions in this situation are apparently reflected less than 1-year-olds' by measures of physical proximity and negative affect. The third study of children of this age contrasting active and passive strangers (Bretherton, 1974) compared the effect of a stranger who initiated interaction by talking and playing, with one who was chatting with mother but who was responsive to the child's advances. Like our subjects, these children looked at and played with the active stranger more, but no difference in smiling or vocalizing was observed. The difference between studies here may be procedural (their passive strangers were responsive) or may possibly reflect real differences of increasing sensitivity to social cues and selectivity in use of social skills and participation in social interaction. One-year-olds may vocalize to a noninterventive adult as much as to an active one, while 2½-year-olds may be more likely to save their vocalization—which by this age is real speech—for conversation initiated by the partner. (We are making the assumption here that the passive stranger in the Bretherton study, although chatting with the mother and relatively passive with regard to interaction with the child, was at least looking at and not deliberately ignoring the child.)

One final study that examines variation in this aspect of the mode of strangers' behavior is the Connolly and Smith (1972) study of children in nursery school. These investigators observed more approaching, smiling, and talking to an observer who talked briefly than to one who merely looked and smiled, although the last two differences did not reach statistical significance. It seems likely that the reason our effects were more striking and significant was that the active stranger in the present study did more than "talk briefly"; she engaged in sustained playful interaction.

The results of all these studies make it impossible to deny that children, like the rest of us, are more sociable and interactive when their partners are—even when that partner is a stranger. The next question that might be asked, then, is whether various specific modes of stranger activity have differential effects on children's behavior.

Talking and playing. To explore this question in the present study, strangers' behavior was further divided into particular modes of activity: talking to the child, playing with a toy, and talking and playing with the toy. No attempt was made to control the strangers' smiling; they all behaved in a pleasant, friendly way during the interactions with the child. Table 5 presents the results of this analysis. Differences between stranger talk, play, and talk-play conditions were situationally logical: there was more play involving objects in the play conditions, more vocalizing in the stranger talk conditions. Most interesting, however, there was no difference in children's positive affect or visual attention associated with these variations in strangers' behavior. Any mode of distal social interaction appears to be equally attractive to children of this age.

Distal versus proximal interaction. The most common investigation of modes of interaction between children and adult strangers has been to compare strangers' distal social behavior with proximal interaction (particularly touching, picking up, and carrying). The evidence from

Table 5
Differences in Children's Social Behavior
Related to Stranger's Mode of Interaction

| | Mean Scores | | | |
| | Stranger Behavior | | | |
Child's Social Behavior	Talks	Plays	Talks and Plays	F^b
Looks at stranger	11.0	9.1	11.0	0.33
Vocalizes to stranger	10.6	6.3	8.0	3.50*
Positive affect to stranger	4.0	4.1	3.9	0.09
Plays with stranger	2.4	6.1	6.7	10.03**

[a]Assessed at home at 30 months.
[b]Analysis of variance for repeated measures; df 2, 26.
*$p < .05$
**$p < .001$

these investigations seems clear: physical contact with a stranger leads to greater wariness or more negative reaction when compared with the behavior of a stranger who looks at, talks to, or plays distally with the child (Ainsworth, 1973; Bronson, 1972; Campos et al. 1975; Gordon et al., 1973; Goulet, 1974; Lewis and Brooks, 1975; Morgan, 1973; Rand and Jennings, 1974; Roedell and Slaby, 1977; Waters, Matas, and Sroufe, 1975), at ages ranging from 3 to 19 months.

Since it did not seem appropriate to "pick up" a 2-year-old in the present study to investigate the effect of physical contact, strangers were instructed to put their arm around the child, take him or her on their lap if the child was willing, cuddle him or her, and engage him or her in a physical game of this-little-piggy, horsie, or tickly. The comparison of this mode of interaction with stranger talk-play is presented in Table 4.

With 2½-year-olds, as well as infants, there was a tendency ($p <$ .10) for more negative affect to be expressed during physical contact with the stranger than when the stranger interacted distally. It does not follow, however, that the children simply reacted with fear to physical contact with an unfamiliar adult. In the first place, the term "fear" is too strong; in the present study no concomitant increase in contacting or appealing to the mother was observed during the physical play episodes—behaviors that one might expect from frightened children. Second, in other studies as well as this one, negative affect is not *inevitably* observed when the stranger initiates physical contact with the child. In Rheingold and Eckerman's (1971, 1973) study, for example, only 4 out of 24 children protested being picked up by the stranger, and in the present study, only 5 out of 14 expressed any negative affect in this situation of friendly physical play—and that negative affect was not severe or prolonged. What is more, children showed heightened *positive* affect as well as negative during physical interaction. In fact, the positive affect score for every child in the sample and the overall amount of positive social behavior (goes, smiles, plays, vocalizes, touches affectionately) for the group was greatest during physical interaction of any interactive mode displayed by the stranger. Even the five children who did display negative affect during physical play with the stranger displayed more positive affect during those episodes than they did when the stranger merely looked, talked, or played with a toy.

It has been suggested by Sroufe, Waters, and Matas (1974) that the *magnitude* of positive or negative affect displayed in the presence of a stranger is a function of, among other things, the "salience" of the stranger stimulus. Clearly, close physical contact is the ultimate in salience of any social stimulation. This might account for the heightened affect during physical interaction. Sroufe et al. also suggest, however, that the direction of affect, positive or negative, is determined by the child's "evaluation" of the stranger's behavior, thus implying that children will express *either* positive *or* negative affect. In the present study, they displayed both. These results parallel those of Bretherton (1974) who observed that 1-year-olds faced with a stranger showed various combinations of positive and negative social behaviors, either in succession (crying then smiling) or simultaneously (coy gaze aversion). She, like Eibl-Eibesfeldt (1970), suggests that a stranger activates in most infants two conflicting tendencies—approach and avoidance—and that the infants' behavior is a result of a careful balance between affiliation and wariness, friendliness and fear.

The important question, then, is, what tips the balance toward one side or the other. It may be inferred from the substantial number of studies showing increased wariness when the stranger approaches and picks up the infant that physical contact is the key. Having examined positive as well as negative social behaviors in this situation, we suggest that there is more to it than simply physical contact. Other studies also suggest that it is not physical proximity or physical contact per se that elicits increased negative reactions. A close noncontact game did not lead to negative behavior (Morgan, 1973), and negative affect was equivalent whether the stranger was holding the child or had put the child down after holding him or her (Rand and Jennings, 1974). An alternative explanation for the prevalence of negative or wary reactions observed in the set of studies reviewed here involves not the mode of stranger behavior, but the *style*. This was the final variation in strangers' behavior investigated in the present study.

"Style" of Behavior

The term "style" has not commonly been applied in the study of social interaction. It is a word with a myriad of meanings, a complexity of components, an abundance of elements—but one which may offer valuable ways of conceptualizing and categorizing the behavior of "strangers" in investigations of children's social behavior. It suggests analyses that go beyond the traditional view of stranger *qua* stranger, and further, beyond evaluations of separate modes of strangers' behavior. Since it is a new and unexplored term, these suggestions are, of course, highly tentative.

One element of strangers' style, especially relevant for further analysis of the implications of physical contact with the stranger, is "vigor." Weisberg (1975) asked strangers to be "cuddlers" or "ticklers" (arousal reducing or arousal inducing), and found that 3-year-old children preferred the cuddler, but their preference for the tickler increased as they got older. This example of research that probes more deeply into specific aspects of behavior under the rubric of "physical contact" illustrates the kind of manipulation that has been lacking in most studies of children's reactions to strangers, and that is being recommended here.

Another element of "style" might be the stranger's "playfulness"—an aspect of the stranger's behavior suggested by Bretherton (1974) to be the appealing feature for children of social interaction with a stranger. Whether the stranger approaches the child quickly or gradually—her "pace" or "tempo"—is another element of style, and evidence suggests that children do differentiate among variations on this dimension, responding more positively to a slower style of approach (cf. Ainsworth, 1973; Ricciuti, 1974; Ross and Goldman, 1977).

Another description of style might focus on its "naturalness." It has been suggested recently that children respond negatively not to the stranger per se but to her "strange" behavior (Cairns, 1977; Haith and Campos, 1977; Morgan, 1973). The effort to simplify and standardize experimental procedures involving strangers has led, it seems, to peculiar, unnatural distortions of adult behavior into artificially simple and arbitrarily stepwise sequences. The unnaturalness of this behavior has been illuminated by Shaffran's (1974) observation that "real people" in an effort to make friends with a baby do not interrupt their approach, pause between activities or isolate their behaviors, use stereotyped sentences ("Hello, baby"), or ignore the child's mother; nor do they limit themselves to a standard period of 1 to 3 minutes of interaction—all behavior patterns common to experimental "stranger" manipulations. Normal, natural, friendly adult behavior toward an unfamiliar child apparently follows a style that is more complex and integrated than that of the adults to whom children have been exposed in empirical investigations.

Observation of the spontaneous interaction of mothers with their infants likewise presents a picture of complex and integrated adult behavior; maternal looking, vocalizing, and making faces at the infant never occur separately (Stern, 1974). Moreover, it has been found that when strangers act like the infant's mother, either naturally (Monahan, 1975), or after training (Rafman, 1974), duplicating her idiosyncratic and complex style of playful interaction, they are less likely to elicit negative reactions from the infant.

The "standardized" stranger sequence, in addition to artificially simplifying behavior, is also characterized by its lack of responsiveness to the child's communicative signals and expressions. Regulatory cues by which people usually control the social stimulation in their environments are ignored by the strange adult automation, who bears down on the child irrespective of his or her attempts to terminate or delay interaction. Other research amply demonstrates that control over stimulation is an important aspect of infants' interactions with mother (Ainsworth, 1973; Clarke-Stewart, 1973; Tronick et al., 1975), with peers (Ross and Goldman, 1977), and even with inanimate objects like toys and mobiles (Gunnar-von Gnechten, 1977; Watson, 1972; Yarrow, Rubenstein, and Pedersen, 1975). The responsiveness of the "partner" in these interactions affects both the infant's immediate affective response and subsequent development. It seems highly plausible that at least some of the negative reactions of infants to strangers are due to the stranger's unnatural and unresponsive style—as a result of its unusualness or its uncontrollability. Some of the infant's "negative" reactions may even be investigators' misinterpretations of behavior that represents the infant's attempt to control the stranger's behavior (e.g., stare, gaze aversion, fret), not the fear or anxiety that has been inferred. Children who are old enough to talk, anecdotes suggest, do try to modify the approach of a "standardized" stranger (Haviland and Lewis, 1975).

The extent to which standardized sequences are followed by strangers in studies of infants' social behavior does seem to be related to the infants' observed behavior. Studies can be divided into three groups according to the flexibility accorded the stranger in the experimental situation. One group has used a strictly standardized, scripted, stepwise procedure, rigorously timed and flawlessly executed: the stranger's behavior and timing are rigidly patterned; she must ignore the infant's signals and not pace her approach or modify her behavior whatever the infant's expression or reaction (Bronson, 1972; Brooks and Lewis, 1976; Gordon et al., 1973; Goulet, 1974; Lewis and Brooks, 1974; Morgan, 1973; Paradise and Curcio, 1974; Rand and Jennings, 1974; Rheingold, 1956; Ricciuti, 1974; Scarr and Salapatek, 1970; Schaffer, 1966; Sroufe, Waters and Matas, 1974; Waters, Matas, and Sroufe, 1975). These studies emphasize infants' negative reactions to strangers. Strangers in a second group of studies, at the opposite end of this continuum, did not follow a standardized sequence; rather, in a free-play situation, they let the infant initiate the approach and then they responded appropriately (Belkin and Routh, 1975; Bretherton, 1974; Connolly and Smith, 1972; Klein and Durfee, 1975; Lewis et al., 1975; Rheingold and

Eckerman, 1971, 1973; Ross, 1975; Ross and Goldman, 1977). These studies demonstrate children's positive reactions to strangers, and their investigators suggest that when the infant is allowed to make the advances, fear disappears. The strangers in a third group of studies achieved a middle ground: within a standard *time* schedule they invited the infant to approach, play, or sit on their lap, rather than imposing interaction on the child (Ainsworth and Bell, 1970; Ainsworth, Bell, and Stayton, 1969; Bretherton, 1974; Brookhart and Hock, 1976; Feldman, 1975; Maccoby and Feldman, 1972; Main, 1975; Stevens, 1971). Reports of these last studies have described both positive and negative reactions of children to strangers.

The procedures in the present study, by design, included the positive aspects of both the latter two groups of studies: frequent opportunities for the child to approach the stranger in free play and for the stranger to behave naturally and responsively, but also standard sequences of specific invitations and instructions to the child. Like these other investigators, we too observed that when strangers acted like "real people" there were only a small number of instances of negative behavior. All our children approached the stranger when invited—if not before—and their behavior was predominantly, though not exclusively, positive and sociable (see, for example, Table 2 for children's behavior to the "nice" stranger).

But the quality of a stranger's responsiveness is not only dictated by the use of a "free" versus a "standardized" procedure. A stranger can intrude uninvited into the child's space and initiate an encounter with or without a standardized script or schedule to follow. Such lack of sensitive responsiveness has been cited as a reason for children's negative reactions to and even withdrawal from strangers (Bronson, 1972; Morgan, 1973), mothers (Ainsworth, Bell, and Stayton, 1969; Tronick et al., 1975), and other caregivers (Robertson and Robertson, 1972). In the present study, as we have mentioned, negative behavior to the stranger was relatively infrequent and of minor concern. To go beyond the assessment of negative behavior, therefore, the effect of the stranger's responsiveness was investigated within the context of positive playful interaction.[7] The stranger was either "stimulating" with a toy: she initiated play and suggested particular activities without regard for the child's interests, preference, or responses; or she was "responsive": she did not make suggestions, but solicited and responded to the child's ideas for play activities. Two strangers played with each child in each of these two styles for 2 minutes. (The order of styles and strangers was counterbalanced.) Children's social behavior toward the stranger in the two different situations of interaction with a stimulating or responsive stranger did not differ in overall amount (Table 6), but when it was later coded into categories of initiating versus responsive, a 2 × 2 analysis of variance (Table 7) for the two kinds of behavior showed that the interaction of child's and stranger's styles was significant. That is, when the stranger was stimulating, the child behaved responsively; when the stranger was responsive, the child took more initiative in the playful interaction.

This finding supports Rheingold and Eckerman's (1975) proposition that infants not only respond to people but also initiate interaction with them. Both initiating and responding are essential parts of social interaction, and children are clearly active as well as reactive participants. Moreover, it suggests that children not only initiate and

Table 6
Differences in Children's Social Behavior
Related to Stranger's Play Style[a]

Child's Social Behavior	Mean Scores		F[b]
	Stranger's Play Style		
	Stimulating	Responsive	
Looks at stranger	16.93	16.29	0.39
Vocalizes to stranger	10.93	11.07	0.07
Positive affect to stranger	5.86	6.57	0.74
Plays toy with stranger	6.93	8.14	0.74
Negative affect, avoids stranger	0.29	0.14	0.62
Goes to stranger	0.36	0.14	1.15
Physical contact with stranger	2.36	2.71	1.16

[a]Assessed at home at 30 months.
[b]Analysis of variance for repeated measures; df 1, 13.
$p < .10$ ($F = 1.77$)

Table 7
Differences in Children's Initiative and Responsiveness
Related to Stranger's Play Style[a]

Child's Social Behavior	Mean Scores		F[b] Stranger Style	F Child Behavior	F S Style x C Behavior
	Stranger's Play Style				
	Stimulating, Initiating	Responsive			
Initiating	8.29	12.21	0.43	0.01	9.93*
Responsive	11.79	9.14			

[a]Assessed at home at 30 months.
[b]Analysis of variance for repeated measures; df 1, 26.
*$p < .01$

respond to social activity, but they do so systematically and appropriately. Their behavior paralleled that of the adult subjects in an experiment by Davis (1962). Those adults who were informed beforehand that their partner in a cooperative task was a dominant kind of person behaved submissively during the task (talked less, did not speak first, reacted rather than suggesting), while those prepared for a submissive partner took the initiative in the interaction. In the present manipulation, although we had deliberately biased the stranger's behavior, we, of course, gave no similar instructions to the child. Yet in the interaction the child behaved in a style that was complementary to the stranger's. The responsive/initiating style of the partner seems to be another behavioral dimension or cue to which 2-year-old children are sensitive.

Other research with children has also looked at the effect of positive responsiveness—from a stranger (Connolly and Smith, 1972; Eckerman, 1973; Eckerman and Rheingold, 1974, Roedell and Slaby, 1977) or the mother (Tronick et al., 1975)—and demonstrated that more positive social behavior on the part of infants and young children is associated with a responsive adult style. These studies, however, have confounded style (responsiveness) with mode (interaction) by comparing the effect of a responsive adult with that of a silent, noninteractive adult. The Tronick et al. study, moreover, confounds responsiveness (mother's still face) with incongruity (still-faced mother is an unusual event). Of interest in the latter study, it should be noted, was the finding that an unsuccessful attempt by the infant to initiate interaction with the mother preceded sobering or wariness (response to unusual or unresponsive event) and several further futile attempts to initiate interaction, before the infant evidenced withdrawal (response to repeated unresponsiveness or frustration). One rule for social interaction seems to be that, given the "opener" of visual regard, one should respond to an advance from the partner, but if no advance is made, initiate something. This "rule" is apparently part of the repertoire of very young children and guides their interaction not only with practiced partners like the mother but with unfamiliar ones like a stranger.

Richards (1974) has suggested that there are three channels of communication used in social interaction: faces, speechlike sounds, and temporal alternating sequences of actions. In the present study we have seen evidence that very young children use and are sensitive to even subtle variations in all three of these channels. From this evidence, preliminary and tentative as it is, it seems obvious that children's behavior with strangers is more complex and "mature" than has been previously realized or at least adequately studied. Children seem to be functioning at a level of sophistication that exceeds the methodology of their investigators. Further study of children's social interaction is needed, but the kind of study called for is one that will apply more complex and sophisticated methods and analyses to the problem.

Variations in Strangers' Characteristics

Most studies on the subject of children's reactions to strangers— when they have gone beyond the notion of stranger solely *qua* stranger—have looked at strangers in terms of variation in what are classified in our conceptual framework as stranger "characteristics"—those relatively long-term features like age, sex, appearance, or history that the stranger brings to the experimental situation. Gewirtz (1972) makes an important point with respect to the study of attachment and dependency when he admonishes investigators to identify whether the phenomena of attachment and play are evoked by *physical* or *behavioral* aspects of interaction. His point may be even more critical for investigations of children's social behavior with strangers. Difficult as it may be to separate physical or classificatory characteristics of strangers from their behavior, it is essential to further our understanding of the processes of social interaction. The tendency in previous research has been to attribute strangers' effects solely to obvious physical characteristics and to ignore the stranger's behavior. It is our contention that many reactions of children to strangers that are currently viewed as related to the physical characteristics of the stranger are in fact behaviorally induced. In this section we will support that contention with reference to several of the currently popular variations in stranger characteristics.

Sex of Stranger

From an early age infants can discriminate between male and female adults (Brooks-Gunn and Lewis, 1975; Zelazo, 1971). When men and women act as strangers in experimental sessions, however, and the issue is more than simple discrimination, differences in children's reactions are not always observed. In studies at ages from 1 to 24 months, no difference was observed by Brooks and Lewis (1976), Cohen and Campos (1974), Goulet (1974), Lord, Lewis, and Brooks (1975), and Ross (1975). Yet in other studies, spanning the age range from 4 months to 3 years, children have been observed to behave differently, reacting more negatively to men (Belkin and Routh, 1975; Décarie, 1974; Lewis and Brooks, 1974; Shaffran and Décarie, 1973; Skarin, 1977), or more positively to women (Greenberg, Hillman, and Grice, 1973, Morgan, 1973; Morgan and Ricciuti, 1969; Weisberg, 1975).

The present study also included an investigation of sex-of-stranger effects at 17 to 18 months. To counteract a methodological problem encountered in many other studies of stranger's sex (e.g., Belkin and Routh, 1975; Goulet, 1974; Lewis and Brooks, 1974; Morgan, 1973; Shaffran, 1974), our investigation involved more than a single stranger of each sex, thus unconfounding individual and sex differences. Six men and five women served as strangers. Each child was visited at home by one male and one female stranger (order counterbalanced) at two visits approximately 3 weeks apart. The stranger spent about 20 minutes with the child in a prearranged sequence of activities like the approach sequence previously described, which allowed considerable latitude in the style of talking and playing. The results of this investigation (Table 8) are consistent with those of research showing more avoidance and negative affect to the male stranger (tendency of $p < .10$) and more positive social behavior to the female (for vocalization $p < .05$). In addition, this study examined and revealed differences in children's behavior to the mother in the stranger's presence. Children vocalized more to their mother when the stranger was a women, and smiled more at her when the stranger was a man.

One explanation for the differences observed in children's reactions to male and female strangers has been that they are related to children's relative familiarity with men and women. Children feel and act more positive and less anxious toward women because of their more frequent interaction with the mother, female babysitter, or the mother's female friends. However, the *pattern* of specific differences in children's behavior to male and female strangers—going beyond merely positive versus negative behavior—is not the same as the pattern of differences in children's behavior to mother versus stranger or to a familiar observer versus a stranger (Clarke-Stewart, 1975). Moreover, the fact that when the stranger was a man children smiled more —even though it was directed at their mother—makes an explanation based on simple stranger anxiety implausible. Another explanation, in keeping with the previously mentioned emphasis on strangers' physical characteristics, has been to attribute differential effects of male and female strangers to their relative size (Brooks and Lewis, 1976;

Table 8
Differences in Children's Social Behavior
to Female and Male Strangers[a]

| Child's Social Behavior | Mean Scores | | F[b] |
	To Female Stranger	To Male Stranger	
Looks at stranger	10.79	10.57	0.17
Vocalizes to stranger	5.22	2.93	4.69*
Positive affect to stranger	20.22	20.50	0.01
Negative affect, avoids stranger	12.86	18.93	3.24†
Physical contact with stranger	5.79	5.15	0.40
Initiates social behavior to stranger	11.19	9.82	0.15
Responsive social behavior to stranger	29.79	26.64	1.20
Looks at mother	14.17	13.72	0.31
Vocalizes to mother	7.50	4.91	10.41**
Positive affect to mother	7.55	10.62	5.67*
Physical contact with mother	34.88	35.25	0.02

[a]Assessed at home at 17/18 months.
[b]Analysis of variance for repeated measures; df 1, 13.
†$p < .10$
*$p < .05$
**$p < .01$

Lewis and Brooks, 1974). Differences in children's reactions have also been observed, however, when male and female strangers were of comparable heights (Skarin, 1977). Results of the research on sex of stranger are perhaps most consistent with a third explanation, based on differences in male and female strangers' *behavior*.

An exploration of the behavioral aspects of sex-or-stranger studies reveals the following facts. Differences in children's reactions to strangers have not been observed when the experimental situation most rigidly constrained the stranger's behavior (e.g., Cohen and Campos's [1974] and Ross's [1975] noninterventive strangers or Lord, Lewis and Brooks's [1975] photographs of strangers). Differences have been observed when the strangers' activity included free play (Belkin and Routh, 1975; the present study) or "natural conversation" (Shaffran and Décarie, 1973; the present study). When the stranger went through a "standardized sequence" results have been mixed. Greenberg, Hillman, and Grice (1973), Skarin (1977), and Morgan and Ricciuti (1969) observed differences; Lewis and Brooks's (1974) difference was not significant; and Goulet (1974) observed no differences.

What this seems to suggest is that the more strangers are allowed to behave "naturally" and to interact freely with the children, the greater are the differences in children's reactions. The differences may, indeed, be related to familiarity—but to the stranger's familiarity with children rather than the children's familiarity with strangers. Although all of the strangers in our study had taken courses in child development, it is likely that the female strangers had had more actual and relevant experience—i.e., familiarity—with young children, since they were currently working as observers and home visitors in other parts of the research project. The trend of men's and women's differential familiarity with children, however, goes beyond the experiences of the particular strangers in our study. In American society the socialization of males and females is biased toward providing girls, and later women, with more frequent and acceptable opportunities for nurturant contact with infants and young children. One recent study (Frisch, 1976) illustrates differences between men's and women's spontaneously adopted play styles that seem to reflect this differential experience. With unfamiliar young children, women selected and played with female-stereotyped toys (doll, mirror, puppet, etc.), were more nurturant and responsive to the children's distress and vocalization, talked to the children more, and used more praise. Men, in the same free-play situation with the same children, chose "masculine" toys (ball, tricycle, etc.) and stimulated children's physical activity.

If strangers are allowed to behave naturally in the strange situation and do tend to follow these different patterns of behavior, it is not surprising that children's reactions to them are different, too. The observation that children respond more positively to female strangers can be accounted for as a response to a "feminine" style of interaction that is more nurturant, positive, and responsive. Children's negative reaction to male strangers might be partially attributed to the "masculine" play style of those strangers. Weisberg (1975), who manipulated the behavior of the stranger as well as looking at the sex of the stranger, could not get many 2-year-old girls in his study to participate in a play session with a male stranger—but particularly with a male stranger who tickled rather than cuddled the child. Tickling is a play style that stimulates activity—a masculine play trait; cuddling is a nurturant—feminine—behavior. The difference observed in men's and women's spontaneous verbalness with young children, moreover, might predictably be reflected by our finding that children vocalized more (to stranger and mother) when the stranger was a woman (a finding supported by Belkin and Routh's [1975] observation that 3-year-olds talked more to a female stranger).[8]

Undoubtedly, children's reactions to strangers are multiply determined, and most likely the more cues there are to differences
between strangers—size, tone of voice, interactive style, etc.—the
greater will be the differences observed in children's reactions. Unfortunately, studies so far have confounded various aspects of "strangerness," particularly by allowing subtle behavioral differences to occur
without recognition. Behavioral differences are especially important
in studies of the effects of strangers' sex. This is borne out by
Morgan's (1973) observation that children's responses to male and
female strangers doing the same thing were more similar than their
reactions to the same stranger doing different things.

Physical Appearance of Stranger

Considering the attention given to explanations of children's reactions to strangers based on strangers' physical attributes, it is perhaps
surprising that so little attention—beyond perceptual research on infants (e.g., Fantz, 1965; Kagan et al., 1966)—has been paid to specific
features of the stranger's physical appearance. One deliberate attempt to manipulate appearance explored the implications of the
specific feature of strangers' size (Brooks and Lewis, 1976), by comparing children's reactions to normal adults and a midget. They
found that in a standardized approach sequence the only effect at-
tributable to size was a difference in looking and orientation to the
stranger. In the present study data from the 30-month visit at home
were also analyzed in terms of the effect of *individual* strangers of the
same age, sex, and race, who had had approximately the same
amount of experience with children. The two strangers were a
moderately tall blond woman who wore glasses and a very tall
brunette without glasses. No significant differences in children's behavior with the two strangers were found (Table 9), confirming the
evidence of other studies that have compared individual, categorically
equivalent strangers (e.g., Bretherton, 1974; Corter, 1973). However,
the interesting thing is that the largest difference recorded in the
present study was in the amount the children *looked* at the two women
($p < .12$). On an appropriately less significant level, this parallels
Brooks and Lewis's finding for a much larger discrepancy in physical
appearance. The point to be made is that differential looking or
orientation seems to be the relevant response for children to make to
differences in physical appearance, and the appropriate level of assessment for research investigating physical characteristics. Had the
differences observed for children's behavior to male and female

Table 9
Differences in Children's Social Behavior
to Individual Strangers[a]

Child's Social Behavior	Mean Scores		F[b]
	To Stranger "A"	To Stranger "B"	
Looks at stranger	43.07	52.29	3.01
Vocalizes to stranger	32.71	23.64	2.40
Positive affect to stranger	14.57	18.29	1.31
Plays with stranger	19.36	12.36	1.98
Negative affect	1.71	0.79	2.09
Goes to stranger	1.21	1.07	0.06
Physical contact with stranger	9.29	4.93	0.38
Responsive, imitates stranger	12.64	16.43	1.00
Looks at, vocalizes to mother	10.14	9.36	0.05
Physical attachment to mother	8.21	8.29	0.00

[a]Assessed at home at 30 months.
[b]Analysis of variance for repeated measures; df 1, 13.
†$p < .10$

strangers involved differential looking, one might be more convinced that for children the major feature of difference between men and women is physical. Visual attention, however, was not among the differences reported in studies of stranger's sex. With respect to the interpretation of differential reactions to strangers, one might also make the point that caution should be exercised in going from the observation of looking behavior to an inference of preference. We cannot conclude from our results that children—or gentlemen—*prefer* blondes, but only that they look at them more. While that may be important to blondes, it should not be all that concerns psychologists!

Age of Stranger

Lewis (Brooks and Lewis, 1976; Lewis and Brooks, 1974, 1976) claims that children's social development is based on their ability to discriminate classes of people—classes like sex and age (child/adult). He supports this position by evidence that infants can, from an early age, discriminate, recognize, and later label variations within such classes (Brooks-Gunn and Lewis, 1975; Shatz and Gelman, 1973). Following this classification theme further, he cites data which suggest that children are more sociable to other children than they are to adults (Brooks and Lewis, 1976; Greenberg, Hillman, and Grice, 1973; Lewis and Brooks, 1974; Lewis et al., 1975). Such evidence leads him to conclude: "It is clear that among strangers, adults are almost never preferred, whereas peers are almost always positively received" (Lewis et al., 1975, p. 57). He then looks for explanations for this conclusion in the same realm that he used to account for sex-of-stranger effects. He suggests that the relevant differentiating criteria between adult and child strangers, like that between male and female strangers, are physical: specifically, size and facial configuration. He offers empirical "support" for this position from his study showing that children's reactions to a midget stranger contain elements in common with their reactions to both a child stranger (same height) and an adult stranger (same facial configuration) (Brooks and Lewis, 1976).

Like gender, however, age is not simply a class but a determinant of specific kinds of behavior. Unfortunately for explanations of age-of-stranger effects, the methods used by investigators of this dimension, too, have not always separated physical from behavioral aspects. In the Lewis et al. study (1975) children were observed to be more sociable to peer than to adult strangers (peer strangers received smiles, close proximity, looking, playing with a toy; adult strangers were ignored). Adult strangers, however, were instructed to be noninterventive; child strangers (who were also subjects), clearly, were not. Quite obviously the conclusion that children inevitably prefer peers is premature, if not incorrect. Children may just prefer action to passivity. There may also be a time limit on the peer preference observed; children may be more interested initially in exploring and interacting with another child, but may soon tire of the challenge such interaction entails.

Supporting the notion that children differentiate according to stranger's age on a finer level than is implied by the classes child/adult, it has also been reported that children, at least by 3½ years, interact in qualitatively different ways with unfamiliar children of different ages, adjusting their conversational level and style according to the age of the listener (Shatz and Gelman, 1973). These authors suggest that this adjustment reflects a simple form of perspective-taking by which children take into account a number of factors about their listeners, including linguistic ability, cognitive level, attentional capacity, status, and size. It is not yet clear, however, *which* factors children consider. Size may be relevant, but data have not been analyzed to test this hypothesis. It seems unlikely that children would modify their behavior solely on the basis of size in this situation any more than in those previously discussed. To explore the issue, one might use retarded children or adults as strangers in an effort to separate linguistic and cognitive ability from size. But it should be cautioned that retarded strangers, like midgets, are atypical stimuli and thus confound size with familiarity. Other characteristics of the listening partner are more likely than size to account for children's differential language. Garvey and BenDebba (1974) offer evidence from a study of same-age pairs of children suggesting that children's language adjustment is not a function of the partner's linguistic ability (words per utterance) or, one might infer, of their cognitive ability. Other aspects of the partner's behavior, however, may affect the child's conversation. The presence or absence of a response—regardless of its linguistic complexity—may be one such behavior. Indeed, Garvey and Ben-Debba did find that children adjusted the *number* of their utterances to approximate that of the partner. Since we know that children's contingent reinforcement can "shape up" adult behavior (e.g., Yarrow, Waxler, and Scott, 1971), it is not unlikely that this mechanism is involved in the interpersonal conversational adaptation observed here. This finding indicates the probable importance of some kind of feedback system between child and partner. It fits with our previous discussion of complementary initiation and response as a basic rule of social interchange, showing in yet another way the importance of interactional (in this case, conversational) turn-taking. Furthermore, it clearly points up the need in future research on children's social development for considering child and stranger as an interactive unit rather than stranger as stimulus, child as responder.

"Familiarity" of Stranger

A final illustration of how behavioral aspects may confound the study of stranger characteristics involves what has been termed the "familiarity" of the stranger. The definition of "familiarity" in the context of children's social development is exceedingly complex. Here, we are restricting our usage to mean the familiarity of the particular individuals to each other (rather than familiarity with the situation or with other similar people). Most investigators who have explored the subject of interpersonal familiarity have considered it as a characteristic of the *stranger* (e.g., Ross, 1975). Actually, as treated in these investigations, it could more accurately be considered a characteristic of the *child* (that is, a function of the child's experience prior to or during the experimental session, which in our conceptual framework falls in the "child characteristics" column). Familiarity *can be* a stranger characteristic in another way, however—that is, as a function of the stranger's experience with the individual child—and, as such, becomes relevant as soon as the experimental session extends beyond initial reactions or the stranger steps outside of rigidly prescribed behavior patterns. As the session or investigation proceeds, the increasing familiarity of child to stranger is matched by that of stranger to child. (This point is similar to, though on a different level from, that made with respect to the stranger's sex.) This increasing familiarity of the stranger with the child and with his or her behavior is relevant in investigations that allow the stranger to behave at all "naturally," and would quite likely be reflected in the stranger-child interaction. Thus the effect of the stranger's familiarity with the child would be recorded as part of the child's social behavior.

A comparison was made in the present study between children's reactions at 30 months to completely unfamiliar strangers and to a somewhat familiar observer whom the children had seen during home observations 12 times before. Strangers and observers each interacted relatively "naturally" with the children, within a schedule of various types of play activity. Individuals serving as strangers and observers had all had experience being both strangers and observers, and had comparable prior experience with children in general, although not with the particular individual child with whom they were paired for this comparison.

The notable finding of this comparison is not that differences in children's reactions were observed (Table 10). That could have been predicted on the basis of various other manipulations of familiarity (Bretherton, 1974; Eckerman, 1973; Eckerman and Whatley, 1975; Rand and Jennings, 1974; Ross, 1975; Sroufe, Waters, and Matas, 1974). The interesting thing is which *particular* social behaviors reflected a difference. No difference was observed in children's interest (looking)—a difference we found to be associated with variation in strangers' *physical* characteristics. There was no difference in social approach behavior (vocalizing, going to, touching)—a pattern associated with variation in the *mode* of strangers' behavior. Nor was there a difference in negative affect, avoidance, or behavior to the mother—behaviors that may be associated with strangers' *style*. The particular difference observed was that children displayed more positive affect, responsiveness, cooperation, and play with the observer than with the stranger.[9]

Clearly, a different pattern of behavior is elicited by familiarity as opposed to other variations in stranger characteristics. Moreover, the pattern displayed seems to implicate the role of the observer's famil-

Table 10
Differences in Children's Social Behavior
to Observer and Strangers[a]

Child's Social Behavior	Mean Scores			F[b]
	To Observer	To Stranger #1	To Stranger #2	
Looks at stranger	43.14	42.42	52.93	2.22
Vocalizes to stranger	33.72	29.00	27.36	0.67
Positive affect to stranger	24.15	14.36	18.50	5.82*
Plays with stranger	30.57	19.79	11.22	6.56*
Negative affect, avoids stranger	1.50	0.93	1.58	0.42
Goes to stranger	0.93	1.36	0.93	0.43
Physical contact with stranger	8.65	12.14	2.08	2.01
Imitates stranger	3.36	0.79	1.21	2.47†
Responsive to stranger	40.22	13.71	13.36	27.10**
Looks at, vocalizes to mother	8.09	12.17	4.25	0.03
Physical attachment to mother[c]	2.25	1.88	2.25	0.28

[a]Assessed in home at 30 months.
[b]Analysis of variance for repeated measures; df 2, 24.
[c]Physical attachment = sum (physical contact, goes to mother).
†$p < .10$
*$p < .01$
**$p < .001$

iarity with the child as well as the child's familiarity with the observer. True, the child's positive affect most likely reflects the child's greater comfort and pleasure with someone he or she has seen and played with before, but a plausible explanation for the highly significant differences observed in the amount of playing and cooperation/responsiveness is that the observer—by virtue of her greater experience and familiarity playing with the child—knew better how to engage the child in play. She could select more appropriate activities, interpret more accurately the child's desires and expressions, and thus be more effective in eliciting cooperative responses.

Our intention is not to suggest that "familiarity" as it is usually conceived—as the child's familiarity with the stranger—is not an important variable. We wish merely to emphasize that in significant social interactions that go beyond mere recognition and initial reactions to strangers performing routine sequences, it is inevitable that differences in the stranger's familiarity with the child will influence the stranger's behavior toward the child, affect their continuing interaction, and thus be reflected in child "outcome" measures of social responsiveness. Once again this highlights the need to consider and study the reactions of children to strangers as an interactive and dyadic phenomenon.

Beyond the Lone Stranger: An Expanded Model of Children's Reactions to Strangers

The findings from the present study of the reactions of 2-year-old children to variations in the characteristics and behavior of strangers can be summarized very briefly in the following set of relations:

Stranger Characteristic/Behavior ⟶ *Children's Behavior*

Affective tone of stranger's interaction with mother ("mood")	Physical proximity to and contact with mother-attachment.
Affective tone of stranger's behavior to child ("manner")	Positive and negative social behavior to stranger—preference, liking, or manner.
Mode of stranger's behavior	Social approach to stranger (looking, vocalizing, going to, touching, playing)— communicative mode.
Style of stranger's behavior	Initiation/responsiveness to stranger— complementary style.
Sex (nurturance, verbalness) of stranger	Affect and vocalization to mother and stranger.
Physical appearance of stranger	Looking at stranger— interest, orientation, or attention.
Familiarity (sensitivity, effectiveness) of stranger	Positive affect, play, responsiveness to stranger—reciprocity.

From even these very preliminary and tentative results it is apparent that children's social behavior is more complex than has been suggested by previous investigations. Their understanding of social interaction is surprisingly sophisticated and clearly revealed in their encounters with strangers. Children as young as 2 years old are sensitive to subtle variations in strangers' behavior and their own behavior seems to reflect an appropriate matching or reciprocity with their partner's.

Variations in strangers' behavior have not previously been investigated or evaluated in research on young children. Moreover, previous investigations have often confounded *assessed* stranger variables or characteristics like sex, age, and familiarity with *unassessed* behavioral variations. One reason for these deficiencies in the research may be that investigators have followed a "single-process approach," searching for Brooks and Lewis's (1976) "process by which the infant categorizes and responds to the social world." They have thus been content to examine or manipulate a single stranger variable that fits into a single theoretical explanation. We would urge expanding the explanatory model and the terminology of research on strangers to look for process*es* of social interaction. It seems reasonable to propose that at least a three-step or three-process model is necessary to account for children's behavior observed with strangers. As a stranger (1) appears, (2) approaches, and (3) interacts with the child, we would suggest, different characteristics of the stranger become salient and different processes are involved.

At the appearance of the stranger, the significant characteristics are likely to be physical. The person is examined visually by the child, presumably recognized as familiar or unfamiliar, or perhaps somewhat familiar ("I haven't seen this person before, but she reminds me of someone I know . . ."). At this point the child may categorize the stranger as male or female, child or adult, blonde or brunette, and his or her affective responses would be influenced by the stranger's physical appearance, familiarity, and perhaps by specific experiences with similar appearing individuals in the past. The most likely response to the stranger at this point is attentive interest and mild or heightened arousal (see also Cairns, 1977; Haviland and Lewis, 1975). Even at this first appearance of the stranger, Cohen's (1972) work on attention suggests there are two processes involved: attention-getting, which is related to the size and movement of the stimulus, and attention-holding, which is related to its novelty and complexity. In the present study this first level of visual attention and recognition was of limited interest. The only "manipulation" related to this step was that of using as strangers individuals who differed in appearance, a manipulation which demonstrated that physical appearance indeed has its greatest effect on children's visual attention.

The next step in the child's encounter with a stranger occurs as soon as the stranger *does* something—she approaches, she smiles, she talks, she invites the child to come and play, she talks to the mother. At this point the child must go a step beyond recognition; he or she interprets the stranger's behavior, in the context of his or her previous assessment of physical/familiarity characteristics. The child may interpret the stranger's behavior as normal, natural, just, meet, and salutary—or unlike anything he or she has ever seen before and therefore arousing and potentially fearsome. The variables of importance at this level included in the present study were the stranger's emotional mood (expressed in her interaction with the mother) and her initial mode of behavior directed to the child. These stranger behaviors were related to whether children approached and initiated interaction.

By this time the child has made some behavioral response to the stranger. This marks the beginning of the third step in the encounter—the stranger and child become an interactive dyad. Now, the most important quality about the stranger may be the responsiveness of her style, the positiveness of her manner, or the mode of her activity. These dimensions were investigated in the present study. They were found to be related to the child's continued willingness to interact, the affect he or she expressed in the interaction, and the kind of interaction which followed. At this point in the encounter it is the "mesh" of the interaction, the adaptability of both participants, that is of concern to the child—and should be to the investigator. It is to this level of social interaction we must proceed if we are to fully understand children's social development and to explain the results of the present study. The processes involved at the first step may be strictly attentional, perceptual, and cognitive. Here the "lone stranger" may serve. But other processes come into play involving social rules and reciprocal interaction at all subsequent steps. It becomes necessary to go beyond the "lone stranger" stimulus—to examine behavior of the *interactive* stranger and child.

In the next section we present the theoretical explanations that have been offered to account for children's reactions to strangers—typically restricted to the first one or two steps of our proposed model for such encounters, discuss their deficiencies, and explore the explanatory possibilities of some other theoretical approaches that do go beyond the limitations of the lone stranger.

Theoretical Explanations

The child's reaction to strangers is an event of interest for a variety of theories in child development, and has been used to explain or support positions of a number of them, but unfortunately at present no one single theory adequately accounts for all aspects of the phenomenon as we have outlined it in the previous section, or explains the data from the present study. Like the predominant empirical focus in the area, most theoretical attention to date has been given to the *negative* aspects of the child's social behavior—especially to the apparently "sudden" appearance in the second half of the first year of wariness, distress, anxiety, or fear when the infant is confronted by a stranger. Stranger distress has been of interest, first, for biological drive theories of child development. To psychoanalysts like Freud and Spitz it represented the onset of object relations with mother: the infant, seeing a stranger, believes that the mother has left him and becomes distressed. Subsequent realization by other psychologists that separation anxiety and stranger anxiety were confounded in this explanation has thrown doubt on this theoretical view, however. In the biological ethological-evolutionary theory of stranger distress (Bowlby, 1969), fear of the stranger is taken as a special case of fear of the strange. This homologue of flight in animals is clearly adaptive since it protects the infant from harmful situations and strengthens attachment to the unstrange mother. Unfortunately, this explanation does not adequately account for behavior actually observed. Infants are able to distinguish between familiar mother and unfamiliar stranger much earlier than they show any fear at that recognition (Brazelton, 1976; Carpenter, 1973; Fraiberg, 1975; Mills and Melhuish, 1974). Moreover, even in the "critical" second half of the first year, infants often explore rather than flee from strangers (Eckerman, 1973; Eckerman and Rheingold, 1974). They show both positive and negative reactions to the same stranger and are inconsistent in their affective reactions over short periods of time (Bretherton, 1974; Shaffran and Décarie, 1973). And finally, they differentiate in their reactions between strangers who are equally unfamiliar, for instance, between child and adult strangers (Greenberg, Hillman, and Grice, 1973; Lenssen, 1975; Lewis and Brooks, 1974, 1976; Lewis et al., 1975). A second ethological mechanism has been postulated to account for this last problem—an innate "baby detector" mechanism that counteracts and inhibits fear of strange infants and children (Bischof, 1975). This postulate may have some merit, but the other problems presented by the data remain.

A second theoretical approach, which has only recently begun to be applied to explaining stranger distress, derives from learning theory. This view suggests that distress may be the result of adult strangers providing a learned cue for forthcoming separation from the mother—the babysitter phenomenon (Lewis and Brooks, 1974)—or the result of specific fears learned in previous encounters with strangers (Bronson, 1972). Unfortunately, the data necessary to support these suggestions—data from longitudinal observations of children's encounters with babysitters and other strangers—are not yet available, so the suggestions must remain tentative, awaiting further evidence.

The most popular theoretical explanations of stranger distress are cognitive. One in particular interprets the phenomenon in terms of incongruity: the stranger is discrepant from the infant's internal representation of the familiar, his or her schema of "mother," and fear is elicited by the novel, the unfamiliar, the incongruous (Bronson, 1972; Hebb, 1946; Hunt, 1963). This explanation has some power—but also some problems. The question arises, for example, of whether incongruity per se elicits fear, or just excitement (cf. Haith and Campos, 1977; Hebb, 1949; Lewis and Brooks, 1976). There is the evidence that novel *objects*, unlike unfamiliar persons, do not cause fear, but rather lead to approach and exploration (Bretherton and Ainsworth, 1974; Bronson, 1972; Eckerman, 1973). Also creating problems for the incongruity hypothesis is the observation that the expression of distress or wariness is significantly affected by the *context* of the experimental situation (Sroufe, Waters, and Matas, 1974). Finally, there are the same problems that face the ethological explanation: evidence that infants do not exhibit distress all the time or to all unfamiliar stimuli, even after it is clear that they can detect novelty. Another problem that also plagues the ethological position is the difficulty of defining what is familiar; that is, what is the schema from which the stranger is discrepant or incongruous. "Mother" obviously is not the only social schema the infant forms. Other schemas are developed for other individuals with whom the infant has frequent and repeated interaction. This problem has led to more complicated alternatives still retaining the notion of schema and to further elaboration of the incongruity hypothesis. The child may compare the stranger with a schema not of mother but of self, for example (Lewis and Brooks, 1974, 1976). This adaptation of the discrepancy position does not account for why boys are more positive to women than to men strangers, however. Alternatively, the child may compare the stranger with a "host of stored schemas," and, in addition, build a new schema of the stranger involving categories like similarity of situation, age, sex, and behavior (Ross, 1975). Because of its generality, this formulation of the incongruity hypothesis, like the others, has little predictive power.

Other cognitive hypotheses related to children's distressful reactions to strangers have also been proposed. One links cognitive level to the onset of fear on the assumption that Piagetian "Stage 4" intelligence is a necessary prerequisite for the exhibition of wariness or fear, since it involves the beginning of cognitive reactions to absent objects and the development of the understanding of the identity of persons and objects in the environment (Décarie, 1974; Schaffer, 1966). So far there is little evidence for this position, either. Children's performance on tests of sensorimotor intelligence is not correlated with the age of onset of stranger distress (Emde, Gaensbauer, and Harmon, 1976; Scarr and Salapatek, 1970) or the likelihood that distress will be exhibited (Brossard, 1974; Goulet, 1974), and, moreover, wariness with a stranger is reported at ages preceding Stage 4 (Sroufe, Waters, and Matas, 1974).

The final two cognitive hypotheses that have been applied to the phenomenon of stranger distress have not been disconfirmed. One suggests that the child "appraises," "evaluates," or "interprets" the stranger's presence according to the context or situation, and that the affect expressed—from slight wariness to outright fear—is determined by the outcome of that evaluation (Schaffer, 1971; Sroufe, Waters, and Matas, 1974). Investigators proposing this hypothesis have been concerned with features of the situation such as the presence or absence of the mother and the sequence of procedures followed; they have clearly demonstrated that such features do indeed· affect children's fear of strangers. The other hypothesis is the "expectancy" hypothesis, which is linked to the early interaction of mother and infant (Bronson, 1972; Lewis and Brooks, 1974). Through reciprocal interaction with the mother (or other caregiver), the infant develops an expectancy of control over his or her environment and the people in it, an expectancy that his or her signals will be responded to. The preprogrammed stranger, like Tronick et al.'s (1975) unresponsive mother, violates this expectancy of the infant, leading to wariness, and if unresponsiveness continues, to withdrawal, avoidance, or perhaps, in the case of the stranger, to fear. To test this hypothesis, observation of infants' regular social interactions at home is necessary, as well as investigation of children's reactions to strangers who systematically vary their responsiveness.

Since disconfirming evidence for the biological, incongruity, and cognitive level hypotheses exists, the three most plausible hypotheses left to account for stranger anxiety at present are the expectancy, specific learning, and context evaluation hypotheses. These await empirical validation. To account for the observations in the present study, however, even these hypotheses, which may explain some aspects of children's fearful reactions to strangers in other studies, are not sufficient. In this study children's negative reactions to strangers were infrequent and when they did occur did not appear to indicate simple anxiety or fear. More negative reactions (to male strangers or to physical contact with the stranger) were accompanied by heightened positive affect in the same episodes (to mother or to stranger). And reactions to "negative" strangers did not include increased contact with mother, which might have suggested that the children were frightened: With a "hostile" stranger children did not go to their mothers for comfort or reassurance; rather, they avoided her. When the stranger was "nasty" to them, although children responded with (appropriately) negative affect, once again, they did not approach or stay near their mother. Clearly, to account for the more complex behavior of children in the present study, we cannot stop with hypotheses about stranger anxiety. We therefore turn to an examination of theorizing about *positive* aspects of children's social encounters.

The positive aspects of children's social behavior with strangers have received less attention than the study of distress, fear, and anxiety. Beyond inquiries into the origins of infants' sensitivity to social stimuli such as the human face, voice, and physical contact, research and theory on positive social development has focused almost exclusively on the child's relation with the mother—with fear of strangers providing a useful flip-side contrast. Nevertheless, the same theories that have been applied to the phenomenon of stranger distress may contribute to our understanding of children's positive social interaction with new people.

Biological theories suggest mechanisms that may provide the motivation for early positive social behavior—instinctual drives (psychoanalysis) or predispositions to be attracted to stimuli provided by human caregivers (ethology). Finding that in the early months infants prefer a face over nonsocial stimuli (Fantz, 1965; Fitzgerald, 1968; Yarrow, 1967), quiet readily to a human voice (Wolff, 1963), and can be soothed by rocking (Ambrose, 1969) and patting (Wolff, 1969), led Bowlby (1969) to postulate that the human infant is genetically biased to respond to social stimuli, and Richards (1974) to state that the infant is preadapted to social life. Human features—physical and behavioral—act as "innate releasing mechanisms" in the ethological view: those of the very young eliciting behavior from adults (Hess, 1970); those of adults releasing behavior in infants (Bowlby, 1969). Such predispositions have clear survival value. This theory may have at least limited utility in explaining the origins of "sociability"— although some (e.g., Lewis and Brooks, 1976) doubt its adequacy even then. It becomes increasingly less appealing, however, as explanations are sought for more mature social behavior patterns. In regard to the results of the present study, this theory does nothing to explain the subtleties of children's discrimination of affective tone in the conversation between mother and stranger or their adoption of a complementary reciprocal style of interaction with the stranger.

Learning theory may also be helpful in explaining children's positive social behavior with strangers. The child's reaction to a stranger may be related to his or her past learning history; his or her initial responses to the stranger may be a function of generalization from other persons he or she has encountered. One test of this hypothesis has not succeeded, however; children's reactions to child, in contrast to adult, strangers were not related to whether or not they had siblings (Brooks and Lewis, 1976; Shatz and Gelman, 1973). Another learning theory hypothesis is that contingent responsiveness of the stranger in the immediate experimental situation reinforces the child's positive social behavior (Eckerman, 1973; Eckerman and Rheingold, 1974; Eckerman and Whatley, 1975). This hypothesis does not adequately account for children's behavior in the present study either. Interaction with the stranger was not merely a function of her responsiveness; noncontingent visual attention increased children's social behavior (mode manipulation), and no difference·in· the frequency of social behavior was observed when the stranger was noncontingently "stimulating" rather than "responsive" (style manipulation).

Applications of cognitive developmental theory to children's positive reactions to strangers have been more common than biological or learning approaches. Many of the cognitive hypotheses suggested to explain stranger distress have been applied to children's positive interactions as well. The incongruity hypothesis is one. Since the established relation between novelty and arousal is curvilinear, the incongruity hypothesis predicts that *moderate* incongruity between the novel (stranger) and the familiar (mother) will lead to attention rather than fear. This could explain why children respond more positively to women (who are somewhat like the mother) than to men strangers (who are highly unlike the mother). We have already suggested the limitations of the incongruity hypothesis for explaining negative reactions to strangers. It is even more difficult to apply to positive behavior. It is almost impossible to define, *a priori*, "moderate" discrepancy and to know which internal referent(s) would be used by the child to make the judgment of "moderate" dissimilarity.

Some investigators (e.g., Bernard and Ramey, 1977) have simply defined the mother as the reference, "moderate discrepancy" as an unfamiliar adult female, and "novel stimulus" as an unfamiliar peer. They take as supportive evidence for the incongruity hypothesis the finding that infants look and vocalize more at photographs of adult females than at photos of mother or unfamiliar peers. Since their finding held only for female subjects and the difference observed between reactions to mother and adult strangers was not significant, however, this "evidence" is far from confirmatory. An alternative explication of the incongruity hypothesis proposes that the child uses a different referent: the child compares the stranger not with his or her schema of *mother* but with his or her categorical concept of *self*, and his or her response is determined by the (in)congruity between stranger and self (Lewis and Brooks, 1976). The unfamiliar child is responded to positively in this account because he or she is "like me." Investigations of this hypothesis, like the mother-schema hypothesis—and perhaps the hypothesis as well—have been overly simple. They have examined variations in certain characteristics of the strangers because they are obvious categories of self (age, size, gender). But although the theory is avowedly constructivist, the methods used are not—denying children the opportunity to actively construct interactions with the strangers. (Strangers are passive to the point of being merely photographs in all these investigations.) The investigators in these studies have also considered children's reactions only in terms of positive or negative affect, visual fixation, or verbal labeling. Moreover, the limited data gathered, even in these restricted situations, do not offer overwhelming support for the self-concept hypothesis. First, results were significant only for female subjects, and second, infants looked at pictures of strange infants and adults more than pictures of strange children. One would expect that if "like me" were the only criterion, pictures of children would be given less attention than those of infants but more than those of adults.

The incongruity hypothesis might be salvaged by incorporating the curvilinear aspect of the novelty/attention relation and applying it to schemas of *both* self and mother, or by giving visual attention more than one interpretation, but the hypothesis then loses its parsimony and still only accounts for a limited aspect of children's behavior with strangers—primarily their behavior at the first step of our proposed model for social encounters. This limitation makes it useless for accounting for data from the present study.

Other cognitive hypotheses that have been advanced to account for children's positive reactions to strangers, as well as for their fear, involve the child's cognitive level or stage of development. While Piaget himself has not given the topic the same detailed attention he has given the study of the physical environment, other theorists have attempted to apply his principles to the social realm. Some suggest that age-related cognitive structures set *limits* on social behavior (Schaffer, 1971). Some explore Piaget's social construct of decentration or the development of self-other perspectives (Shantz, 1975;

Urberg and Docherty, 1976). These notions of social cognition are not useful, however, for explaining the results of the present study, as we suggested in our earlier discussion of the "mood" manipulation.

Still other theorists emphasize the structural similarities between social and cognitive development. The most comprehensive and detailed explication of this last position is offered by Lee (1975), who proposes that interpersonal competence is merely an extension of cognitive competence. The two are inextricably bound: structures and schemes are common to both; only elements and the conditions that influence their development are different. She offers hypotheses about how children acquire interpersonal competence (consistent strategies of interaction through which reciprocity of mutual exchange can be maintained) and construct social schemes (internal representations which allow prediction of social encounters) in the periods from sensorimotor to operational intelligence (2 to 7 years).

In Lee's theory, both cognitive and social schemes have three components: intellective (knowledge), affective (meaning), and enactive (action). When two people meet they assess each other on various dimensions and impute characteristics to the other (intellective); drawing on past experience, feelings are evoked (affective); and each acts accordingly (enactive). Clearly this is a more comprehensive approach than the application of a simple incongruity hypothesis, and thus it is potentially more useful for explaining children's encounters with strangers.

Focusing on the intellective component, Lee proposes that competence in the social domain, as in the physical, involves the child's ability to "conserve," that is, to identify those features of the world that are invariant. In social encounters, she claims, important invariant features of the partner are physical characteristics (variants include sex, age, and race), behavioral state (variants are reading, jumping, cuddling, etc.), emotional state (happy, sad, etc.), and role relationship (father, sister, etc.); important invariant features of the situation are setting (home, laboratory, etc.) and group configuration (size, homogeneity, etc.). In each encounter with a stranger, the child must assess the invariant features of the stranger and the situation. To do this, the child needs to know behavioral/perceptual "cues" that will aid him or her in identifying the variants of social exchange. That is, for example, when a person cries (cue) there is a high probability that he or she is sad (variant), which is an element of emotional state (invariant), unless the context (invariant) indicates he or she is actually happy (variant). Lee suggests that the child acquires such knowledge

from learning language labels and through numerous social exchanges that allow differentiation of behavioral/perceptual cues and
the association of these cues with variants.

In the present study we have seen some evidence for the existence
of such cue systems in children's knowledge about social interaction.
The mood and manner manipulations demonstrated that children
respond to cues of emotional tone. During the angry and happy
dialogues between mother and stranger, children avoided their angry
mother, and stayed .close to happy mom. They seem to be more
sensitive to the mother's cues than those of an unfamiliar adult. In the
manipulation of stranger manner, children responded with negative
behavior to anger directed at them and with positive behavior when
the stranger was nice, again indicating their sensitivity to emotional
cues in social interaction. Most dramatic, perhaps, was the children's
apparent awareness of the import of visual regard. The stranger's
ignoring or excluding the child by reading, looking or turning away, or
talking to someone else led the child to initiate far fewer social
advances to the stranger than when the stranger merely looked at the
child. Eye contact apparently provides a cue for social interaction,
indicating that a person is open to interaction (looking) or not
interested in interaction (not looking). It seems clear that 2-year-old
children have and use at least the cue systems to emotional tone and
social interaction in their encounters with strangers, and that this
accounts for some of their behavior in the present study.

But Lee's theory, too, has some problems in accounting for children's encounters with strangers. Because the preoperational child
can only perceive one property, cue, or element of an encounter at a
time, she suggests, he or she makes superficial assessments based on
the most salient cue. The child does not see how cues within each
variant relate to each other, how variants relate to cues, or how variants relate to each other; nor can he or she take into account, simultaneously, cues from the partner and cues from the context. Other
researchers, however, have found that even these young children do,
in fact, react to both partner and situation simultaneously (Skarin,
1977; Sroufe, Waters, and Matas, 1974). Focusing on the affective
component of social thought, such investigators claim that children's
affective responses to a stranger depend on their evaluation according to the context (Sroufe, Waters, and Matas, 1974), their extraction
of meaning from the situation (Waters, Matas, and Sroufe, 1975), their
expectation of positive consequences (Bronson, 1972), or their ap-
praisal based on previous encounters (Schaffer, 1971). This suggests

that the applications of the Piagetian principle of conservation, which accounts so well for children's behavior in the physical realm, may not completely succeed in explaining children's social behavior.

Other investigators, too, have emphasized the distinctions between the two realms of social and physical knowledge—a distinction Piaget does not make—based on the notion that we know about people in ways we cannot know about things because we ourselves are people (Bearison, 1975; Lewis and Lee-Painter, 1972). Bearison has been particularly systematic in distinguishing the two kinds of knowledge. He suggests that social knowledge is marked by relatively greater variability, is more labile and situation-specific. While the adage "A rose is a rose is a rose" and even " a rose by any other name . . ." may hold true in the physical world, when we are talking about people, a Rose is not necessarily a Rose—and certainly not if she changes her name! The reason social knowledge is different from physical, Bearison claims, is that in social relations the knower is in a mutually reciprocal relationship with the known—each is simultaneously both knower and known—and their interaction is dynamic and equilibratory. This distinction, although it seems obvious, has apparently not significantly influenced thinking about social development. It suggests most clearly that we must go beyond a static, physicalistic model of children's reactions to strangers—such as the incongruity hypothesis, and possibly the conservation hypothesis—in order to study and understand social phenomena. It further points out the folly of trying to understand the ways children come to understand the thoughts and feelings of others by extension of (Piagetian) models of the development of physical knowledge.

This is a major point made by the present study. While physical models may account for the initial reaction of the child to the stranger as a noninteractive physical stimulus, as soon as the stranger acts—or does *not react* to the child—the child's behavior becomes interactive with the stranger's. This interactiveness was demonstrated in the present study by the social behavior of children with strangers who behaved "naturally" and "responsively." The point is not new. It has been made before by investigators of the social psychology of adults; by Stone (1962), for example, who stressed that every social transaction must be broken down into at least two analytic components or processes: appearance and discourse, and by Heider (1958) and Jones and Gerard (1967) who stated:

> The important attributes of social objects are not usually revealed by physical states and changes; they are revealed by patterned communications that bear an almost arbitrary relation to the apparent physical struc-

ture of their source. . . . The stimulus patterns basic to person perception are usually more extended over time than those relevant to thing perception (Heider, 1958). . . . [In] the formation of impression, we feel that the most central process is that involved in moving from behavioral cues to inferences about enduring dispositions [pp. 259, 261].

The point also needs to be emphasized in the study of children's social encounters.

The usefulness of adult social psychology perspectives to studies of children does not stop with this contribution. Research and theorizing about social development in childhood, being primarily concerned with origins, has tended to focus on the abilities of infants. More adequate theorizing to account for the behavior of our 2-year-old subjects and to enrich theory about the origins of social knowledge can be attained if one also looks at adult outcome and end-states. Particularly in the study of social development the perspectives of adult psychology can be useful, since adult social psychologists have been more concerned with the discourse aspect of social interaction and less influenced by models for the development of physical knowledge, and less biased toward accounting for all behavior in terms of strong emotional drives.

One current perspective in social psychology and sociological theorizing that may be useful in accounting for children's behavior in encounters with strangers is the symbolic interactionist, dramaturgical position of Erving Goffman (1967, 1974). His view is that:

On every occasion when two or more persons are in one another's immediate physical presence, a complex set of norms will regulate the commingling. These norms pertain to the management of units of participation, territoriality, display of relationships, and the like. And if talk occurs, then, of course, norms will apply regarding organization of turns at talking and initiation and termination of the encounter [1974, p. 495]. In any society, whenever the physical possibility of spoken interaction arises, it seems that a system of practices, conventions, and procedural rules comes into play which functions as a means of guiding and organizing the flow of messages [1967, pp. 33–34].

Goffman further notes that the rules of conduct depend on obligations and expectations and differ according to the intimacy of the relation between the interactors. In a nonfamiliar relation, he suggests, actors must show circumspection in approach. Inappropriate hugging and kissing or otherwise invading the recipient's privacy is not following the rules of conduct. This notion of social norms and rules may also illuminate the behavior of children in their encounters with strangers. Young children may have formulated some of the rules of social interaction. In the experimental procedures that characterize most studies of children and strangers, especially those demonstrating stranger distress, however, children are seldom given an opportunity to answer the three basic questions which must be solved in any encounter with an unknown person—who is the stranger, is he friendly, and what is his status? (Harré, 1974)—before they are confronted by an unresponsive and intrusive stranger who, following some arbitrary script, enters the room, and after a brief "Hello, baby" or a measured stare, rushes over and embraces the child. The stranger is obviously not following the norm of circumspection. Any evidence of fear on the child's part may be a result of the stranger's violation of the "rules" of social interaction.

Goffman himself sticks to cataloguing the rules of adult interaction (which, he admits, are not necessarily the same as those for children). Some suggestions for simpler rules that might guide children's behavior may be gleaned from the literature on children's encounters with strangers (although they have not typically been articulated as "rules"). Lewis and Brooks (1974) suggest that one rule may be "stay and attend to a distant event; avoid or approach a close event." Another rule may be "speak when you're spoken to" (Garvey and BenDebba, 1974) or "if you hear a question, respond—even if your answer is irrelevant" (Lewis, 1976). Perhaps an early rule is "take turns with your partner" (Ross and Goldman, 1977). Who knows, maybe other "grandmotherly" dicta—like "children should be seen and not heard," "look at me when I'm talking to you," and "don't talk to strangers"—are also rules that influence children's behavior.

The present study found evidence for two of the foregoing "rules." The observation that children talked significantly more when the stranger was more talkative (in verbal versus other modes of interaction or with female versus male strangers) illustrates the rule of "speak when spoken to." The rule of taking turns was suggested by the results of the initiating versus responsive stranger style manipulation. Children responded in reciprocal, complementary fashion to the stranger's style; they were responsive to the stranger's advances, but, if the stranger made no advances, took the initiative. This notion of reciprocity or turn-taking as a determinant of children's reactions in social encounters with strangers has not been included in the hypotheses applied to reactions to strangers thus far. It may be useful to consider it as a basic social "rule" governing dyadic interaction.

The problem, then, is to account for the *development* of such social rules. For the rules and rituals that concern sociologists, the explanation offered, based on evidence that adult rituals and conventions vary from culture to culture, is that they are learned through early socialization (Goffman, 1974). Since some form of turn-taking is apparent in the rhythmicity and reciprocity of infants' interaction with mother from the very early days of life (Brazelton, Koslowski, and Main, 1974; Fogel, 1976; Kaye, 1977), however, it seems likely that this social "rule"—and perhaps others—has some element of "nature" as well as "nurture." We cannot resolve that issue here.

One might propose that later, more elaborate adult rituals evolve from basic cue systems and primitive rules like turn-taking learned early in life and evident in the behavior of young children. Early encounters with strangers may prepare the way for the later archetypal solution to an unavoidable confrontation between adult strangers meeting on a narrow path: each catches the other's eye; a slight smile and eyebrow flash are exchanged; each (now acknowledged as a social actor) makes incipient ushering motions; one passes; each makes an acknowledging head bow (Harré, 1974). One of the few theoreticians who has been concerned with the development of social rules and the capacity to manage ceremonial acts, however, denies that this relationship is likely.

While others, following Bowlby (1969), have suggested, without satisfactory evidence, that adult social interaction evolves out of the child's early relation with the mother, Harré (1974) dismisses this view as naive and sentimental. Most adult encounters, he says, are motivated not by emotional forces but by following rules. Not only is the early development of attachment irrelevant for adult behavior, but that social relationship must perish before adulthood is possible. Adult social competence, with its sets of personas, rules, and arbiters for each scene encountered, he asserts, does not even begin to develop until the child is of school age.

We would propose, rather, that the proper study of the development of adult rules and rituals is the behavior of children, not with their mothers, but with strangers. Precursors of adults' everyday social behavior may indeed not lie in the child's attachment to mother, but may be evident in his or her interaction with unfamiliar persons.[10] Thus they may exist prior to the demise of attachment which Harré suggests is necessary for mature development. In fact, both authentic expressions of deep emotion ("face") and public ritual behavior ("mask") may be exhibited throughout the life span—although the experiences of childhood may emphasize the former, while adult opportunities most often require expression of the latter.

Dramaturgical sociologists have been criticized for emphasizing the "mask" of human behavior to the exclusion of "authentic" expressions, and for assuming that people are actors who are always "on stage" (Messinger, Sampson, and Towne, 1962). They have also been criticized for their view that social rules are normative structures "out there" which actors follow automatically (Mehan and Wood, 1975). In the ethnomethodological view that is presented by the latter authors social rules are not structures but structur*ings*. After actors make a judgment about what kind of situation they have entered, their actions not only index the external world but reflexively alter it. Rules *do not exist* independent of actors and situations. For Garfinkel (1967), the rule ("scenic practice") includes in it an "*et cetera*" provision which indicates that the rule is to be used under certain particular circumstances, while Cicourel (1974) suggests that "interpretive procedures" enable the actor to articulate general normative rules with immediate interaction scenes. These ethnomethodological "practices" and "procedures" allow the actor to choose and to make sense of appropriate substantive rules or social norms. They govern the sequencing of interaction and establish conditions for evaluating and generating behavioral displays in novel or familiar situations.

Ethnomethodological conceptualizations go beyond Goffman's notion of normative rules by suggesting that rules can be both more *general* (the normative approach only lists particular norms and thus can never be complete) and more *specific* (taking into account the particular situation or context). The significance of these conceptions is to integrate the notion of social rules with the data showing contextual effects on the behavior of adults and children, and to provide a mechanism whereby an individual can determine the appropriateness of exhibiting "face" or "mask." These ethnomethodological notions, therefore, seem more satisfactory than simple normative rules for explaining social knowledge.

Cicourel suggests that the interpretive procedures emerge developmentally: "The child initially acquires simple properties of interpretive procedures and surface rules which permit him to detect restricted classes of normal forms in voice intonation, physical appearance, facial expressions, cause and effect, story beginning and endings, simple games, and the like." But, he adds, "We have little or no solid empirical information or even consistent and imaginative theoretical formulations about children's acquisition of the properties of interpretive procedures" (1974, p. 50). The results of the present study are not sufficient to resolve the theoretical issues he is concerned with, but they suggest that studying children's encounters with strangers is not irrelevant to the issue. Future work on the social development of young children should explore these ideas further.

It is apparent from this discussion of theoretical explanations for children's reactions to strangers that no single theory, as presently formulated, is completely adequate to account for the data from this—or any other—stranger study. Different theories offer explanations for different stages of development—of the child or the interaction. For understanding the behavior of the newborn, the concept of "innate releasing mechanisms" to physical or behavioral cues may be useful; for later behavior in infancy, the concept of "expectations" developed through interaction with responsive caregivers; still later, the notion that children's behavior is guided by social "rules" or "procedures" may apply.

To explain the behavior of our 2-year-olds in their rather sophisticated interactions with strangers, all three explanations are helpful. Young children recognize physical characteristics and are sensitive to behavioral cues; they apparently have expectations about the probability of reciprocal social participation; and they behave in accordance with basic rules of social exchange. In addition, their behavior with the stranger seems to be influenced by their partner's *salience* (closer and more vigorous physical contact leading to heightened affect— both positive and negative), *manner in prior interaction* (effect of partner's mood and manner carrying over into subsequent, neutral "approach" sequence), and *interactive style* (children at this age being attracted by a style that is relatively "natural" and spontaneous, positive and playful, active but gentle, receptive, and responsive).[11] They clearly understand what it means to be a social partner, and their social behavior with a stranger is affected by that knowledge; their relation with even a totally unfamiliar person is a real and responsive partnership in social interaction.

A guide for further research

As we have suggested, the study of children's early social relations has suffered from a restrictive emphasis on exploring the phenomenon of "fear of strangers." The interest may be shifting now to investigating positive aspects of social interaction with unfamiliar persons. Therefore, in order to guide these investigators through the quagmires that beset earlier attempts, a few general suggestions are offered here.

First, investigators must appreciate the complexity of children's behavior in encounters with strangers. (That complexity is demonstrated by both the results of the present study and its conceptual framework, Figure 1.) Then, they should recognize that the stranger is not just a physical stimulus for the child, but an interactive partner with the child. They must therefore take the stranger's behavior into account and not confound behavior with physical characteristics. Finally, they must assess strangers' behavior and children's reactions with the sophistication they deserve and demand.

Child measures. The full range of children's social behavior should be assessed (not just "positive" or "negative" affect, but indices of fear, exploration, affiliation, attachment) (cf. Eckerman, 1973), using detailed recording of specific kinds of behavior (not just categories), separated across modalities, time, situations, and direction of affect (cf. Morgan and Bennett, 1975; Rheingold and Eckerman, 1973), and including physiological indices as well as behavioral ones (cf. Campos et al., 1975; Sroufe, Waters, and Matas, 1974; Waters, Matas, and Sroufe, 1975).

Stranger measures. No longer should studies analyze effects merely of the stranger per se. They should clearly separate strangerness (a new and unfamiliar person) from strangeness (an unusual person like a midget or an unnatural encounter that is "scripted"). The stranger's behavior in the assessment situation should be given the same detailed attention as the child's. It is essential to specify exactly who the stranger is (including physical features and background experiences) and to clearly separate the stranger's physical characteristics from his or her behavior. It is important either to specify with exquisite precision the procedures to be followed by the stranger, or, preferably, to meticulously observe the stranger's actual behavior with the child and then analyze the effects of various *kinds* of behavior, rather than combining across modality, time, or situation. Interaction between stranger and child should be submitted to the same kind of microanalysis currently being applied to the interaction between mother and infant (e.g.; Brazelton et al., 1974, Fogel, 1976; Kaye, 1977; Stern, 1974)—clearly going beyond the notion of "the lone stranger" as an inert and noninteractive stimulus to which the child merely responds.

Background factors. Knowledge of processes of social development will also be significantly enhanced by the study of relevant background factors. Longitudinal observation of the child's social experiences is needed—observation of the child's interactions with persons inside and outside the family, regular acquaintances and strangers, children and adults, men and women. Linking the child's social behavior to his or her other characteristics—like sex, temperament, culture, and cognitive level—would also be valuable.

Real-life correlates. It would also substantially advance our knowledge to study children's social behavior in the "real world." We can do this by minimizing the artificial or laboratorial aspects of our procedures—conducting our assessments in the child's home, following more "natural" sequences, letting the child and stranger get acquainted over longer periods of observation—and by correlating experimental results with observations or reports of children's real-life encounters with strangers—at home, on the playground, in the supermarket.

Questions for investigation. Particular questions that need to be investigated include the following:

What characteristics of other people—physical and behavioral—are children sensitive to at different ages?

Are there basic "rules" of social exchange that children follow in their interactions with other people? If so, what are they and how do children know or learn them?

Do these rules appear in a developmental sequence from infancy to adulthood, and if so, in what order?

How do rules of social interaction differ according to the individual partner of "class" of partners? How are rules for interacting with mother different from those for an acquaintance or for a stranger; how are rules different for interacting with a child or an adult?

What is the short-term developmental course of social interaction, that is, how and when is a stranger transformed into a friend?

Are there individual differences among children in social skills or competence and how do they develop? To what other individual differences are these related (language, cognition, attachment, etc.)?

What factors in the child's social environment influence his or her social development (interactions in the social network of mother, father, siblings, caregivers, babysitters, adult and child acquaintances)?

An integrative approach. Finally, we need to re-evaluate, and perhaps to replace, our entire approach to research on social development. In the past the most popular approach to conceptualizing and investigating social development seems to have been to invent simple constructs that would account for observed or inferred behavior, constructs that could be uniquely defined, unambiguously delineated, and theoretically justified. Such memorable constructs as "attachment," "sibling rivalry," "the Oedipus complex," "fear of strangers," and "stranger anxiety" were the result. For a time, these constructs served a useful purpose. They identified and brought attention to interesting developmental phenomena; they provided a useful and vivid shorthand for particular patterns of social behavior; they raised issues that challenged theories of development. But the picturesque labels were perhaps too appealing; the images they evoked, too compelling. They became so widely accepted, so commonly cited, that children's every social behavior was interpreted in terms of these constructs. This limited investigators' view of children's social competence, and their awareness of parallel patterns of behavior across the life span. It now appears that these constructs are inadequate to explain the variety and complexity, the range and richness of children's social behavior and development. By leaning solely on polar constructs of attachment and stranger anxiety, in particular, we have missed the *continuum* of social relations and the *continuity* of social development that more accurately characterizes children's social behavior. The narrowness of these constructs has obscured the broader picture of children's developing, changing, and varied social interactions.

Work has already begun that is forcing us to rethink and modify notions about children's attachment to mother; research on children's relations with their fathers (Clarke-Stewart, 1977a; Kotelchuck, 1973; Lamb 1976), regular babysitters, and day-care workers (Clarke-Stewart, 1977b; Ricciuti, 1974) is rapidly expanding this concept. Even more dramatic expansion of the stranger anxiety construct can follow from the study of children's reactions to unfamiliar persons. If children's reactions to strangers are studied in relation to variations in the context of the encounter, the familiarity, naturalness, and responsiveness of the stranger, and the identity and behavior of the social partner, the construct of stranger anxiety will undoubtedly be discarded in favor of a continuum of social interaction and affiliation. I would urge researchers to take this direction, so that we may soon hear the familiar cry, "Hi, ho, Silver, away . . ." as the vanishing "Lone Stranger" of research on social development is replaced by a large and varied cast of interactive partners.

Notes

1. Rheingold and Eckerman's stranger, in fact, was someone whom the child had met before the experimental sessions began.
2. During the biased interaction, but not during the approach sequence, children did look at the silent stranger significantly less than at the happy or hostile strangers, but this difference more accurately reflects a difference in stranger activity rather than a difference in mood.
3. A recent study of children's recognition of situational aspects of adult facial expressions (Abramovitch, 1977) supports this conclusion that

children were responding differentially to cues from mother and a stranger. In that study, 4-year-old children were able to tell from silent videotapes whether their own mother was interacting with a friend or with a stranger, but they could not so identify the interactive partner of an unfamiliar mother.

4. Order of nice and nasty stranger counterbalanced.

5. Studies of the effects on children's performance of continuous nurturance versus nurturance withdrawal (Ascione, 1975) are not comparable to the present manipulation of stranger's manner, since in those studies non-nurturant adults have merely ignored the child rather than displaying negative affect to him or her.

6. The order of presentation of various modes of stranger's behavior was counterbalanced, and measures of children's social behavior were calculated on the basis of equal time segments for each mode.

7. In this positive playful situation negative behavior to the stranger was too infrequent to analyze.

8. There is a possibility that the stranger's presence or behavior also influenced the mother's behavior in the situation, especially since children were observed to talk more to their mother as well as to the stranger when the stranger was a woman. Mothers, however, were instructed to remain silent and noninterventive though responsive in this situation. It is unlikely that the mother's behavior accounts for the differences observed—except as it is in response to the child's. Unfortunately, we did not record maternal behavior in the situation.

   The observation in the present study that children smiled more at their mothers when the stranger was a man might also fit with a masculine play style that is more vigorous, since it is then more exciting.

9. A similar pattern of differences was observed in a comparable investigation of these same children's behviavior at 14 months, reported by Clarke-Stewart (1975).

10. The most basic elements of adult social rules, being fundamentals of social interaction (e.g., turn-taking, look-and-listen), obviously are part of the infant's early and continued interaction with the mother (as well as with other social partners). The distinction being made here is between the strong emotional aspect of the infant's relation with mother (attachment) and less emotional interchanges with casual acquaintances. Since idiosyncratic and emotional aspects of the mother-infant relation may confound or camouflage expression of the child's knowledge of social rules, it is suggested that the study of children's interactions with strangers may demonstrate more continuity with adult social behavior than the study of attachment or interaction with mother.

11. These observations are based particularly on the results of the sex and mode manipulations in the present study.

References

Abramovitch, R. Children's recognition of situational aspects of facial expression. *Child Development*, 1977, *48*, 459–463.

Adamson, L., Als, H., Tronick, E., and Brazelton, T.B. Social interaction between a sighted infant and her blind parents. Paper presented at the biennial meeting of the Society for Research in Child Development, Denver, 1975.

Ainsworth, M. D. S. The development of infant-mother attachment. In B. M. Caldwell and H. N. Ricciuti (Eds.), *Review of Child Development Research*, Vol. 3. Chicago: University of Chicago Press, 1973, pp. 1–94.

Ainsworth, M. D. S., and Bell, S. M. Attachment, exploration, and separation: Illustrated by the behavior of one-year-olds in a strange situation. *Child Development*, 1970, *41*, 49–67.

Ainsworth, M. D. S., Bell, S. M., and Stayton, D. J. Individual differences in strange-situation behavior of one-year-olds. Paper presented to study group on "The Origins of Human Social Relations" sponsored by the Center for Advanced Study in the Developmental Sciences and the Ciba Foundation, London, July, 1969.

Ambrose, L. *Stimulation in Early Infancy*. New York: Academic Press, 1969.

Ascione, F. R. The effects of continuous nurturance and nurturance withdrawal on children's behavior: A partial replication. *Child Development*, 1975, *46*, 790–795.

Bearison, D. J. The comparative development of social and physical knowledge. Unpublished manuscript, Graduate School of City University of New York, 1975.

Belkin, E. P., and Routh, D. K. Effects of presence of mother versus stranger on behavior of three-year-old children in a novel situation. *Developmental Psychology*, 1975, *11*, 400.

Bernard, J. A., and Ramey, C. T. Visual regard of familiar and unfamiliar persons in the first six months of infancy. *Merrill-Palmer Quarterly*, 1977, *23*, 121–128.

Bischof, N. A systems approach towards the functional connections of fear and attachment. *Child Development*, 1975, *46*, 801–817.

Bloom, K. Social elicitation of infant vocal behavior. *Journal of Experimental Child Psychology*, 1975, *20*, 51–58.

Borke, H. Interpersonal perception of young children: Egocentrism or empathy? *Developmental Psychology*, 1971, *5*, 263–269.

Bowlby, J. *Attachment and loss*, Vol. 1. *Attachment*. New York: Basic Books, 1969.

Brazelton, T. B., Koslowski, B., and Main, M. The origins of reciprocity: The early mother-infant interaction. In M. Lewis and L. A. Rosenblum (Eds.), *The Effect of the Infant on Its Caregiver*. New York: Wiley, 1974, pp. 49–76.

Brazelton, T. B., Tronick, E., Adamson, L., Als, H., and Wise, S. Early mother-infant reciprocity. *Parent-Infant Interaction*. New York: Elsevier Excerpta Medica North Holland, 1975.

Bretherton, I. Making friends with one-year-olds: An experimental study of infant-stranger interaction. Unpublished doctoral dissertation, Johns Hopkins University, 1974.

Bretherton, I., and Ainsworth, M. D. S. The responses of one-year-olds to a stranger in a strange situation. In M. Lewis and L. A. Rosenblum (Eds.), *The Origins of Fear*. New York: Wiley, 1974, pp. 131–164.

Brody, S., and Axelrad, S. Maternal stimulation and social responsiveness of infants. In H. R. Schaffer (Ed.), *The Origins of Human Social Relations*. New York: Academic Press, 1971, pp. 195–210.

Bronson, G. W. Infants' reactions to unfamiliar persons and novel objects.

Monographs of the Society for Research in Child Development, 1972, *37*, (3, Serial No. 148).

Brookhart, J., and Hock, E. The effects of experimental context and experimental background on infants' behavior toward their mothers and a stranger. *Child Development*, 1976, *47*, 33–340.

Brooks, J., and Lewis, M. Infants' responses to strangers: Midget, adult, and child. *Child Development*, 1976, *47*, 323–332.

Brooks-Gunn, J., and Lewis, M. Person perception and verbal labeling: The development of social labels. Paper presented at the annual convention of the Eastern Psychological Association, New York, April, 1975.

Brossard, M. D. The infant's conception of object permanence and his reactions to strangers. In T. G. Décarie (Ed.), *The Infant's Reaction to Strangers*. New York: International Universities Press, 1974, pp. 97–116.

Cairns, R. B. Beyond social attachment: The dynamics of interactional development. In T. Alloway, P. Pliner, and K. Krames (Eds.), *Attachment Behavior*. New York: Plenum, 1977, pp. 1–24.

Campos, J.J. Possible operational definition of "fear" and recent studies of "fear of strangers." Unpublished manuscript, University of Denver, 1975.

Campos, J. J., Emde, R. N., Gaensbauer, T., and Henderson, C. Cardiac and behavioral interrelationships in the reactions of infants to strangers. *Developmental Psychology*, 1975, *11*, 589–601.

Carpenter, G. Mother-stranger discrimination in early weeks of life. Paper presented at the biennial meeting of the Society for Research in Child Development, Philadelphia, March 1973.

Cary, M. Non-verbal initiation of conversation. Colloquium presented at the University of Chicago, December, 1976.

Cicourel, A.V. *Cognitive Sociology*. New York: Free Press, 1974.

Clarke-Stewart, K. A. Interactions between mothers and their young children: Characteristics and consequences. *Monographs of the Society for Research in Child Development*, 1973, *38*, (6–7, Serial No. 153).

Clarke-Stewart, K. A. Sociability and Social Sensitivity: Characteristics of the stranger. Paper presented at the biennial meeting of the Society for Research in Child Development, Denver, April, 1975.

Clarke-Stewart, K. A. The father's impact on mother and child. Paper presented at the biennial meeting of the Society for Research in Child Development, New Orleans, March 1977. (a)

Clarke-Stewart, K. A. Variations in early child-care arrangement. Work in progress, Chicago, 1977. (b)

Cohen, L. B. Attention getting and attention holding processes of infant visual preferences. *Child Development*, 1972, *43*, 869–879.

Cohen, L. J., and Campos, J. J. Father, mother, and stranger as elicitors of attachment behaviors in infancy. *Developmental Psychology*, 1974, *10*, 146–154.

Connolly, K., and Smith, P. K. Reactions of pre-school children to a strange observer. In N. Blurton Jones (Ed.), *Ethological Studies of Child Behavior*. Cambridge, England: Cambridge University Press, 1972, pp. 157–172.

Corter, C. M. A comparison of the mother's and a stranger's control over the behavior of infants. *Child Development*, 1973, *44*, 705–713.

Davis, K. E. Impressions of others and interaction context as determinants of social interaction and perception in two-person discussion groups. Unpublished doctoral dissertation, Duke University, 1962, Cited in E. E. Jones and H. B. Gerard, *Foundations of Social Psychology*. New York: Wiley, 1967.

Décarie, T.G. *The Infant's Reaction to Strangers*. New York: International Universities Press, 1974.

Deutsch, F. Female preschoolers' perceptions of affective responses and interpersonal behavior in video-taped episodes. *Developmental Psychology*, 1974, *10*, 733–740.

Deutsch, F., and Madle, R. A. Empathy: Historic and current conceptualizations, measurement, and a cognitive theoretical perspective. *Human Development*, 1975, *18*, 267–287.

Eckerman, C. O. Competence in early social relations. Paper presented at symposium on "Early competence: Data and Concepts" at the annual convention of the American Psychological Association, Montreal, August, 1973.

Eckerman, C. O., and Rheingold, H. L. Infants' exploratory responses to toys and people. *Developmental Psychology*, 1974, *10*, 255–259.

Eckerman, C. O., and Whatley, J. L. Infants' reactions to unfamiliar adults varying in novelty. *Developmental Psychology*, 1975, *11*, 562–566.

Eibl-Eibesfeldt, I. *Ethology: The Biology of Behavior*. New York: Holt, Rinehart and Winston, 1970.

Emde, R., Gaensbauer, T. J., and Harmon, R. A. Emotional expression in infancy: A biobehavioral study. *Psychological Issues*, 1976, *43* (No. 1).

Fantz, R. L. Visual perception from birth as shown by pattern selectivity. *Annals of the New York Academy of Science*, 1965, *118*, 793–814.

Fein, G. G. Children's sensitivity to social contexts at 18 months of age. *Developmental Psychology*, 1975, *11*, 853–854.

Feldman, S. S. Some possible antecedents of attachment behavior in two-year-old children. Unpublished manuscript, Stanford University, 1975.

Fitzgerald, H. E. Autonomic pupillary reflex activity during early infancy and its relation to social nonsocial visual stimuli. *Journal of Experimental Child Psychology*, 1968, *6*, 470–482.

Fogel, A. Gaze, face and voice in the development of mother-infant interaction. Unpublished doctoral dissertation, University of Chicago, 1976.

Fouts, G., and Atlas, P. Attachment and stranger anxiety: Mother and stranger as reinforcers. Paper presented at the annual convention of the American Psychological Association, New Orleans, 1974.

Fraiberg, S. The development of human attachments in infants blind from birth. *Merrill-Palmer Quarterly*, 1975, *21*, 315–334.

Frisch, H. Effects of infants' real and designated sex on adult-infant play. Unpublished doctoral dissertation, University of Chicago, 1976.

Gaensbauer, T. J., Emde, R. N., and Campos, J. J. "Stranger" distress: Confirmation of a developmental shift in longitudinal sample. *Perceptual and Motor Skills*, 1976, *43*, 99–106. Cited in M. Haith and J. Campos, Human infancy, *Annual Review of Psychology*. Palo Alto: Annual Reviews, 1977.

Garfinkel, H. *Studies in Ethnomethodology*. Englewood Cliffs, N.J. Prentice-Hall, 1967.

Garvey, C. and BenDebba, M. Effects of age, sex, and partner on children's dyadic speech. *Child Development*, 1974, *45*, 1159–1161.

Gessell, A., Ilg, F. L., and Ames, L. B. *Infant and Child in the Culture of Today*. New York: Harper and Row, 1943.

Gewirtz, J. L. Attachment, dependence, and a distinction in terms of stimulus control. In J. L. Gewirtz (Ed.), *Attachment and Dependency*. New York: Winston-Willey, 1972.

Girgus, J. S., and Wolf, J. Age changes in the ability to encode social cues. *Developmental Psychology*, 1975, *11*, 118.

Goffman, E. *Interaction Ritual*. Garden City, N.Y: Doubleday, 1967.

Goffman, E. *Frame Analysis*. Cambridge, Mass.: Harvard University Press, 1974.

Gordon, I. J., Beller, E. K., Lally, J. R., Yarrow, L., Moreno, P., Rand, C., and Freiberg, K. Studies in socio-emotional development in infancy. Final Report to the Office of Child Development, Grant No. OCD-CB-268, November, 1973.

Goulet, J. Conception of causality and reactions to strangers. In T. G. Décarie (Ed.), *The Infant's Reaction to Strangers*. New York: International Universities Press, 1974, pp. 59–96.

Greenberg, D., Hillman, D., and Grice, D. Infant and stranger variables related to stranger anxiety in the first year of life. *Developmental Psychology*, 1973, *9*, 207–212.

Gunnar-von Gnechten, M. R. Changing a frightening toy into a pleasant one by allowing the infant to control it. Paper presented at the biennial meeting of the Society for Research in Child Development, New Orleans, March, 1977.

Haith, M. M., Bergman, T., and Moore, M. J. Eye contact and face scanning in early infancy. *Science*, in press.

Haith, M. M., and Campos, J. J. Human infancy. In *Annual Review of Psychology*. Palo Alto: Annual Review, 1977.

Harré, R. The conditions for a social psychology of childhood. In M. P. M. Richards (Ed.), *The Integration of a Child into a Social World*. Cambridge, England: Cambridge University Press, 1974, pp. 245–262.

Haviland, J. M., and Lewis, M. Infants' greeting patterns to strangers. Paper presented at the Human Ethology Session of the Animal Behavior Society, Wilmington, North Carolina, May, 1975.

Hebb, D. O. On the nature of fear. *Psychological Review*, 1946, *53*, 259–276.

Hebb, D. O. *The Organization of Behavior*. New York: Wiley, 1949.

Heider, F. Perceiving the other person. In R. Tagiuri and L. Petrullo (Eds.), *Person Perception and Interpersonal Behavior*. Stanford, Cal.: Stanford University Press, 1958, pp. 22–26.

Hess, E. Ethology and developmental psychology. In P. Mussen (Ed.), *Carmichael's Manual of Child Psychology*. New York: Wiley, 1970, pp. 1–38.

Hunt, J. McV. Piaget's observations as a source of hypotheses concerning motivation. *Merrill Palmer Quarterly*, 1963, *9*, 263–275.

Jones, E. E., and Gerard, H. B. *Foundations of Social Psychology*. New York: Wiley, 1967.

Jones, E. E., Gergen, K. J., and Davis, K. E. Some determinants of reactions to being approved or disapproved as a person. *Psychology Monographs*, 1962, *76* (No. 521).

Kagan, J., Henker, B., Hen-Tov, A., Levine, J., and Lewis, M. Infants' differential reactions to familiar and distorted faces. *Child Development*, 1966, *37*, 519–532.

Kaye, K. Toward the origin of dialogue. In H. R. Schaffer (Ed.), *Studies in Mother-Infant Interaction*. London: Academic Press, 1977, pp. 89–118.

Klein, R. P., and Durfee, J. Infants' reactions to strangers vs. mothers. Paper presented at the biennial meeting of the Society for Research in Child Development, Denver, April, 1975.

Kotelchuck, M. The nature of the infant's tie to his father. Paper presented at the biennial meeting of the Society for Research in Child Development, Philadelphia, April, 1973.

Kreutzer, M., and Charlesworth, W. Infants reactions to different expressions of emotions. Paper presented at the biennial meeting of the Society for Research in Child Development, Philadelphia, 1973.

LaBarbera, J. D., Izard, C. E., Vietze, P., and Parisi, S. A. Four- and six-month-old infants' visual responses to joy, anger, and neutral expressions. *Child Development*, 1976, *47*, 535–538.

Lamb, M. E. *The Role of the Father in Child Development*. New York: Wiley, 1976.

Lee, L. C. Toward a cognitive theory of interpersonal development: Importance of peers. In M. Lewis and L. A. Rosenblum (Eds.), *Friendship and Peer Relations*. New York: Wiley, 1975, pp. 207–221.

Lenssen, B. Infants' reactions to peer strangers. Paper presented at the biennial meeting of the Society for Research in Child Development, Denver, 1975.

Lévy-Schoen, A. *L'image d'autrui chez l'enfant*. Paris: Presses Universitaire de France, 1964. Cited in M. Lewis and J. Brooks, Infants' social perception: A constructivist view. In L. Cohen and P. Salapatek (Eds.), *Infant Perception*. New York: Academic Press, 1976.

Lewis, M. Socioemotional development in the opening years of life: Considerations for a new curriculum. Invited address, American Educational Research Association, San Francisco, April, 1976.

Lewis, M., and Brooks, J. Self, other and fear: Infants' reactions to people. In M. Lewis and L. A. Rosenblum (Eds.), *Origins of Fear*. New York: Wiley, 1974, pp. 195–227.

Lewis, M., and Brooks, J. Infants' social perception: A constructivist view. In L. Cohen and P. Salapatek (Eds.), *Infant Perception*. New York: Academic Press, 1975.

Lewis, M., and Lee-Painter, S. An infant's interaction with its social world: The origin of meaning. Paper presented at the annual convention of the Canadian Psychological Association, Montreal, 1972.

Lewis, M., Young, G., Brooks, J., and Michalson, L. The beginning of friendship. In M. Lewis and L. A. Rosenblum (Eds.), *Friendship and Peer Relations*. New York: Wiley, 1975, pp. 27–66.

Lord, S., Lewis, M., and Brooks, J. Person perception: Infants' responses to pictures. Paper presented at annual convention of the Eastern Psychological Association, New York, April, 1975.

Maccoby, E. E., and Feldman, S. S. Mother-attachment and stranger-reactions in the third year of life. *Monographs of the Society for Research in Child Development*, 1972, 37 (1, Serial No. 146).

Main, M. Exploration, play, cognitive functioning and the mother-child relationship. Paper presented at the biennial meeting of the Society for Research in Child Development, Denver, April, 1975.

Marvin, R. S., and Abramovitch, L. I. An ethological study of the development of coy behavior in young children. Paper (revised) presented at the biennial meeting of the Society for Research in Child Development, Philadelphia, March, 1973.

Maudry, M., and Nekula, M. Social relations between children of the same age during the first two years of life. *Journal of Genetic Psychology*, 1934, *54*, 198–215.

McCluskey, K. W., Albas, D. C., Niemi, R. R., Cuevas, C, and Ferrer, C. A. Cross-cultural differences in the perception of the emotional content of speech: A study of the development of sensitivity in Canadian and Mexican children. *Developmental Psychology*, 1975, *11*, 551–555.

Mehan, H., and Wood, H. *The Reality of Ethnomethodology*. New York: Wiley, 1975.

Messinger, S. E., Sampson, H., and Towne, R. D. Life as theatre: Some notes on the dramaturgic approach to social reality. *Sociometry*, 1962, *25*, 98–110. Reprinted in D. Brissett and C. Edgley (Eds.), *Life as Theatre*. Chicago: Aldine, 1975, pp. 32–42.

Mills, M., and Melhuish, E. Recognition of mother's voice in early infancy. *Nature*, 1974, *252*, 123–124.

Monahan, L. C. Mother-infant and stranger-infant interaction: An ethological analysis. Unpublished doctoral dissertation, Department of Psychology, Indiana University, 1975.

Morgan, G. A. Determinants of infants' reactions to strangers. Paper presented at the biennial meeting of the Society for Research in Child Development, Philadelphia, April, 1973.

Morgan, G. A., and Bennett, C. Implications of various methods of scoring infants' reactions to unfamiliar adults. Paper presented as part of symposium on "Infants Reactions to Unfamiliar Adults: A Discussion of Some Important Issues" at the biennial meeting of the Society for Research in Child Development, Denver, April, 1975.

Morgan, G. A., and Ricciuti, H. N. Infants' responses to strangers during the first year. In B. M. Foss (Ed.), *Determinants of Infant Behavior*, Vol. 4. London: Methuen, 1969, pp. 253–272.

Morris, E. K., and Redd, W. H. Children's performance and social preference for positive, negative, and mixed adult-child interactions. *Child Development*, 1975, *46*, 525–531.

Odom, R. D., and Lemond, C. M. Developmental differences in the perception and production of facial expressions. *Child Development*, 1972, *43*, 359–369.

Paradise, E. B., and Curcio, F. Relationship of cognitive and affective behaviors to fear of strangers in male infants. *Developmental Psychology*, 1974, *10*, 476–483.

Rafman, S. The infant's reaction to imitation of the mother's behavior by a stranger. In T. G. Décarie (Ed.), *The Infant's Reaction to Strangers*. New York: International Universities Press, 1974, pp. 117–148.

Rand, C. S., and Jennings, K. D. The function of infant crying in stranger situations. Paper presented at the biennial Southeastern Conference of the Society for Research in Child Development, Chapel Hill, North Carolina, March, 1974.

Raven, B. H., and Rubin, J. Z. *Social Psychology: People in Groups*. New York: Wiley, 1976.

Rheingold, H. L. Modification of social responsiveness in institutional babies. *Monographs of The Society for Research in Child Development*, 1956, *21*, (2, Whole No. 63).

Rheingold, H. L., and Eckerman, C. O. Fear of the stranger: A critical examination. Paper presented at the biennial meeting of the Society for Research in Child Development, Minneapolis, April, 1971.

Rheingold, H. L., and Eckerman, C. O. Fear of the stranger: A critical examination. In H. W. Reese (Ed.), *Advances in Child Development and Behavior*, Vol. 8. New York: Academic Press, 1973, pp. 185–222.

Rheingold, H. L., and Eckerman, C. O. General issues in the study of peer relations: Some proposals for unifying the study of social development. In M. Lewis and L. Rosenblum (Eds.), *Friendship and Peer Relations*. New York: Wiley, 1975, pp. 293–298.

Ricciuti, H. N. Fear and the development of social attachments in the first year of life. In M. Lewis and L. A. Rosenblum (Eds.), *The Origins of Fear*. New York: Wiley, 1974, pp. 73–106.

Richards, M. P. M. First steps in becoming social. In M. P. M. Richards (Ed.), *The Integration of a Child into a Social World*. Cambridge, England: Cambridge University Press, 1974, pp. 83–97.

Robertson, J., and Robertson, J. Quality of substitute care as an influence on separation responses. *Journal of Psychosomatic Research* (Oxford), 1972, *16*, 261–265.

Roedell, W. C., and Slaby, R. G. The role of distal and proximal interaction in infant social preference formation. *Developmental Psychology*, 1977, *13*, 266–273.

Ross, H. The effects of increasing familiarity on infants' reactions to adult strangers. *Journal of Experimental Child Psychology*, 1975, *20*, 226–239.

Ross, H. S., and Goldman, B. D. Establishing new social relations in infancy. In T. Alloway, P. Pliner, and L. Krames (Eds.), *Attachment Behavior*. New York: Plenum, 1977, pp. 61–80.

Scarr, S., and Salapatek, P. Patterns of fear development during infancy. *Merrill Palmer Quarterly*, 1970, *16*, 53–90.

Schaffer, H. R. The onset of fear of strangers and the incongruity hypothesis. *Journal of Child Psychology and Psychiatry*, 1966, *2*, 95–106.

Schaffer, H. R. Cognitive structure and early social behavior. In H. R. Schaffer (Ed.), *The Origins of Human Social Relations*. New York: Academic Press, 1971, pp. 247–267.

Shaffran, R. Modes of approach and the infant's reaction to the stranger. In T. G. Décarie (Ed.), *The Infant's Reaction to Strangers*. New York: International Universities Press, 1974, pp. 149–186.

Shaffran, R., and Décarie, T. G. Short term stability of infants responses to strangers. Paper presented at the biennial meeting of the Society for Research in Child Development, Philadelphia, March, 1973.

Shantz, C. U. The development of social cognition. In E. M. Hetherington (Ed.), *Review of Child Development Research*, Vol. 5. Chicago: University of Chicago Press, 1975, pp. 257–324.

Shatz, M., and Gelman, R. The development of communication skills: Modifications in the speech of young children as a function of listener. *Monographs of the Society for Research in Child Development*, 1973, *38* (5, Serial No. 152).

Skarin, K. Cognitive and contextual determinants of stranger fear in six- and eleven-month-old infants. *Child Development*, 1977, *48*, 537–544.

Spitz, R. Anxiety in infancy: A study of its manifestations in the first year of life. *International Journal of Psycho-Analysis*, 1950, *31*, 138–143.

Sroufe, A. L. Waters, E., and Matas, L. Contextual determinants of infant affective response. In M. Lewis and L. A. Rosenblum (Eds.), *The Origins of Fear*. New York: Wiley, 1974, pp. 49–72.

Stern, D. Mother and infant at play: The dyadic interaction involving facial, vocal, and gaze behaviors. In M. Lewis and L. A. Rosenblum (Eds.), *The Effect of the Infant on its Caregiver*. New York: Wiley, 1974, pp. 187–213.

Stevens, A. G. Attachment behaviour, separation anxiety, and stranger anxiety in polymatrically reared infants. In H. R. Schaffer (Ed.), *The Origins of Human Social Relations*. New York: Academic Press, 1971, pp, 137–144.

Stokes, N. A., and Dabbs, J. M. Sequential analysis of visual and verbal behavior during dyadic conversation. Paper presented at the annual convention of the American Psychological Assocation, Washington, D.C., September, 1976.

Stone, G. P. Appearance and the self. In A. Rose (Ed.), *Human Behavior and Social Processes*. Boston: Houghton-Mifflin, 1962, pp. 86–118. Reprinted in D. Brissett and C. Edgley (Eds.), *Life as Theatre*. Chicago: Aldine, 1975, pp. 78–90.

Tagiuri, R., Blake, R. R., and Bruner, J. S. Some determinants of the perception of positive and negative feelings in others. *Journal of Abnormal and Social Psychology*, 1953, *48*, 585–592.

Tautermannová, M. Smiling in infants. *Child Development*, 1973, *44*, 701–704.

Tiryakian, E. Existential self and the person. In C. Gordon and K. J. Gergen (Eds.), *The Self in Social Interaction*. New York: Wiley, 1968.

Tizard, J., and Tizard, B. The social development of two-year-old children in residential nurseries. In H. R. Schaffer (Ed.), *The Origins of Human Social Relations*. New York: Academic Press, 1971, pp. 147–161.

Tronick, E., Adamson, L., Wise, S., Als, H., and Brazelton, T. The infant's response to entrapment between contradictory messages in face-to-face interaction. Paper presented at the biennial meeting of the Society for Research in Child Development, Denver, 1975.

Urberg, K. A., and Docherty, E. M. Development of role-taking skills in young children. *Developmental Psychology*, 1976, *12*, 198–203.

Walters, R. H., and Parke, R. D. The role of the distance receptors in the development of social responsiveness. In L. P. Lipsitt and C. C. Spiker (Eds.), *Advances in Child Development*, Vol. 2. New York: Academic Press, 1965, pp. 59–96.

Waters, E., Matas, L., and Sroufe, L. A. Infants' reactions to an approaching stranger: Description validation, and functional significance of wariness. *Child Development*, 1975, *46*, 348–356.

Watson, J. S. Orientation-specific age changes in responsiveness to the face stimulus in young infants. Paper presented at the annual meetings of the American Psychological Association, Chicago, 1965.

Watson, J. S. Smiling, cooing, and "the game." *Merrill-Palmer Quarterly*, 1972, *18*, 323–340.

Weisberg, P. Developmental differences in children's preferences for high-

and low-arousing forms of contact stimulation. *Child Development*, 1975, *46*, 975–979.

Wolff, P. H. Observations on the early development of smiling. In B. M. Foss (Ed.), *Determinants of Infant Behavior*, Vol. 2. New York: Wiley, 1963, pp. 113–138.

Wolff, P. H. The natural history of crying and other vocalizations in early infancy. In B. M. Foss (Ed.), *The Determinants of Infant Behavior*, Vol. 4. London: Methuen, 1969, pp. 81–110.

Yarrow, L. J. The development of focused relationships during infancy. In J. Hellmuth (Ed.), *Exceptional Infant*, Vol. 1. Seattle: Special Child Publications, 1967, pp. 428–442.

Yarrow, L. J., Rubenstein, J. L., and Pedersen, F. A. *Infant and Environment: Early Cognitive and Motivational Development*. New York: Wiley (Halsted Press), 1975.

Yarrow, M. R., Waxler, C. Z., and Scott, P. M. Child effects on adult behavior. *Developmental Psychology*, 1971, *5*, 300–311.

Young-Browne, G., Rosenfeld, H. M., and Horowitz, F. D. Infant discrimination of facial expressions. *Child Development*, 1977, *48*, 555–562.

Zelazo, P. Smiling to social stimuli: Eliciting and conditioning effects. *Developmental Psychology*, 1971, *4*, 32–42.

5 Social Skills in Action: An Analysis of Early Peer Games

BARBARA DAVIS GOLDMAN AND HILDY S. ROSS

The ability to interact synchronously with their mothers has been well established for preverbal children under the age of 2 (Brazelton, Koslowski, and Main, 1974; Bruner and Sherwood, 1976; Schaffer, Collis, and Parsons, 1977; Stern, 1974), and the ability to engage in a coherent conversation with a peer is clearly documented for children above the age of 2 (Garvey and Hogan, 1973; Keenan, 1974; Mueller, 1972). Further, the skills underlying such interactional competence have been studied for infants with their mothers and older children with their peers. However, though there are indications of interactional competence in much of the research on *early* peer interaction, these skills have generally not been dealt with in any detail. That is our purpose here. We shall describe the structure and content of early peer games, a special and complex form of peer interaction. From the games, the explicit and implicit social skills will be specified, and then compared to those found in the interactions of infant with adult, child with child, and adult with adult.

In the 1930s considerable research was conducted on early peer interaction (Buhler, 1933; Maudry and Nekula, 1939; Shirley, 1933).

According to most current sources, these studies indicated that peer interaction is nonexistent, or generally negative, until children are past the age of 2. For example, Lewis *et al*. (1975, p. 34) conclude that "a review of these early studies reveals an asocial or antisocial infant." Mueller and Lucas (1975, p. 223) note that prior studies of unacquainted toddlers "reported little achievement of peer interaction before the age of two"; and Dragsten and Lee (1973, p. 9) state that "these researchers found very little social behavior other than watching among infants 13 to 14 months and thus concluded that social behavior is largely absent in young infants." Moreover, these early studies generally have been contrasted with more recent research which reveals that peer interaction is both positive in nature and reasonably frequent. However, a careful reading of both the frequently cited research and the less well known studies (Mallay, 1935a, 1935b; Mengert, 1931) reveals that there *was* evidence of positive peer interactions, including interactions that were called "games." Thus there is continuity, rather than contrast, between earlier and current research.

Perhaps contemporary workers are not entirely to blame for the bias toward emphasizing the absence of or negative features of peer interaction found in these older studies; the researchers themselves often called more attention to a lack of interaction, or to the presence of "negative" interactions such as object struggles, than to the more friendly overtures. These "negative" interactions, or the absence of interaction, were presented as normative social behavior even though the experimental situations were often highly contrived. Shirley's (1933) "baby parties" with 10-month-old infants illustrate both the bias toward the negative and the artificiality of the settings.

"Baby party" is a misnomer, as what actually occurred was a series of six 1-minute "tests" which seemed designed to elicit conflict between the pairs of infants. In two of these tests novel toys were placed between the two infants or given to both of them. Though the predominant activities were simply attempts to contact and manipulate the toys, Shirley repeatedly referred to this as *aggression* and clearly viewed the babies as adversaries. Moreover, despite one infant's offering a doll to another outside the test situation, she concluded only that "aggressive social behavior has begun by the age of 10 months" (p. 78).

In a section separate from the "baby party" data, positive interaction was noted among the two sets of twins in her sample:

> At 21 weeks Freddie turned and reached for Winnie, who was lying beside him on the bed. Accidentally he stuck two fingers in her mouth, and she chewed on them, much to his amusement. In their 51st week,

according to the mother's report, Freddie was sitting on the bed playing with two safety pins clasped together. *He held them out to Winnie, who was sitting beside him. Just as she reached and touched them he jerked them away, and both babies laughed; they continued this for some time.* [pp. 83–84, emphasis added].

Although infants under 1 year, albeit twins, were described as playing what we will later classify as a game, Shirley's work is cited as revealing only a lack of social interest (Dragsten and Lee, 1973; Lewis et al., 1975).

The ambitious experimental study of Maudry and Nekula (1939) is also generally cited as indicating a lack of positive social interaction among infants. To establish normative levels of early peer interaction, 24 children, aged 6 to 24 months, were observed with from four to twelve different partners. The children were in temporary institutional care, and the pairs were composed of partners separated in age by not more than 3 months. The experimental "play" situation consisted of a series of five 4-minute trials. In the first, the infants were placed facing each other in a small playpen. In subsequent trials, they were given hollow cubes, a bell, a drum with one drumstick each, and a bell. A running record of the social behavior of each child was made and then coded for analysis. The first social reactions to the partner in each trial were categorized as either "positive" or "negative."

Maudry and Nekula did state that "the social attitude is a negative one between 9 and 13 months" (p. 201). It seems more accurate, however, when looking at their data, to note that positive and negative initial reactions were approximately equal, with the positive being *slightly* more, whereas, in the younger and older age groups, the positive reactions were *much* more likely. Further, it was chiefly when objects were involved that there were negative reactions to the partner. As these authors noted themselves, "This negative attitude, however, is not due to a genuine hostility, but to the predominant interest in material, to the acquisition of which the partner is often a hindrance" (p. 203). Only 3.4% of the behavior of the 9- to 13-month-olds was categorized as *personal* aggression, in contrast to the high (45.3%) incidence of struggles over novel toys.

The presence of complex sequences of positive social behavior that Maudry and Nekula called "games" was also documented, and, in fact, one sequence involving the drum was included in their illustrative protocol. But, as with Shirley's (1933) data, it was the fights, or more accurately, object struggles, that were cited, not the games.

Bridges's (1933) detailed observational study of social development in institutionalized children has more often been acknowledged as containing positive social reactions to peers (Blurton-Jones, 1974; Mueller and Lucas, 1975), but even her observations of games involving imitation in 11- to 15-month-old children are rarely cited.

Charlotte Buhler's work, however, may provide the most striking example of the contemporary failure to acknowledge the positive social interaction observed. It is true that she originally employed the highly artificial paradigm used by Maudry and Nekula (1939) and Shirley (1933), and her data *did* reveal the similar preponderance of object struggles. However, in her three major works available in English (1930, 1933, 1935), positive reactions of infants to one another were also noted from 6 months onwards. In her 1933 review article, which included results from her original 1927 investigation, infants from 6 to 10 months were described interacting in the following ways with unfamiliar peers: "active seeking of contact," "touching," "exchanging toys" (p. 375), "making cooing sounds," and "cooperating in play" (p. 378).

In this same review she wrote, "As the earliest evidence of leadership in the first year of life, we indicated the initiative of a child who performs and demonstrates a game which the other then takes up or imitates" (p. 383). Examples of such games among infants residing temporarily in an institution are included in *The First Year of Life* (1930):

> B (boy) 50 (10 months) looks attentively at G (girl) 44, offers her again the rattle. G44 takes it back again, holds it out again—and so on.
> B53 (10 months) drums lustily on the night table. His neighbour B73 (11 months) stands up opposite him in his crib and beats on the railing of his crib with "da da" which B53 always immediately imitates. [p. 59].

Her strongest statements of the highly positive interactions, including games, which are possible among infant peers are contained in a rarely cited source, *From Birth to Maturity* (1935):

> At six and seven months the infant tries eagerly to include anyone who is present in its play. Objects are given and received from others and the child enjoys especially those games that include a partner, hide and seek, exchange of toys, etc. [Reference is made to photographs of infants exchanging toys and contacting the same object simultaneously.] The partner's gestures are observed at the latest in the fifth month and at eight months there is an astonishing capacity for interpreting and understanding them. Children of this age have been observed trying to comfort a frightened or crying child [pp. 55–56].

Thus it seems obvious that more than a cursory reading of these studies would indicate that early peer interaction was an interesting and potentially important area in which to study social skills in action.

Yet, for some reason, the research ceased, until its revival approximately 40 years later. According to Lewis and Rosenblum (1975), this apparent loss of interest stemmed from the dual influence of psychoanalytic theory, with its emphasis on the parent-child relationship, and Piagetian theory, which presumes that important interaction between two partners who are both still in the sensorimotor stage is implausible. These authors also account for the resurgence of interest in early peer interaction and its possible impact on social development by recourse to theory: both psychoanalytic and Piagetian theory are now being questioned, hence one can now study areas the theories ignored. Appolloni and Cooke (1975) postulate nontheoretical reasons: the lack of naturally occurring peer groups of infants and toddlers, in other than residential institutions, prevented research by "applied behavioral scientists" who only investigate naturally occurring phenomena. In their view, the advent of infant day care has allowed peer interaction to be studied in "natural environments." Dragsten and Lee (1973) explain the lack of research as at least "partially due to the conviction of many that social interaction between very young children is essentially nonexistent" (p. 1). Blurton-Jones (1974) blames Parten's categories of parallel and cooperative play, and presumably her data (1932), for creating that impression. Dragsten and Lee, like Appolloni and Cooke, point to the increase in infant day care as increasing the importance of the study of infant social behavior.

Most probably there are a number of explanations for both the suspension of research on early peer interaction and its recent popularity. In any case, the sheer amount of early peer research in the last few years is impressive. Perhaps the assumption that the studies from the 1930s failed to find evidence of positive peer interaction has led current workers to focus on demonstrating the presence, and, in general, the positive nature of early peer interaction. Subjects for these demonstrations have been unacquainted children brought together for a short period (Bronson, 1975; Eckerman, Whatley, and Kutz, 1975; Lenssen, 1975; Lewis et al., 1975), a group of infants and toddlers raised together (Vincze, 1971, 1974), and those who were together regularly in a day-care facility (Durfee and Lee, 1973) or play group (Mueller and Lucas, 1975; Mueller and Rich, 1976). Several studies have focused on the differences in interaction patterns between children with their peer friends and with strangers (Dragsten and Lee, 1973; Young and Lewis, 1975) in an attempt to assess the effect of familiarity and the potential for forming relationships that transcend a brief session in the laboratory.

Others who have studied peer interaction among infants and

toddlers have chosen to address additional issues. Rubenstein and Howes (1976) have demonstrated that the extensive interaction which occurred when a peer friend was present increased the level of complexity of play with toys among 19-month-olds. Among 6- to 11-month-olds, Finkelstein, O'Brien, and Ramey (1974) found that *removing* the toys normally present in a day-care center resulted in an increase in peer contacts, and the increase was maintained even after the toys were reintroduced. Apparently the younger infants needed the toy-distractors removed in order to fully discover the potential of peer interaction, whereas, for the older infants, a peer was necessary for the full exploitation of the potential of toys. Individual differences have been studied by Lee and her colleagues, in terms of the strategies or overtures used by individual infants (Lee, 1973) and in terms of the interactions between different dyads (Snipper and Lee, 1974). Theoretical questions about the relationship between cognition and peer-directed social behavior have received considerable attention (Bronson, 1974; Kagan, Kearsley, and Zelazo, 1975; Lee, 1975). Finally, more applied issues, such as the peer interaction patterns of Down's syndrome toddlers integrated with nondelayed toddlers, are also beginning to receive some research attention (Chekel and Tremblay, 1974; Ray, 1974, 1975).

Games have been a part of the interactions of infants and toddlers observed in contemporary work as well; however, most current researchers have merely noted their presence or counted them along with other types of complex interaction. Games, or attempts to initiate games, are mentioned by Durfee and Lee (1973) as occurring among infants under 1 year of age. Eckerman, Whatley, and Kutz (1975) include them in their highest category "coordinate play," and Rubenstein and Howes (1976) include games as part of their category "play." Lewis et al. (1975) employ a category "game-play," defined as "peek-a-boo" or "lead-chase;" Bronson's (1975) classification system also seems to include games embedded within other categories. However, in these studies the primary method of data analysis has generally consisted of tabulating frequencies of specific behaviors within specific intervals; as a result, games, or any other complex, extended interaction cannot be studied in any detail. It is also possible that early peer games are acknowledged as interesting phenomena, but that their rarity in certain studies argued against further analysis, even when videotapes of the play sessions would allow it. For example, though Lewis et al. (1975) include a photograph of a 12-month-old playing tag with a peer friend, their category "game-play" was only scored for a total of four 5-second periods out of 5,040. Others, however, have observed much more extensive and extended games (e.g., Rubenstein and Howes, 1976), but their use of global categories has precluded anything except anecdotal description.

Detailed descriptions of games are not entirely lacking however. Vincze (1974) has provided evocative descriptions of peer games among infants less than 1 year old who were reared together in a residential nursery. In infants as young as 4 months, repeated mutual hand-patting, accompanied by mutual smiling and vocalizing, occurred. Five- and six-month-olds engaged in laughing games. Imitation games, consisting of vocalizing in various intonations, shouting, and a wide variety of movements, began at 8 months, and were often performed rhythmically, with the children acting either simultaneously or in alternation. Peek-a-boo was first observed in infants around 10 months of age, but was most common between 1 and 2 years. Hide-and-seek and chasing/romping games also began at around 10 months, and often included five to six infants, though most activities involved only a pair. It seems quite likely that the experience of being reared together, while being well cared for by adults, contributed to the early emergence of complex interactions with peers. Nevertheless, Vincze provides good evidence that very young children *can* possess sufficient social interaction skills to create games with each other.

Mueller and his colleagues have also been concerned with a developmental progression in early peer interaction, including games, but they have focused on the structure, rather than the content, of the interactions (Mueller and Lucas, 1975; Mueller and Rich, 1976). Five firstborn 1-year-old boys participated twice weekly in a play group for 3 months; play group interaction was videotaped weekly.

Games were noted briefly by Mueller and Rich (1976), though apparently they did not occur within the context of the play group prior to the third month of its existence, and then only particular pairs of children played games. Social interactions of lesser complexity, especially object-centered interactions, occurred from the first session onwards, however. The developmental analysis of Mueller and Lucas (1975), based on the interactions among play group members, especially between two boys with extensive prior contact, traced the evolution of interaction through three stages.

In Stage I, interactions were object-centered rather than social, presumably because the 1-year-olds without experience with peers lacked the appropriate skills for regulating interaction with other children. Mueller and Lucas acknowledged that a turn-alternation pattern might appear to be present in these interactions, but they asserted that the nonsimultaneity of actions stemmed from the act/ watch rhythm of interaction with objects and that any turn alternation was accidental.

Stage II interactions, however, were social. Both partners repeated their actions if their peer responded, and both shared responsibility for maintaining the interaction. Turn alternation was real, not illusory. These interchanges (previously labeled "games" by Mueller and Rich) were either simple or complex, but were predominantly imitative. Role reversal, as in ball games, marked Stage III.

As this developmental progression was based primarily on the changing interactions of one dyad, confirmation of the ordinality of the stages awaits replication. Nevertheless, the analysis of the structure of the interaction is worthy of attention; especially intriguing are the gradual changes in turn alternation, the relationship between the roles of the partners, and the possibility of a general game-initiating signal being developed by peers afforded repeated contact.

Considering both the current and the earlier research on peer interaction, there is evidence that very young children, under the age of 2, can and do interact with each other. However, the studies which report or describe extended, patterned interaction sequences or games are predominantly those whose subjects are familiar with each other. Establishing that very young, *unacquainted* children can play games would constitute additional evidence of their sociability. As complex extended interactions, games are perhaps a more persuasive argument than documentation of the presence of more frequent, but simpler, social behaviors such as smiling and offering a toy. Moreover, examination of the structure of the game interactions and of the ways the partners engaged each other in games provides important evidence, not just of social inclinations, but of the considerable repertoire of social skills possessed by children between their first and second birthdays.

Method

Subjects

Forty-eight normal, full-term infants within 2 weeks of 12, 18, or 24 months were subjects of the current study. Sixteen infants were in each of the three age groups; half were male and half were female.

Each 18-month-old participated in two sessions, one with a 12-month-old and the other with a 24-month-old same-sexed peer. (Concerns about the sensitivity to developmental status a toddler, specifically one who is 18 months old, might demonstrate in his encounters with peers who are 6 months older or younger than himself, led to this aspect of the design.) The two sessions were a week apart and half of the 18-month-olds of each sex were paired with a younger and half with an older child on their first visit.

The infants' families seemed roughly representative of the middle-class, industrial community from which the sample was drawn, judging from the wide range of occupations reported for the fathers (e.g., fireman, teacher, truck driver, dentist, builder). Only nine of the mothers were employed, and with one exception their employment was part-time and generally in the evenings when their husbands would care for the children. Eighteen infants were first born (five with younger siblings); 17 had one older sibling; and 13 came from homes with two, three, and, in one case, four other children.

Mothers were asked how frequently the subjects played with other children their own age. Thirty answered not at all, infrequently, or about once a week or less; 12 stated that their infants had "some" peer contact or that they played with others two or three times each week; only six mothers reported frequent or daily peer contact for their infants.

Mothers were also asked if their infants showed any interest in their peers when they encountered them. Three reported little interest in peers; 21 noticed some peer interest as evidenced by friendly overtures such as pointing, waving, watching, or vocalizing; 24 mothers described their infants' enthusiastic reactions to peers, including combined responses of smiling, waving and saying "hi," grabbing and hugging, and delighted screams of "I want baby."

Experimental environment

The current study was conducted in an unfurnished room measuring 3.8 × 5.0 m. A large one-way-vision window spanned the length of one wall, and video cameras were mounted in the two opposite corners. The primary camera was equipped with a wide-angle lens which enabled recording from approximately two-thirds of the room. A barrier, .76 m. high, blocked access to the remainder of the room, resulting in an area of 3.8 × 3.25 m. in which the children could play.

A second camera focused on a small blind spot in the primary camera's range, next to the barrier. Both pictures could be integrated with the use of a special-effects generator which enabled split-screen recording.

The two mothers sat on cushions on the floor against the wall opposite the barrier and .6 m. from one another. Two rows of five toys each were located 1.8 m. in front of the mothers, between the mothers and the barrier. Two similar sets of ten toys were used, one for each visit of the 18-month-old, and the order of use of the toy sets was balanced across the other factors (sex, visit number, order of peers). The toys were selected to be of interest to children in the age range, sufficiently numerous and diverse to maintain the children's interest throughout the sessions, amenable to joint play, and capable of being divided into two similar sets. Three toys were used in both sets (wooden blocks, two toy telephones); three in each set were highly similar (two books, two balls, two pull-apart puzzle pull toys); four items in each set were roughly parallel (a shoe house with little people who fit in it or a house with little bears that fit inside; a xylophone or a dog, both of which made noise as they were moved along the floor; an hourglass or a bell that were similar in size, shape, and made noise when shaken; a plush stuffed dog or walrus).

Procedure

On arrival, each mother and infant were conducted to a separate interview room where the mother learned more about the study and answered some questions about her infant, while the infant played with some toys. The mother was asked to carry her child into the experimental room, to sit on the cushion, and to allow her child to remain near her or to move around the room as he pleased. She was asked to interfere as little as possible, neither directing her child's activity nor engaging him in extensive play sequences; she was asked to interfere only if she felt the children might harm themselves or each other. Mothers were encouraged to talk to one another and the children, and to respond appropriately to the initiatives of the children.

The 18-month-old and mother entered the experimental room first; the other infant and mother followed within 1 minute, and the door was closed. The trial began on the entry of the second child and lasted 25 minutes.

The entire session was recorded on videotape. To supplement the videotape record, two independent observers dictated a verbal account of the activities of each of the children on two-channel audiotape.

Preparation of Transcripts

Each videotape was viewed and a preliminary notation was made of all interactions that involved or pertained to the other partner. On the basis of these descriptions, a set of exhaustive categories of peer interaction was developed. An Esterline-Angus 20-channel event recorder was then used to record the time of occurrence and duration of all peer-directed social behaviors. Two separate recordings were made for each play session; for each, the observer focused on one partner while viewing the videotape and listening to the previously dictated commentary. For each recording, some responses of the other partner were also indicated, to allow the two records to be appropriately synchronized into a single sequence of all interactive behavior. With this sequence as an outline, each videotape was repeatedly viewed both with and without the accompanying narrative on the audiotape to produce a detailed transcript of the entire session. At this point, the decision was made to focus on the set of extended, complex, patterned interactions that seemed to be, or resemble, games.

This larger set of possible games was then repeatedly viewed, and more detailed transcripts were developed. A search for commonalities among interactions that seemed unequivocally to be games established four features or criteria that were then applied to all possible games to establish the set of games discussed here. The four features were *mutual involvement* by both partners, *alternation of turns*, successive *repetition* through at least four turns, two by each partner, and *nonliterality*. In addition, signs of any type of negative affect had to be absent.

Mutual involvement was the most general feature; each child performed some action in response to an action of his partner. Alternation of turns at acting followed from, and allowed for, mutual involvement. Each partner had his own turn, and turn alternation regulated the interaction such that both could act but not interrupt each other. Repetition of at least a two-turn sequence was the feature that was responsible for the appearance of a "pattern" in the game interactions, as opposed to an extended interaction which was not predictable. Nonliterality was the feature that distinguished games from other repetitive interactions regulated by turn alternation; games contained indications that the actions or content of the game were not to be interpreted as they ordinarily would be, that is, the particular content did not define the goal of the interaction, as it would in a nonplay or literal exchange. The apparent goal of the interaction was to play a game, and the apparent goal of the game was to interact.

Subsequent to the establishment of a set of games which fulfilled these criteria, the relevant sections of the videotapes were again viewed repeatedly to provide additional detail. The tables that supplement the text provide some indication of the nature of the resultant transcripts, which are the source of all results to be reported.[1]

Inter-observer Reliability

A second, independent observer viewed the videotapes of two game sequences and developed transcripts of the interaction which occurred. These were then compared to the original transcripts, and the exact agreement on the activity and object of the activity between the two records was calculated. A total of 160 action-object items were judged, and the percentage of interobserver agreement was 84% and 88% for the two transcripts.

Results and Discussion

The Games

Twenty-eight interaction sequences were identified as games.[2] Based on the relationship between the roles of the two partners, the games were designated as *reciprocal*, when the roles repeatedly were reversed; as *imitative*, when one partner's turns were highly similar or identical to those of the other; or as *complementary*, when each partner's turns complemented or completed the turns of the other. All reciprocal games involved the ball being rolled or thrown, chased or caught, by each partner in turn, and will thus be referred to simply as ball games. The three types of games were represented approximately equally in the sample of 28.

The nine ball games, though essentially similar in form, differed in the particular manner the partners chose to exchange the ball—rolling, throwing, bouncing it off the walls. The eight imitation games featured a physical action, a vocalization, or a combination of the two. The "content" of these games included kicking the barrier, rhythmic foot taps, vocalizing "da" and swiping at the partner's face, and several variations of faked laughter. The 11 games with roles that were complementary differed considerably from one another, though there were three that involved the placing of a leg across the partner's lap. The content of the other games included repeatedly removing blocks from the mouth of the partner after their insertion, pushing a toy dog into the partner who moved around the room, and touching actions, including tickling.

Table 1 illustrates the three types of role relationships, the clear alternation of turns, and the content of the turns, using two-turn sequences from three games.

The length or duration of the games can be indicated in two ways, by the number of turns, which formed the basis of the games, and by the actual duration between the beginning and end of the game. Both measures, however, are not as straightforward as might be assumed, as decisions must be made whether to include repeated overtures prior to involvement by the partner, whether to include sometimes lengthy prethrow signaling, and when to declare that a game is completed, given attempts to re-engage a distracted or no longer interested partner.

Thus, despite the fact that games often evolved and subsided, criteria were designated to indicate the points at which games were considered to start and stop. The overture, or the first of a series of attempts which eventually resulted in a game, was designated as the start; games were considered to have ended when both partners ceased their attempts to re-engage one another in the game, and/or turned to other activities.

The duration of the individual games varied widely, from a brief 8 seconds to over 4 minutes. In our sample, the nine ball games were the longest, averaging about 111 seconds, with a range from 39 to 280 seconds. The 11 games with complementary roles averaged about 60 seconds, with a range of 10 to 222 seconds. The eight imitation games were the briefest, averaging 32 seconds, ranging from 8 to 95 seconds. The combined duration of the 28 games was almost 32 minutes, 4% of the time available to all 32 dyads, but approximately 12% of the play sessions which included at least one game.

The average number of turns in the three types of games combined was 12.2, with a range of 4 to 31 turns. Ball games averaged 11.8 turns, complementary games averaged 13.7, and imitation games averaged 10.4 turns. The total number of turns in all 28 games was 341.

The 28 games were contributed by 11 of the 32 dyads in the study. Of these 11, six dyads contributed one game each to the sample, three contributed two each, one dyad played three games, and one remarkable pair played 13 games (six imitative, six complementary, and one ball game). Three of the 18-month-olds, two boys and one girl, played games during both play sessions. Thus 19 of the 48 children involved in the study were participants in games during the relatively brief period that they were observed. Six of the game-playing dyads were

Table 1
Illustrative two-turn sequences from three games

Reciprocal Roles

18 walks over to the ball,
turns toward and looks at 12
while holding his arm outstretched toward the ball,
picks up the ball, turns to
look at 12, holds up the ball
while looking at 12, *throws*
the ball directly to 12,
continues to watch 12,
immobile

                                   12 looks at and *contacts the*
                                   ball as it rolls to him, looks
                                   up at 18

(18 smiles at 12, continues
to watch, immobile)

                                   12 continues to look at 18 for
                                   two seconds, then *rolls the ball*
                                   back to 18, looks up at 18

Imitative Roles

18 reaches out toward 24
with a block in her hand
and *swipes at 24's face and*
vocalizes "da," sits back
and drops her arm to her
side

                                   24 bends forward and reaches out
                                   toward 18's face (without a
                                   block in her hand) *and vocalizes*
                                   "da" as she swipes, leans back
                                   and drops her hand to her side

---

Complementary Roles

                                   24 looks around the floor,
                                   approaches and *picks up another*
                                   block, places it in her mouth,
                                   and turns to look at 18, con-
                                   tinues to watch, immobile

18 *approaches, pulls the*
block from 24's mouth and
vocalizes, backs away, continues to watch, immobile .

male and five female; four of the dyads were composed of an 18- and a 12-month-old, the remaining seven of an 18- and a 24-month-old. The most numerous (17), longest, and most varied games were played by the older female dyads, the least frequent and briefest (a single ball game with the mothers' help) by the younger female dyad. The younger and older male dyads played four and six games, respectively.

The 18-month-olds initiated half (14) of the 28 games; the 24-month-olds initated 13, and one 12-month-old initiated an imitation game. Considering the 18-month-old as either the younger or older member of the dyad revealed differential patterns in the initiation of the three types of games. Ball games were initiated equally (5 to 4) by the older and younger member, whereas almost all (6 of 8) of the imitation games were initiated by the younger partner. Almost all (10 of 11) of the complementary games were initiated by the older partner.

There were no consistent relationships between the presence of siblings or the extent of prior interaction with peers, as reported by the mother, and the playing of games with an unfamiliar peer. Some of the toddlers and infants who played games had extensive prior contact with other children, but some had none at all; others who had similar prior experience played no games. Maternal reports of interest in unfamiliar peers encountered when shopping, in the park, and so forth also failed to differentiate game players from the others.

Games tended to occur during the middle of the 25-minute play session, with 13 of the 28 starting during the middle third (the ninth to the sixteenth minutes). Six occurred during the first 8 minutes; two of these, both ball games, were begun within 4 minutes after the two partners met. Nine began during the last third.

No consistent pattern emerged when the amount and type of interaction preceding and following the occurrence of games was examined. For example, three games occurred after 10 to 20 minutes of minimal social interaction, whereas others were preceded by extensive interaction, including other games. Ball games were followed by unsuccessful ball game overtures in four of the six dyads who played them, and one dyad engaged in several object struggles after playing a game. In contrast, two dyads played two or three ball games, and in two other dyads imitation and complementary games followed one another within seconds. Considering all 11 dyads, two reasonable assumptions, that games, as complex forms of interaction, might be preceded by extensive, albeit less complex, interaction, and that the occurrence of a game would predispose the partners to continue to interact positively and frequently, were given no consistent support.

The Skills

To exist, games must begin. One might assume that to begin a game, the initiating child would indicate what is to be the content of the game while signaling his intentions of nonliterality, that "this is to be a game." He would also indicate that this is to be a *social* game, by signaling the completion of his turn and inviting his partner to take *his* turn. Thus, some games might start with a clear game overture (ball games especially), while others might evolve more slowly, such that only after the second partner responded to an act of the first, by imitating it, or laughing, or whatever, would a game clearly be in progress. Nonliterality and turn-yielding signals might then be found to occur first in the partner's turn or in the initiator's repetition of his own turn. In both cases, as the partners were unfamiliar with each other, they would have to use signals that would be commonly understood, or they would have to negotiate shared meanings. As the partners were essentially preverbal, they would have to communicate through the pattern of their actions. As the games continued, they had to retain their nonliteral quality and the turns should continue to alternate. Thus signals of both kinds might be expected to continue to occur, though perhaps less obviously as the partners learned more about the content and structure of the games they were developing and playing.

Nonliterality. To signal game intentions, specifically that the co-occurring act was meant nonliterally, one most obvious and likely candidate would be smiles and/or laughter, especially when part of the overture. (The incidence of smiles and laughter, but especially smiles, is most likely underrepresented because of the difficulty of seeing the partners' faces at all times, when observed either live or on videotape. Further, problems with the audio portion of some of the videotapes may have obscured brief laughter.) Smiles and/or laughter were recorded for 20 of the 28 games (smiles only in nine, laughter only in six, and both smiles and laughter in five). More important, in 15 of the 20 games, smiles and/or laughter were observed during the first two complete turns. In five of these 15 games, smiles and/or laughter were part of the first turn or overture. In three more, which happened to be ball games, the initiators smiled or laughed after the first exchange—that is, after their partners had contacted or retrieved the ball; their partners immediately returned the ball. In an additional seven games, the first smiles or laughter came from the partner as he took his first turn. (In many games it was the partner's response which seemed to define the interaction as a game.) Thus it does seem that smiles and/or laughter may serve a metacommunicative function, to signal "I mean (or meant) this act to serve as the basis for a game."

Of course, smiles and laughter do not exclusively serve to signal nonliterality. They also indicate enjoyment or amusement and serve as social overtures or responses. Considering the entire sample of 32 play sessions, 67% of all laughter but only 19% of all smiles occurred within the context of games. Thus the infants and toddlers had to employ additional means to communicate their intentions to play games.

The particular content of the overtures may have facilitated a game interpretation in two ways. It seems reasonable to assume that most, if not all, of the partners had played ball games with their parents, siblings, or others. As recipients, they might thus recognize a ball game overture as such. Whether the initiating partner made such assumptions is debatable—he may simply have attempted a ball game because it was one *he* knew how to play. Regardless, the choice of the familiar ball game as content would seem quite fortuitous.

In addition, the content of the overture might serve as a cue of nonliterality through its irrelevancy as literal interaction. Interpretation of an action as nonliteral seems more likely when literal interpretations are unlikely. (Even ball game overtures may include this cue—if a ball is meant simply to be exchanged, it is unlikely one would throw it across the room, then turn to the partner). Except as attention-getting devices, there seems to be no literal goal or possible reason for many of the behaviors which comprise the content of the complementary and imitation games—holding an elbow near the face of the partner, foot tapping, faked laughter, vocalizing "da," or flapping one's tongue repeatedly over one's front teeth. But these, and the other actions, do not seem to have been performed to obtain the attention of the partner, as in 12 of the 19 complementary and imitative games the partner was already watching the initiator immediately prior to the overture. Since six of the eight games without any accompanying smiles or laughter were imitative or complementary, and in five of these the partner responded to the first overture, it seems that such irrelevancy can be employed and interpreted as a signal of game intentions. Whether it is a reliable signal cannot be assessed, as there is no way to calculate how many other acts, performed once and receiving no response, were meant as overtures.

During the course of the interaction, each partner's repetition of his own actions reinforced the interpretation of the acts as nonliteral, as vehicles for a game. Repetition of the overture, beyond the apparent purpose of securing the involvement of the partner. and inducing him to take his turn, also served to signal nonliterality, or game intent. The use of this signal was apparently necessary in almost one-quarter of the games (6 out of 28) in which the partner did not respond with his turn until the overture had been repeated from one to five times. Several kinds of evidence support the interpretation of repetition signaling a game overture and not just being the common way of obtaining a partner's attention. In all cases, the partner was either already attending or had started to do so at the time of the first overture. Further, three of the six were ball game overtures without smiles or laughter by the overturing child, and thus might have required clarification of their intent before the partner responded. Most telling, however, is the pattern of repetition in the three other games. In these, the overturing act was repeated, essentially identically, but with an interesting and consistent variation: the overturing turn immediately prior to the first complete game turn by the partner was an elongation of the basic turn. All three became imitation games, though the partners initially were responding without imitating. Further, once the partner was imitating, there was a rapid exchange of turns, whereas during the overture, the overturing turns were more widely spaced. The insistent repetition of the overture thus seemed to signal both that a game was intended, and that an imitation game was what the initiator had in mind. Table 2 illustrates this multiple use of repetition with transcripts from two imitation games.

Table 2
The use of repetition to signal an imitation game overture

Prior to the game, the 18-month-old is sitting in the corner near her mother, holding a book and facing the 24-month-old. The 24-month-old is sitting in the center of the room among the toys, facing toward the 18-month-old and her mother, but looking at the toys.

	Time	
18 *vocalizes* fake laugh to 24 "ahhaha"	0	
	2	24 *looks up at 18 and says* "hi"
18 *repeats fake laughter* "haha"	3	
		24 continues to watch 18
18 glances up at her mother, looks back at 24 and *repeats fake laughter* "ahahaha"	7	

Table 2
The use of repetition to signal an imitation game overture
(*continued*)

	Time	
	8	24 *vocalizes a fake laugh* "*haha*," looks at her mother, looks back at 18
18 *vocalizes a fake laugh* "*aha*"		
	12	24 *vocalizes a fake laugh* "*aha*"
18 *vocalizes a fake laugh* "*ha*"		
	14	24 *vocalizes a fake laugh* "*ha*"
18 continues to watch 24		
	17	24 runs up to 18 (start new game)

Prior to the game, the 18-month-old is sitting on his mother's cushion, between her legs, looking around the room and occasionally looking at and vocalizing to the 12-month-old. The 12-month-old is sitting on the floor in front of his mother, his torso oriented toward the 18-month-old and playing with his mother's shoes. His legs are straight out in front of him.

	Time	
	0	12 looks at 18, at his own feet, *taps his foot twice* by lifting his leg off the floor and letting it drop, looks up at 18, and continues to watch, immobile
18 turns to look at 12, engages in extended mutual visual regard for 13 seconds, looks down at his own shoes and moves his feet slightly		
	18	12 looks at his mother, *taps his foot once*, looks up at 18
18 turns to look at 12, looks at his own shoes and touches them, vocalizes "ma," points out the toys to 12		
	29	12 *taps his foot once* while looking at it, looks up at 18
18 turns to look at 12, looks at his own knees and pats them, looks at the toys, then		

Table 2
The use of repetition to signal an imitation game overture
(*continued*)

	Time	
at his own shoes and vocalizes		
	36	12 *taps his foot once* while looking at it, looks up at 18
18 continues looking away from 12, then points at the camera and vocalizes, looks at 12, then looks around the room		
	47	12 *taps his foot twice while looking at 18*, continues to watch, immobile
18 smiles at 12, moves his feet		
	54-55	12 *taps his foot three times* while looking at 18, continues to watch, immobile
18 smiles at 12 and *taps his foot once* while looking at 12, smiles again at 12, looks at his own feet	58	
	63	12 *taps his foot twice* while looking at 18, continues to watch, immobile
18 smiles, looks at 12, *taps his foot*, pauses for 3 seconds, and *taps his foot again while looking at 12*, looks at his shoes and touches them	65-68	
	70	12 *taps his foot twice* while looking at 18
18 looks up at 12, *taps his foot twice*, looks at and touches his shoes, glances at 12, looks at and touches his shoes	72	
	82	12 *taps his foot twice* while looking at 18
18 turns to look at 12, smiles at 12, looks away, coughs, looks at 12, looks at his own shoes		
	95	12 *taps his foot twice* while looking at 18, turns to look at his mother (the game ends)

Thus, it appears that laughter and/or smiles, familiar game content, irrelevancy, and repetition *can* be employed metacommunicatively by infants and toddlers to signal game intent or nonliterality.

In most games, these metacommunicative cues were coupled with spontaneously created content. In seven games, however, instead of creating the content, the children were able to use these cues and others such as exaggeration to transform a previously occurring literal act, their own or their partner's, or an accidental event, into a game. For example, the mother of an 18-month-old removed a block from her daughter's mouth, saying "Get that out of your mouth. Dirty." This literal interaction between mother and child was transformed into a game; the 24-month-old repeatedly put blocks into her own mouth, and the 18-month-old repeatedly pulled them out, not because dirty blocks are a health hazard, but simply to engage in an interaction. In another dyad, the 24-month-old was accidentally bumped by the 18-month-old who was pushing a toy dog along the floor. After backing away slighty, she stopped, laughed, looked at her mother who laughed, then waited to be bumped again. As with the spontaneous overtures, the transformation may be effected by one partner, but the other has to understand and accept it.

Turn alternation. Games were thus begun in several ways. But games must not only be begun, they must be played, by both partners. Though games are possible where both partners consistently take their turns simultaneously, in all the games in this sample the partners alternated turns to achieve mutual involvement and to regulate the interaction. To alternate turns, two abilities are required: indicating to the partner that it is now time for him to act, and giving him enough time, to both start and complete his turn.

The most common turn-yielding signal, which occurred in every game, was looking at the partner or continuing to look at him, often accompanied by immobility, following completion of the turn. This pattern also characterized the behavior of the partners between their own turns, that is, they most often remained immobile and visually attentive while their partner was taking *his* turn. As a turn-yielding signal, it was more or less apparent depending on the length of time between the end of one partner's turn and the beginning of the other's turn; as between-turn behavior, it was most striking when the partner's turns were quite long. Given that these games might be described as behavioral dialogues, it seems appropriate that behavioral silence—immobility—functioned analogously to silence in conversation.

In several ball games, partners waited, immobile, 16, 24, 28, and 33 seconds to have the ball returned to them after their own throw, roll, or offer. In a foot-tap imitation game, the initial overtures of the 12-month-old were separated by 18, 11, 7, 11, and 7 seconds. Thus, infants and toddlers can wait. Waiting so long for a partner's response indicates more than the ability to do so, however; it also suggests the very real desire of the infants and toddlers to secure mutual involvement and thus to play a game.

Other turn-yielding signals were related to the specific game. In ball games the direction of visual gaze was used not only to signal a turn-yield, but also to indicate the content or referent of the turn. In several instances, after throwing the ball, a toddler would alternately look at his partner, look at the ball, and look back at his partner again, until the partner retrieved the ball. Other signals during ball games, which often had long intervals between retrieving and throwing, as well as between throwing and retrieving, encouraged the partner to complete his turn by alluding to the content of it: backing away, holding the arms up ready to catch; patting the floor between outstretched legs to indicate where to roll the ball; and bringing one's arm down forcefully, as if pantomiming a throw. Withdrawal, in a manner that was specific to the particular content of the turn—for example, sitting back and dropping the arm following a reach toward the partner's face, backing away from the barrier after kicking it, or lifting one's hand away from the ball and stepping back—served as a turn-yielding signal after at least one turn in 17 of the games, including seven of the eight imitation games. All imitation games were either predominantly vocal, had a vocal component, or at least produced sound (kicking the barrier, foot tapping). In these then, silence was also a turn-yielding cue. Complementary games were not so consistently marked by sound cues. In these, maintaining a posture, a kind of immobilized action, occurred in nine of the 11 games—holding out an object, holding one's head thrust forward with a block in one's mouth, or placing one's face within three to six inches of the partner's face, upside down.

Further, not only could the partners hold an action posture, but some at least could do so for an extended period of time when necessary. For example, in one complementary game involving repeated exchanges of blocks, the interval between an offer and its acceptance ranged from 2 to 20 seconds, with the offering partner continuing to hold out her arm for the full time.

Apparent violations of turn alternation. Though alternation of turns was a consistent feature of every game in the sample, two kinds of apparent violations of the alternating-turn pattern occurred: simultaneous turns and one partner taking two turns in a row (excluding repetition in the overture as discussed above). These instances are informative as they reveal not a lack of skill or awareness of the "rules of the game," but rather provide additional evidence of both.

There were seven instances of simultaneous turns, which occurred in four ball games by three different dyads. Each involved both partners attempting to retrieve the ball at the same time. In one of these, the dyad was not yet fully involved in a game—one of the mothers rolled the ball to the barrier and both children started to chase it; the 24-month-old deferred, stopping and watching the 18-month-old get the ball. In two, one partner was having difficulty retrieving the ball when the other partner started to act, perhaps to help. In both, the second moved back as the first succeeded in retrieving the ball. In one of the remaining four instances, both partners approached, and then withdrew simultaneously, with the partner who originally threw the ball reapproaching and throwing again. Given the large number of turns in the ball games (107), it is interesting that only seven simultaneous "retrieves" occurred. More important, however, is the fact that in four of the seven, one or both partners gave a turn-yielding signal, deferring to the other through stopping his chase to watch, immobile; withdrawing his arm; or sitting back. That the partners employed such signals not only at the end of a turn, but also in situations where they found themselves taking turns simultaneously, further reveals their awareness of both the necessity of alternating turns and the nonliterality of the exchange. One defers when it really doesn't matter *who*, at that moment, has possession of the ball; maintaining the interaction is more important.

The most obvious and consistent display of turn-yielding signals in the midst of simultaneous turns was not included in the above, as it constitutes a special case. There were two games by one younger male dyad which were based on a turn structure unique to this dyad—partly simultaneous and partly alternating turns. The 18-month-old would throw the ball across the room and wait; the 12-month-old would chase after the ball; then the 18-month-old would start to chase the ball so that both would run together, often side by side. Then the 12-month-old would stop, and even lift up his hands if near the ball, and the 18-month-old would get the ball and repeat the sequence. As the ball was not exchanged, and the roles were never reversed, these were designated as complementary, rather than reciprocal ball games. Though the 18-month-old apparently did not intend for the roles to be reversed, or for the ball actually to be exchanged, the 12-month-old did seem to be attempting to play a traditional ball game. However, it appeared that his own awareness of ball game structure, and perhaps a bit of intimidation, caused him repeatedly to cease acting when simultaneous turns occurred. Thus two games, albeit unusual ones, were created out of the violation of the alternating-turn structure and its remedy.

The second kind of apparent violation of the alternating-turn structure, where one partner took several (two to four) turns in a row (excluding overtures), occurred 14 times in the 28 games, with ten instances during ball games, two in complementary games, and two instances in imitation games. Only two of these violations however resulted from one of the partners simply not waiting long enough for his partner to take his turn; both of these were in ball games. In the remaining 12, when the toddlers took multiple turns, mutual involvement appeared to be their goal, not the contrary, In six cases, one partner waited, essentially giving only a turn-yielding signal, following an incomplete or inadequate turn by his partner: The partner then adequately performed his turn, and mutual involvement was again achieved. In the remaining six cases, the multiple turns occurred when one partner failed to respond; his partner would then retake his own turn, and yield again, thereby providing yet another chance to respond. To illustrate, during a complementary game, the partner whose role was to pull the block from the mouth of the other couldn't, as her partner failed to put one in her mouth. Rising to the challenge, she took a block from her own mouth and held it to her partner's mouth, then pulled it away, essentially repeating her own role, and yielded. Her partner, suitably primed, then got another block, put it in her mouth, and the game continued. Of the six instances of this type, two were successful, i.e., they occurred in the middle of a game. Four were not, occurring at the end of games as attempts to re-engage the partner.

Thus, 12 of the 14 turn-alternation violations were more apparent than real; in them the infants and toddlers further revealed their awareness of the potency of a turn-yielding signal and the many uses of repetition.

Game endings. Further evidence of the importance of alternating turns and mutual involvement is found in an examination of how the games ended. Sixteen ended when one partner failed to take his turn, apparently having lost interest in the game; five more ended after a partner took his turn, and then lost interest, as evidenced by either turning away or performing some action unrelated to the game. Mothers intervened in two games, essentially directing one partner not to take his turn. In one case, one partner apparently took too long to take his turn, and his partner was distracted. In four, one partner redefined the interaction as literal, keeping the object rather than relinquishing it, accompanied in two games by "No, mine," or a scream when the partner reached for it.

In nine of the 28 games, following either a turn-taking failure or a redefinition of the interaction as literal, the games simply stopped, and the partners went their separate ways. In ten, there was at least one attempt to re-engage the partner after he indicated a loss of interest, which might be either before or after his turn, but only in three games was there more than one attempt. Following nine of the attempts to re-engage, interaction ceased; in one, interaction continued though the game did not. Thus in 18 cases, termination of the game resulted in termination, for the moment at least, of interaction. After the remaining ten games however, including the one noted above, interaction did not cease. In three cases, a new game was begun and in the other seven, other nongame interaction continued; in no case was there an attempt to reinstate the original game. The partner who actually ended the game and the other member of the dyad each initiated half of the subsequent interactions.

Unsuccessful game overtures. So far we have dealt only with games and with overtures that resulted in games. Since multiple skills and constraints are involved in beginning and continuing a game, it should not be surprising if previously unacquainted infants and toddlers do not always achieve the interactions they try to start. An additional perspective on the skills involved in employing the various signals to indicate game intent and to regulate the alternation of turns is thus provided by an analysis of unsuccessful overtures.

To ensure that the interactions were, in all likelihood, game overtures instead of literal social behaviors, and to provide enough similar instances for a comparison, only ball game overtures were selected for study.[3] Peer-directed patterns designated as ball game overtures included rolling or throwing the ball directly to the partner; rolling or throwing the ball across the room, but with visual attention to the partner immediately before, after, or during the throw; chasing the ball just thrown; saying "catch" and/or gesturing to receive the ball.

Thirty-three sets of such overtures were identified. The overtures consisted of from one to eight discrete attempts in each, with an average of 2.4. Their mean duration was 28 seconds, ranging from 4 to 135 seconds. Fifteen dyads contributed from one to five overtures, with a mean of 2.2. Of these 15 dyads, six also had at least one ball game, and three more played at least one other kind of game, while the remaining six played no games.

There were no overtures by 12-month-olds, 20 by the 18-month-olds (8 to 12-month-olds and 12 to 24-month-olds), and 13 by 24-month-olds. Fourteen of the initiators were female, and 19 were male, a distribution highly similar to that of the ball games (four played by females, five by males). The older female dyads contributed 13 overtures; the older males, 12; the younger males, seven; and the younger females, one.

Ball game attempts were distributed in a pattern opposite to the pattern of games; there were seven in the middle third, and 13 in both the beginning and last 8 minutes. Twenty-one occurred prior to any game, eight were after a ball game had already occurred, and four after imitation or complementary games. In the overtures themselves no pattern was discernible that depended on whether the overture occurred before or after a game, or occurred in a play session without any games whatsoever. Individual style was occasionally apparent, as repeated overtures by the same member of the dyad were often quite similar.

Possible reasons for the failure of the overtures were varied. In three of the 33 overtures, the partner was facing away at the time and thus did not see the attempts. In an additional overture, the partner was facing away during the early attempts within the overture. In four, the signaling itself may have been somewhat ambiguous. But in 25 of the 33, the original throw, roll or request for the ball was seen and clearly marked as a ball game overture through prethrow signaling (holding the ball over the head or shoulder for an extended period while looking at and often approaching the partner), verbalizations, gaze direction, and/or gaze alternation. Twelve of these were also repeated from one to seven times.

The various factors which seemed to contribute to the failure of these "good" overtures to result in ball games provide additional evidence of the multiplicity of skills in playing games. Though several overtures had more than one possible flaw, the most likely single reason for these 25 failures is listed in Table 3. The diversity of flaws is apparent.

As in any reciprocal interaction, it is often difficult to fault only one partner. Some failures do seem to be the responsibility of the initiator, such as not giving enough time, or the recipient, such as keeping the ball after an apparently nonliteral exchange. But many are equivocal—the partner could simply expend more effort in retrieving if the ball is not thrown directly to him, or he could put aside his other toys if a less-than-opportune moment had been chosen. The importance of the partner in not only responding to the overture, but in potentially overcoming its faults becomes obvious. *Mutual* interest,

Table 3
Probable cause of failure of ball game overtures
despite adequate signaling of game intent

Probable Cause of Failure	Number of instances
Recipient treats exchange as literal, and keeps the ball or gives it to his mother	5
Recipient is busy with other toys at the time of the overture	3
Recipient is not occupied with other toys, but neverthe-less does not play	5
Recipient waits too long to take his turn and the initiator becomes distracted	3
Recipient becomes distracted as he retrieves or is about to retrieve the ball	2
Initiator does not give enough time to recipient to retrieve the ball before retrieving it himself	4
Initiator does not throw the ball near enough to the recipient	2
Initiator becomes distracted while retrieving the ball after it was returned	1
Total	25

cooperation, and compensation are perhaps what is lacking in the unsuccessful overtures, and what enabled nine ball games to develop even though some of their overtures were similarly flawed.

Summary and Conclusions

In summary, a careful look at the 28 games played by these infants and toddlers has revealed a considerable repertoire of interactional skills. These include the ability to coordinate their respective turns in three different ways (reciprocal, complementary, and imitative); the ability to spontaneously create game content; the ability to transform literal events into nonliteral vehicles for games; the ability to signal game intent or nonliterality through laughter and/or smiles, familiar game content, irrelevancy, and repetition; the ability to alternate turns, through turn-yielding signals that are both general, e.g., pausing after turn completion, and specific to game content; the ability to wait, even for protracted periods, for the partner to take his turn; the ability to resolve the problem of simultaneous turns or "interruptions"; and the ability to employ "violations" of the turn-alternation pattern of re-establish mutual involvement. These skills may be viewed as the possession of the individual partners, though not all games, nor all game players, displayed all skills. Clearly, however, the game belongs to the dyad.

We might first consider why these infants and toddlers chose to play games, or to attempt them, given the multiplicity of skills involved and the apparent difficulty in obtaining and maintaining mutual involvement. Despite their complexity, the function of games may be to provide a comparatively easy way for the partners to extend their interaction. Given their apparent goal of interaction, the repetitive structure of games allows the partners to focus on maintaining the interaction rather than on formulating the content of each turn. The repetition even allows for the turn-yielding signals to become superfluous; when the content of the partner's turn is known in advance, one knows when it is complete, even without a turn-yielding signal. The structural feature of turn alternation precludes any ambiguity about whether one will have a turn; it becomes simply a question of when.

Further, it is their structure that not only allows these previously unacquainted children to play games, but it also allows us to call their play a game. The feature consistently employed by those who differentiate "games" from "play" is the presence of rules. The following quotations are illustrative: "Play is unrestricted, games have rules" (Opie and Opie, 1976, p. 394); "children play verbal games—to be distinguished from verbal play by the existence of rules . . ." (Cazden, 1976, p. 607); "true games, with articulate and specifically agreed upon rules . . ." (Reynolds, 1976, p. 627); and "In the case of the very simplest social game, on the contrary, we are in the presence of rules . . . (Piaget, 1965, p. 13). Commonly, those who clearly distinguish between games and play also insist that the rules must be explicit and transmitted verbally from one partner to the other. If prior verbal agreements must be made, then the interactions of these infants and toddlers would not qualify as games. However, this distinction seems unnecessarily rigid; rather, what appears critical is the *presence* of rules.

Given one turn by each partner, it is quite easy to specify, through a rule, the content of the subsequent turns. Even in imitative vocalization games where the exact phrase may be different each time, the second partner's turn is always a repetition of the first partner's turn.

Further, the rules of game content are specified, to an extent, in the overture itself: in complementary games the nature of the second partner's turn is specified by its integral relationship with the first partner's turn; in ball games the presence of one ball generally dictates reciprocal roles; and in imitation games repetition of an act without a complement or reciprocal, followed by a pause, seems to signal imitation. In addition, the alternation of turns and the content of the game can both be seen as rule-governed, given that reactions to their violation may precipitously terminate the game. An additional source of evidence of the rule-governed nature of these interactions is that, while the partners themselves did not express the rules verbally, the mothers did so. Instructions such as "You wait and Jackie will throw it for you" and "Now, throw it back to Jackie" not only helped the partners play a game, they also made explicit the rules involved.

We are not alone in employing the designation "games" based on the *presence* of an apparently rule-governed structure. Bruner and Sherwood (1976) especially make a strong case for the importance of infant games in *learning* about rules, and others as well employ the phrase "the rules of the game," implicitly indicating their presence (e.g., Hayes, 1976). Still others apply the label "games" without recourse to explicit rules; a recurring pattern of contingencies is sufficient (e.g., Bretherton, 1974; Piaget, 1962; Stern, 1974; Watson, 1972). Thus, though some researchers (e.g., Cazden, 1976; Garvey, 1974) conservatively label merely as "play" various interaction sequences that we, and others, would call games, the clear, if implicit presence of rules seems to justify the appellation.

The presence of a rule-governed structure, however, does not require that the infants and toddlers had decided exactly how the games were to be played beforehand. To the extent that a particular game was a creation, rather than a re-enactment, the partners understood and were guided by the rules only in the process of playing the games. As Shotter (1974) has stated, "Any rules there might be in the child's play are not formulated in advance, but issue in the course of playing with others in a co-ordinated way, i.e., they issue in the invention of a game" (p. 234). That these infants and toddlers, unfamiliar with each other, seemed to negotiate the rules of their games as they played them does not mean that all early peer games are thus "invented" and "negotiated." Rather, it is most likely that, given repeated opportunities to be together, they might develop games which could be played without ongoing negotiation; the rules would be known by both partners, in advance, and such games would be initiated whenever mutual involvement was sought in a manner similar to that of mothers and infants (Bruner and Sherwood, 1976; Ross, Goldman, and Hay, 1976). Even during their initial encounter, however, there were indications that the partners possessed and shared an emerging concept of "the game," including an awareness of its rules, and even perhaps, its name. The insistent repetition of overtures to some of the imitation games and yet in other cases the immediate response to overtures, the responses to rule violation, and the similarity of the ball game overtures, all seem to indicate a prior understanding of game structure. But perhaps the most telling fragment of evidence occurred during a game which took place after the official end of the session. Following her partner's refusal to relinquish the ball during her turn, the 24-month-old, in a tone of voice conveying both request and command, simply repeated "Play ball. Play ball." Here, we do not have to assume, or interpret, or treat "as if"—the player herself was clearly aware of, intended, and even named the interaction.

Documenting the abilities of infants and toddlers to engage each other in rule-governed games is important. What is also significant, from a developmental perspective, is the strong resemblance to other games, other rules, and other interactions. The *content* of the games themselves, including the three different role relationships of reciprocal, imitative, and complementary turns, greatly resembles that of games between infants and adults, be they strangers or parents (Bretherton, 1974; Piaget, 1962; Ross, Goldman, and Hay, 1976). Slightly older peers engage in highly similar imitation and complementary games (Garvey, 1974; Keenan, 1974; Lee, 1975), and of course, also play ball. The turn-alternating structure of the games, including the gazing at the partner while pausing after turn completion, is highly similar to interactions spanning the age range of infancy to adulthood. Identical turn-yielding signals structure reciprocity or mutual involvement through alternating turns in mother-infant feeding situations (Kaye, 1977b), mother-infant conversations (Bateson, 1975; Brazelton, Koslowski, and Main, 1974; Richards, 1974; Schaffer, Collis, and Parsons, 1977; Trevarthen, 1974), experimental attempts to elicit infant imitation (Kaye, 1977a; McCall, 1975; Rodgon and Kurdek, 1975), and conversation among children (DeLong, 1974) and adults (Duncan, 1972, 1973; Kendon, 1967; Sacks, Schegloff, and Jefferson, 1974). Nonliterality, or game intent, was signaled by the infants and toddlers in the same manner that 4-year-olds signal "pretend" (Garvey, 1974; Garvey and Berndt, 1975) and rough-and-tumble play and games (Blurton-Jones, 1974). Moreover, the signals of smiling and/or laughter, irrelevancy, and repetition are employed not only by humans, but also with an identical purpose, and often in an identical manner, by the young of other species (Bekoff, 1972; Bruner, Jolly, and Sylva, 1976; Wilson, 1974), indicating a developmental continuity beyond the single life span. Given the predominance of nonliteral, playful "fighting" in these other species, and the commonality of rough-and-tumble play in slightly older children, the ability to signal play intent and to understand such signals is critical; more is at stake for the individual than just the exchange of a ball. Thus the early development and practice of the various signals of nonliterality in play and games that are devoid of any hint of agonism would seem quite adaptive. Further, given that play, including games, is necessary from the perspective of both evolution and individual development (Bruner, Jolly, and Sylva, 1976), the proficient signaling of nonliterality is a most important ability. Early peer games then, while not overwhelmingly frequent, may be highly functional, as they both allow and require the participants to practice interaction skills, not with their more competent mothers, but with peers. Apparently, they will continue to employ these same skills, with peers and others, for the rest of their lives.

Our sample of previously unacquainted infants and toddlers was thus able to interact competently and creatively, and in a rule-governed manner. Their games appear as well formed, and as complex, as those of acquainted children in the same age range (Mueller and Lucas, 1975; Vincze, 1971, 1974). Certainly the frequency is greater than in other studies with unacquainted children (Bronson, 1974; Eckerman, Whatley, and Kutz, 1975; Lewis et al., 1975), providing firm evidence of the possibility of peers engaging each other in complex, reciprocal interactions without prior "practice" with the particular partner, or, in some cases, prior experience with peers. Perhaps the provision of specific toys, such as the ball, facilitated such interactions. (Nelson [1973] lists ball as one of the first ten words acquired by her sample, presumably because of the infants' great interest in this object.) That one partner was 6 months older than the other may also have contributed significantly, for while skills may be possessed by one partner, they only become operative with the cooperation of the other. This factor may partially explain why the 18-month-olds in this study played games, but did not, for example in the study of Eckerman, Whatley, and Kutz (1975) when they were paired with a same-age peer. However, as the 18-month-olds managed to play games even with the 12-month-olds, other factors seem to be involved. Konner (1975) has strongly asserted that a peer group of age-mates is highly artificial, as only a mixed-age peer group occurs in the human environment of evolutionary adaptedness; infants' interactional skills would thus have been selected for that type of interaction. He implies that it is the interaction with older, more skillful children that allows for interaction, as opposed to "parallel play" in very early childhood. But it is possible that it is not only the presence of an older, more competent partner that facilitates interaction. The difference could work both ways, such that the presence of an obviously younger partner might elicit more explicit signals, more patience in waiting for the other to take his turn, and greater efforts at accommodation. Differences in developmental status might also obviate the frequently apparent need to establish dominance; it becomes a given, and the dyad can then engage in other kinds of interactions.

In conclusion, this study documents early sociability with peers, in that the infants and toddlers chose to play games with each other. That they were unfamiliar with each other indicates that each partner had been able to independently abstract general and universal rules of interaction from his prior interactions, and was able to negotiate specific game rules, as required. In these particular games, the cardinal rule of interaction, that of reciprocity, was enacted through turn-yielding signals which allowed the partners to smoothly alternate turns and thus maintain mutual involvement. Finally, the rules they followed and the signals they used to create and regulate their games are employed throughout the life span; though still preverbal, by the second birthday they are well on their way toward interactional competence.

Notes

This study was submitted as an M.A. thesis by the senior author to the Department of Psychology of the University of Waterloo, 1976. The support of a Canada Council Research Grant (H.S.R.) is gratefully acknowledged. The authors are indebted to Donna Robinson for her expert assistance in conducting the play sessions, and to Jerome Goldman, Michael Ross, Dale Hay, and Jeremy Anglin for their encouragement and thoughtful criticism of earlier drafts of this chapter. We would also like to thank the 48 infants and toddlers who entertained and enlightened us, and the 48 mothers whose cooperation made this study possible.
1. Copies of the transcripts may be requested from Barbara Davis Goldman, Department of Psychology, University of Waterloo, Waterloo, Ontario, Canada, N2L 3G1.
2. The number of games (28) did not allow the use of inferential statistics to compare among experimental groups; the numbers reported are thus descriptive of our sample, but are not intended to be the basis for inferential predictions to other samples.

3. Transcripts of the unsuccessful ball game overtures were developed in a manner analogous to that employed for the games.

References

Appolloni, T., and Cooke, T. P. Peer behavior conceptualized as a variable influencing infant and toddler development. *American Journal of Orthopsychiatry*, 1975, *45*, 4–17.

Bateson, M. C. Mother-infant exchanges: The epigenesis of conversational interaction. *Annals of the New York Academy of Sciences*, 1975, *263*, 101–113.

Bekoff, M. The development of social interaction, play, and metacommunication in mammals: An ethological perspective. *Quarterly Review of Biology*, 1972, *47*, 413–434.

Blurton-Jones, N. G. Ethology and early socialization. In M. P. M. Richards (Ed.), *The Integration of a Child into a Social World*. London: Cambridge University Press, 1974, pp. 263–294.

Brazelton, T. B., Koslowski, B., and Main, M. The origins of reciprocity: The early mother-infant interaction. In M. Lewis and L. Rosenblum (Eds.), *The Effect of the Infant on Its Caregiver*. New York: Wiley, 1974, pp. 49–76.

Bretherton, I. Making friends with one-year-olds: An experimental study of infant-stranger interaction. Unpublished dissertation, Johns Hopkins University, 1974.

Bridges, K. M. B. A study of social development in early infancy. *Child Development*, 1933, *4*, 36–49.

Bronson, W. C. Competence and the growth of personality. In K. J. Connolly and J. Bruner (Eds.), *The Growth of Competence*. New York: Academic Press, 1974, pp. 241–264.

Bronson, W. C. Developments in behavior with age mates during the second year of life. In M. Lewis and L. Rosenblum (Eds.), *Friendship and Peer Relations*. New York: Wiley, 1975, pp. 131–152.

Bruner, J. S., Jolly, A., and Sylva, K. (Eds.). *Play—Its Role in Development and Evolution*. London: Penguin Books, 1976.

Bruner, J. S., and Sherwood, V. Peekaboo and the learning of rule structures. In J. S. Bruner, A. Jolly, and K. Sylva (Eds.), *Play—Its Role in Development and Evolution*. London: Penguin Books, 1976, pp. 277–285.

Buhler, C. *The First Year of Life*. New York: John Day, 1930.

Buhler, C. The social behavior of children. In C. A. Murchison (Ed.), *A Handbook of Child Psychology*, Vol. 1. New York: Russell and Russell, 1933, pp. 374–416.

Buhler, C. *From Birth to Maturity*. London: Routledge and Kegan Paul, 1935.

Cazden, C. B. Play with language and metalinguistic awareness: One dimension of language experience. In J. S. Bruner, A. Jolly, and K. Sylva (Eds.), *Play—Its Role in Development and Evolution*. London: Penguin Books, 1976, pp. 603–608.

Chekel, M. I., and Tremblay, A. The study of play in delayed children. Paper presented at the conference of the American Association on Mental Deficiency, Toronto, June 4, 1974.

DeLong, A. J. Kinesic signals at utterance boundaries in preschool children. *Semiotica*, 1974, *11*, 43–73.

Dragsten, S. S., and Lee, L. C. Infants' social behavior in a naturalistic versus experimental setting. Paper presented at the annual convention of the American Psychological Association, Montreal, August, 1973.

Duncan, S., Jr. Some signals and rules for taking speaking turns in conversations. *Journal of Personality and Social Psychology*, 1972 *23*, 283–292.

Duncan, S., Jr. Toward a grammar for dyadic conversation. *Semiotica*, 1973, *9*, 29–46.

Durfee, J. T., and Lee, L. C. Infant-infant interaction in a daycare setting. Paper presented at the annual convention of the American Psychological Association, Montreal, August, 1973.

Eckerman, C. O., Whatley, J. L., and Kutz, S. L. Growth of social play with peers during the second year of life. *Developmental Psychology*, 1975, *11*, 42–49.

Finkelstein, N., O'Brien, C., and Ramey, C. T. The influence of toys on social interaction. Paper presented at the third biennial meeting of the Southeastern Society for Research in Child Development, Chapel Hill, North Carolina, March 7, 1974.

Garvey, C. Some properties of social play. *Merrill-Palmer Quarterly*, 1974, *20*, 163–180.

Garvey, C., and Berndt, R. The organization of pretend play. Paper presented at the symposium on "Structure in Play and Fantasy," American Psychological Association, Chicago, September, 1975.

Garvey, C., and Hogan, R. Social speech and social interaction: Egocentrism revisited. *Child Development*, 1973, *44*, 562–568.

Hayes, C. The imaginary pulltoy. In J. S. Bruner, A. Jolly, and K. Sylva (Eds.), *Play—Its Role in Development and Evolution*. London: Penguin Books, 1976, pp. 534–536.

Kagan, J., Kearsley, R. B., and Zelazo, P. R. The emergence of initial apprehension to unfamiliar peers. In M. Lewis and L. Rosenblum (Eds.), *Friendship and Peer Relations*. New York: Wiley, 1975, pp. 187–206.

Kaye, K. Infants' effects on their mothers' teaching strategies. In J. C. Glidewell (Ed.), *The Social Context of Learning and Development*. New York: Gardner Press, 1977, pp. 173–206. (a)

Kaye, K. Toward the origin of dialogue. In H. R. Schaffer (Ed.), *Mother-Infant Interaction*. London: Academic Press, 1977, pp. 89–118. (b)

Keenan, E. D. Conversational competence in children. *Journal of Child Language*, 1974, *1*, 163–183.

Kendon, A. Some functions of gaze-direction in social interaction. *Acta Psychologica*, 1967, *26*, 22–63.

Konner, M. Relations among infants and juveniles in comparative perspective. In M. Lewis and L. Rosenblum (Eds.), *Friendship and Peer Relations*. New York: Wiley, 1975, pp. 99–129.

Lee, L. C. Social encounters of infants: The beginnings of popularity. Paper presented at the International Society for the Study of Behavioral Development, Ann Arbor, August, 1973.

Lee, L. C. Toward a cognitive theory of interpersonal development: Importance of peers. In M. Lewis and L. Rosenblum (Eds.), *Friendship and Peer Relations*. New York: Wiley, 1975, pp. 207–221.

Lenssen, B. G. Infants' reactions to peer strangers. Paper presented at the annual meeting of the Society for Research in Child Development, Denver, 1975.

Lewis, M., and Rosenblum, L. A. Introduction. In M. Lewis and L. Rosenblum (Eds.), *Friendship and Peer Relations*. New York: Wiley, 1975, pp. 1–9.

Lewis, M., Young, G., Brooks, J., and Michalson, L. The beginning of friendship. In M. Lewis and L. Rosenblum (Eds.), *Friendship and Peer Relations*. New York: Wiley, 1975.

Mallay, H. A study of some of the techniques underlying the establishment of successful social contacts at the preschool level. *Journal of Genetic Psychology*, 1935, *47*, 431–457. (a)

Mallay, H. Growth in social behavior and mental activity after six months in nursery school. *Child Development*, 1935, *6*, 303–309. (b)

Maudry, M., and Nekula, M. Social relations between children of the same age during the first two years of life. *Journal of Genetic Psychology*, 1939, *54*, 193–215.

McCall, R. B. Imitation in infancy. Paper presented at the annual meeting of the Society for Research in Child Development, Denver, April, 1975.

Mengert, I. G. A preliminary study of the reactions of two-year-old children to each other when paired in a semi-controlled situation. *Journal of Genetic Psychology*, 1931, *39*, 393–398.

Mueller, E. The maintenance of verbal exchanges between young children. *Child Development*, 1972, *43*, 930–938.

Mueller, E., and Lucas, J. A developmental analysis of peer interaction among toddlers. In M. Lewis and L. Rosenblum (Eds.), *Friendship and Peer Relations*. New York: Wiley, 1975, pp. 223–257.

Mueller, E., and Rich, A. Clustering and socially directed behaviors in a playgroup of one-year-old boys. *Journal of Child Psychology and Psychiatry*, 1976, *17*, 315–322.

Nelson, K. Structure and strategy in learning to talk. *Society for Research in Child Development Monographs*, 1973, *38* (1–2).

Opie, I., and Opie, P. Street games: Counting-out and chasing. In J. S. Bruner, A. Jolly, and K. Sylva (Eds.), *Play—Its Role in Development and Evolution*. London: Penguin Books, 1976, pp. 394–412.

Parten, M. B. Social participation among pre-school children. *Journal of Abnormal and Social Psychology*, 1932, *27*, 243–269.

Piaget, J. *Play, Dreams and Imitation in Childhood*. New York: W. W. Norton, 1962.

Piaget, J. *The Moral Judgment of the Child*. New York: Free Press, 1965.

Ray, J. S. Ethological studies of behavior in delayed and non-delayed toddlers. Paper presented at the annual meeting of the American Association on Mental Deficiency, Toronto, June, 1974.

Ray, J. S. Free-play behavior of normal and Down's syndrome toddlers. Paper presented at the annual meeting of the Animal Behavior Society, Wilmington, North Carolina, May 24, 1975.

Reynolds, P. C. Play, language and human evolution. In J. S. Bruner, A. Jolly, and K. Sylva (Eds.), *Play—Its Role in Development and Evolution*. London: Penguin Books, 1976, pp. 621–635.

Richards, M. P. M. First steps in becoming social. In M. P. M. Richards (Ed.),

The Integration of a Child into a Social World. London: Cambridge University Press, 1974, pp. 83–98.

Rodgon, M. M., and Kurdek, L. A. Vocal and gestural imitation in children under two years old. Paper presented at the annual convention of the American Psychological Association, Chicago, August, 1975.

Ross, H. S., Goldman, B. D., and Hay, D. F. Features and functions of infant games. Invited address to the annual meeting of the Canadian Psychological Association, Toronto, June, 1976.

Rubenstein, J., and Howes, C. The effects of peers on toddler interaction with mother and toys. *Child Development*, 1976, *47*, 597–605.

Sacks, H., Schegloff, E. A., and Jefferson, G. A simplest systematics for the organization of turn-taking for conversation. *Language*, 1974, *50*, 696–735.

Schaffer, H. R., Collis, G. M., and Parsons, G. Vocal interchange and visual-regard in verbal and pre-verbal children. In H. R. Schaffer (Ed.), *Mother-Infant Interaction.* London: Academic Press, 1977, pp. 291–324.

Shirley, M. *The First Two Years: A Study of Twenty-Five Babies*, Vol. II. Minneapolis: University of Minnesota Press, 1933.

Shotter, J. The development of personal powers. In M. P. M. Richards (Ed.), *The Integration of a Child into a Social World.* London: Cambridge University Press, 1974, pp. 215–244.

Snipper, A. S., and Lee, L. C. Social encounters of infants: Individual status and interactive styles. Paper presented at the annual meeting of the American Psychological Association, Washington, D. C., September, 1974.

Stern, D. N. The goal and structure of mother-infant play. *Journal of the American Academy of Child Psychiatry*, 1974, *13*, 402–421.

Trevarthen, C. Conversations with a two-month-old. *New Scientist*, 1974, 230–233.

Vincze, M. The social contacts of infants and young children reared together. *Early Child Development and Care*, 1971, *1*, 99–109.

Vincze, M. Patterning of common activities in a group of infants, 1974. Unpublished translation of Az egyuttes tevekenyseg alakulasa egy egyutt nevelkedo csoportban 3 honapos kortol 2-1/2 eves korig, *Pszichologiai Tanulmanyok, 10*, 289–295.

Watson, J. Smiling, cooing and "the game." *Merrill-Palmer Quarterly*, 1972, *18*, 323–340.

Wilson, S. Juvenile play of the common seal *Phoca vitulina vitulina* with comparative notes on the grey seal *halichoerus grypus. Behaviour*, 1974, *48*, 37–60.

Young, G., and Lewis, M. Friends and strangers: Peer relations in infancy. Paper presented at the annual meeting of the Animal Behavior Society, Wilmington, North Carolina, May, 1975.

6 Ownership and Permission Among Nursery School Children

DENIS NEWMAN

In his classic study on language and thought, Piaget (1955) reported that much of the speech of young children is not communicative. Recent work on children's use of language in ordinary social situations (Garvey and Hogan, 1973; Shatz and Gelman, 1973) has challenged this view by providing convincing evidence that much of what nursery-school-aged children say is responsive and adaptive to listeners even if it fails to display the particular kind of social rationality Piaget was looking for. Concomitant with this view of the child as socially responsive, research on the social functions of language and on children's verbal skills involved in social interaction, i.e., on their communicative competence, has begun to flourish (Mitchell-Kernan and Ervin-Tripp, 1977). Far from being uninteresting in its social consequences, children's speech is currently providing important insights into the nature of children's social development.

This chapter reports a study which examined the use of language by a group of nursery school children in their construction of a small piece of social organization, a particular spontaneous play group which lasted about 20 minutes before dispersing. The detailed analysis of the children's speech, as well as their gestures and

213

movements recorded on videotape, made possible the investigation of how, at the level of social interaction, they were able to keep their play group together and on course from one moment to the next. Insofar as the children's speech served to communicate shared understanding of the organization they were producing, it was seen that the production of social organization was one of its communicative functions. The children's verbal utterances were part of what constituted the organization they were producing and, as will be demonstrated, derived much of their significance, both for the children and for the investigator, from their place in it. Thus it can be argued that studying the social functions of language cannot proceed independently of studying the social organization that results from the use of language. This view, that one of the functions of language is to produce social organization, has implications both for studying the kinds of organization children produce and for studying the various verbal means by which they produce it. This chapter focuses on the latter question, using one particular piece of organization as an illustration.

Much of the current research on the kinds of social interactive skills that are pertinent to this study has been restricted to dyadic interaction, often in an isolated playroom (Garvey, 1974; Keenan, 1974). In a nursery school setting, however, spontaneous play groups of more than two often occur. With more than two children playing together, social organizational possibilities and problems arise which do not occur in dyadic encounters. For example, alliances may be formed, some children may be excluded from an ongoing play episode or others may ask permission to join. Within a large group, such as a nursery school class, a smaller group of children playing together may have the problem of defending their property against unwanted outsiders while maintaining the internal coherence of their own play. By examining a group of children playing within a larger aggregation, the study reported here illustrates the group's management of some of these problems. At the same time, the children's use of language in dealing with these problems is compared with the findings from studies of the interactive skills found in dyads. By examining the role of language in a nursery school play group, the study extends the findings concerning the young child's verbal interactive skills into the realm of skills for managing more complicated social organizations.

In the study reported here, ownership serves as a focus for the illustration of children's social organization. In a nursery school, ownership presents particularly interesting problems for the children since the toys, chairs, and other objects are "officially" the property of the school, not of an individual child. Transitory ownership occurs, however, but it often becomes the source of considerable negotiation and dispute. A particular instance of ownership remains as a state of affairs only so long as it is recognized by the children concerned. The transitory and negotiated nature of ownership allows it to serve as an illustration of the temporally organized production of social facts by the children.

In order to clarify the framework for viewing the childrens' social activities, some terms require definition. Insofar as ownership is dependent on sustained recognition by the participants, it can be considered a *social fact* as opposed to a physical state or a mental state, both of which are usually considered to have an existence independent of people's recognition of or agreement to them. "Social fact," then, refers simply to any recognized state of affairs for which shared recognition is a necessary condition. The term "social episode" (or simply, "episode") can be used to refer to the temporal duration of some social fact or set of related social facts. Ethnomethodological studies of the achievement of social facts in the course of social interactions (Garfinkel, 1967; Garfinkel and Sacks, 1970; Sudnow, 1972; Turner, 1974) show that such an episode can be considered as a unit of social interaction, i.e., as a sequence of interactive events during which a state of affairs is displayed and recognized as being in effect. This definition for episode is similar to Goffman's (1974). His notion of an encounter or face engagement (1963), for example, refers to one rather basic kind of social episode in which there is shared recognition of the fact that "we are engaged (in some activity, conversation, etc.)."

The paradigmatic case of playing a conventional game illustrates the concept of episode considered as the duration of a set of related social facts. During a game of Monopoly, for instance, the rules of Monopoly can be appealed to as relevant for resolving certain kinds of disputes. Shared acceptance of the rules is a state of affairs recognized as obtaining for the duration of the game but not between games. Other transitory facts also attach to the same particular episode. For example, each player is assigned a particular token and he owns it until the game's end but not beyond. Aside from these facts which are dependent on the episode, the episode's being in progress is itself a fact the recognition of which must be maintained among participants and others. An episode may simply disintegrate due to distraction, in which case the rules of Monopoly and the token assignments would become irrelevant. To avoid disintegration, participants must continually display their attentiveness. But the episode should not be considered in any way causal of the subordinate facts. In a Monopoly game, for instance, making his moves in accordance with the rules and with his own token are some of the more obvious means by which a participant shares his recognition of the episode, thereby sustaining it as a joint venture. The episode is simply the occasion for the relevance to the participants of these other facts.

The concept of episode as illustrated here has the following usefulness in accounting for the presence of social facts. Facts which can be found to be dependent on the existence of the episode can be considered as sustained in the maintenance of the episode as a whole. Thus, for example, one player's reminding another that it is his turn helps to maintain both the game as an ongoing joint enterprise and the episode-specific assignment of tokens.

With regard to episodes of young children's play, the fact of temporary ownership of the play objects by the participants can be seen as a subordinate fact in relation to children's maintenance of their engagement in play. That is, as long as the children maintain the coherence of their play, they maintain authority over the objects as well. A consequence of this coterminality is that the children's efforts, for instance, to maintain topical coherence in the play can also be seen as their maintenance of ownership.

The episode of play to be illustrated is essentially a dichotomous organization. It provides, as the basis of ownership, for the classification of children in the classroom as participants or as outsiders. Among coparticipants the objects being played with are owned jointly. As long as engagement in the episode is maintained, all participants have the right to play with the objects.

Evidence for ownership, as well as for the episode as a whole, can be found in the children's verbal utterances. For example, their shared recognition of ownership can be seen in their consistent use of possessive pronouns (mine, yours, etc.). Less obviously, but of considerably more interest, the children's recognition of ownership is shown in the occurrence of requests by outsiders to participants for permission to use the owned objects or to join in the play. An important condition for the appropriateness or "felicity" (Austin, 1962) of such a request is that the requestee have authority or rights over the thing for which permission is being requested. Searle (1969) has argued that in performing a speech act such as this, the speaker *implies* that such conditions are met. Thus, when an outsider asks permission of the participants, he can be seen as recognizing the requestee's rights, or, even more strongly, as bestowing rights on the requestee. To say it is a bestowal of rights is warranted since, in recognizing the rights, the outsider is "playing by the rules" and thus helping to construct the episode to which the rights 'of ownership are attached. In general, whenever a social fact is one of the conditions for a speech act, the fact also becomes a consequence of the act. It is important to notice that in a nursery school classroom, the production of an episode is a cooperative venture not only of the participants but, to some extent, of the outsiders as well. The episode is not so powerful an institution that it can withstand the attacks of an outsider who refuses to remain excluded. The episode, then, must be seen as constructed both from the inside and from the outside.

It will be clear that the particular segment of interaction analyzed in this study is not adequate as a basis for secure generalizations about the nature of child behavior or about the structures of knowledge that may underlie it. The immediate interest is to consider the possibility of describing some of the social functions of young children's verbal utterances which occur in the course of producing social organization.

Data and Methods

The Data

Four boys and three girls from middle-class English-speaking homes attended a nursery school at The Rockefeller University three hours each morning, three days a week for a period of seven months. At the end of this period the children ranged in age from 37 to 42 months.

Although the teacher regularly initiated snack times and various crafts activities, she allowed a large proportion of the time for child-initiated play where she was as unobtrusive as possible. She also conducted various language tests with individual children in the room during periods of free play.

The sessions were regularly videotaped by means of cameras mounted in each corner of the room which could be selected and adjusted for direction and angle by remote control. Sound was picked up by microphones and transmitters sewn into the children's jackets. For each session one child was selected as the target, and the camera direction and angle was adjusted to capture this child and those with whom he was interacting.

A sample of approximately four hours (one continuous hour from each of the last four months) was transcribed. These transcripts and the corresponding videotapes were the basic data for the present study.

Selection and Transcription

The entire four hours was viewed about a dozen times and the transcript read extensively in the course of prior projects, before a continuous 16-minute segment was selected for more detailed analysis in this study. At all times, the videotapes were viewed at normal speed.

For convenience of presentation here, the segment was retranscribed, omitting utterances by children or the teacher when they were not engaged in the interaction of interest. This transcription, which includes descriptions of nonverbal actions, is reproduced in the appendix to this chapter. Numbers next to the examples presented in the text refer to the line numbers in the appendix. To maintain anonymity, the names of the children were changed. The transcription conventions used in the examples were the following:

1. Loudness of the utterance varies in degree from normal to shout, indicated by No, *No*, NO, *NO*. Words in an utterance marked as a degree louder are stressed.

2. Inaudible portions of an utterance are indicated by empty parentheses ( ). Words in parentheses indicate what the portion sounded like.

3. Brackets spanning two lines of dialogue indicate that the utterances overlap.

4. Whenever a speaker glanced or looked at the addressee just before or during his utterance, the addressee's initial is given in brackets immediately after the speaker's. A "?" in the brackets means that the speaker's gaze could not be determined from the videotape.

5. A hyphen indicates an utterance or word was cut short.

6. No attempt was made to represent variations in the pronunciation of recognizable words.

Interpretation

The children's behavior recorded on the videotape displays an orderliness. It was the goal of this study to document this order by using the children's utterances, gestures, and movements as evidence. The repeated viewing of the videotape results in a fitting together of the separate events into a consistent account. This coherent whole is the evidence for the existence of the episode as a unit of social interaction. The coherence further makes possible the interpretation of any event in relation to the others. Permission requests, as one set of events, were identified, provisionally, on the basis of the grammatical form exemplified by "Can I try it?" which is literally a request for permission (Fillmore, 1973), assuming "can" to be an acceptable variation of "may." As will be seen, this strict linguistic criterion proved inadequate since the form was found to have more than one function. The various functions that utterances have for the management of an interactive episode can be identified only when they can be seen to have a systematic relationship to the organization being constructed. This is not to say that all child interaction has an identifiable orderliness. But, when it does, the coherence that the children produce provides the investigator with a means for identifying the functional elements as well as for studying the production of order itself.

Given the dependence of the procedure of interpretation on the investigator's judgments of coherence, some further comments are called for in regard to the validity of the description. It is the essential differences between children and adults that both motivate developmental studies and result in warnings against overreliance on facile interpretations of children's speech (Ryan, 1974). What can be recommended is a consideration of the peculiarities of the child's "problem solving." Confronted with a conflict, a problem, or a failure to achieve some intended result, the child uses whatever resources he has available to repair the situation. Since these solutions often display procedures or skills peculiar to the child, what the investigator produces on the basis of this evidence can be clearly seen as a description of what the child is actually doing. Thus, by attending to the particular way the child comes to terms with problems, the tendency to interpret his behavior as though he were "just like an adult" can be avoided.

The consideration of motivated problem solving allows for the inclusion of more events in the coherent whole. This is the case because many problems are found to arise in the course of the child's management of an episode or are found to have a solution in the establishment of an episode. The interpretation of any solution, however, requires an initial interpretation of how the child views the problem he is confronting. The results of this study consist of a series of arguments about what the child's response implies about what he can be said to be (or interpreted as) doing. Without this initial premise, however, any such argument cannot be made. Interpretation of the conflict must either be derived from the coherent-account-so-far or be simply accepted by the reader as not too farfetched. In either case judgments of coherence and reasonableness are the only criteria that can be proposed for judging descriptions of child behavior.

Results

The following presentation of results is divided into four sections. The first section illustrates the children's orientation to or awareness of the notion of episode in the course of some conflicts and their resolution. The second section deals with the way children establish episodes. Some research on children's dyadic conversations and verbal play is reviewed. These studies suggest that children's repetition of each other may be a way of establishing episodes. Examples of interaction are presented to illustrate the same phenomenon and its implications for a play group within a larger group. The third section shows how repetition can be combined with announcements to maintain, direct, and re-establish the interactive episode. The final section examines the children's use of permission requests with regard to taking turns with an episode-related toy. Throughout the presentation sufficient narrative is added and the examples are arranged so that the sequence of events remains clear.

Orientation to Episodes of Ownership

The kind of episode to be illustrated is constituted by the shared recognition that some group of children jointly owns some play objects. The following examples provide evidence that members of the classroom recognize this as an episode.

The teacher often encourages the children to articulate their reasons for asserting ownership, as in the following example which forms part of the background for the segment to be examined in detail below. Don and Kevin are playing with three wooden boxes (see Figure 1). Their play consists of a number of games in which the boxes are lined up first as a train, then as a diving board, etc. At one point Steven tries to sit on one of the boxes and the following interaction between Steven, Don, and the teacher takes place:

D [S]: Nope. Nope.
T [D]: Tell him why.
D [S]: Nope, because we made this all by ourselves.
T [S]: Okay, you have to get ( ) with something else.

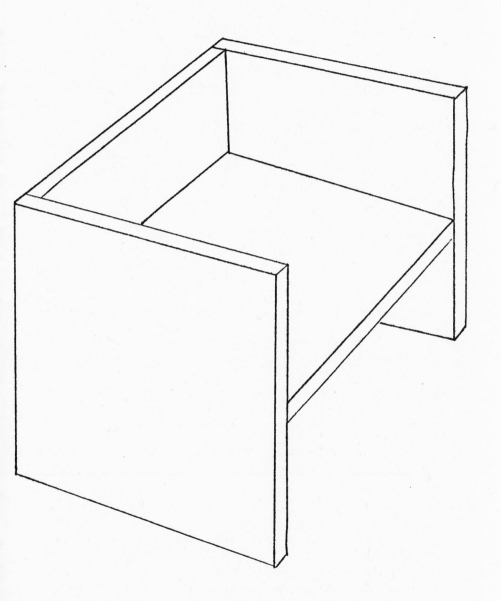

Figure 1. A wooden box. Size: approximately one foot cube.

Having "made this" is the reason for their ownership. The phrase "all by ourselves" indicates the joint ownership arising from having worked together. Don speaks on behalf of them both.

Sometime after this interaction, Don and Kevin leave the boxes to decorate Easter eggs. The segment begins as they finish at the craft table. They go off to a corner and put on Batman capes. While this is going on, Steven, alone, begins "sawing" on the boxes with a plank. Noticing Steven, Don, followed by Kevin, runs over to the boxes.

(1) D [S]:   Nooo, I, I didn't, ah. We got that for Christmas.
(2) K: We got that for Christmas.
(3) D: *Yeah.* . . .

While getting something for Christmas is clearly a way that ownership is established in families, the assertion compares unfavorably in reasonableness to the earlier one to the same challenger. Don's choice of a somewhat magical claim instead of a reapplication of the earlier successful argument can be explained if the notion of episode is part of his understanding of ownership. While it is still the case that Don and Kevin have "made this" configuration of boxes, there has been an extended and voluntary lapse since their earlier activity. The earlier play can be considered an episode, now over, to which ownership of the boxes had attached. Having arranged boxes in a certain way produces ownership only for the duration of the activity for which they are so arranged. The best Don can do under the present circumstances is to display his determination, which alone might cause Steven to retreat.

Steven, however, continues sawing. Rather than pursuing his claim, Don goes to get a plank. Vanessa, who has been nearby, also picks one up. Vanessa and then Don begin sawing.

(4) S [V]:   I'm *making* something. No you don't *saw*
    [D]:   I'm I am *sawing*.
(5) D [S]:   I'm sawing *too*.

In (4), Steven asserts that he is engaged in an activity. Don does not accept Steven's assertion as being adequate grounds for having the boxes to himself and sets up a parallel activity of his own. Steven may not have any objection to playing with Don, but may only be concerned with not being displaced himself. In any case, they appear to reach a tacit compromise with Steven's taking an end of Don's saw and their working together until the plank slides down between the boxes. Steven's actions toward Don contrast with those toward Vanessa. While talking with Don, Steven simply pushes Vanessa's saw off the boxes without looking up. Moments later Vanessa's box and plank are taken from her again without negotiation. Clearly physical force as well as negotiation are used by the children. Nevertheless, the negotiations that do occur are numerous and of considerable complexity.

Don and Steven look down at the boxes holding their saws.

(10) S: Now you're going to build something with that.
(11) D: Yeah.
(12) S: To build something. We have to *build* something *new*.

Steven makes a proposal or suggestion to Don. Simultaneous with (12), Don and Steven begin building. (12) is not a proposal since the work is already in progress. It is more like a formulation of what it is that is in progress, i.e., a description of or rationale for the joint activity. It is significant that as the work begins the pronoun becomes "we," since for reference to be correct, the formulation must be heard to be of a joint activity and not of two separate projects or even of a project in which Steven was simply a helper. "New," which is tagged on at the end of (12) after a slight pause, does not help to specify the kind of object to be built, but rather helps to formulate the activity as a whole, i.e., that it is a new activity or project as opposed to what Don or Steven might have been doing in the past.

During this interaction, Kevin and Vanessa have been talking about using the planks as "skis." Vanessa begins sawing the third box.

(14) V [K]: Let's do, let's do our own, okay?

Kevin walks off to get a plank. (It is not clear whether he intends to join Vanessa or the other boys.) Vanessa is making a proposal of a joint activity to Kevin. What the activity might be is not specified in the utterance (although her sawing action gives some indication). What it is that would be *their own* does not have to be specified for the utterance to be an intelligible proposal since "our own" could be heard to contrast with Don and Steven's *own* activity which is already clearly in progress. She is proposing to work with boxes and planks in the same way but separately. Her use of "own" might be considered to signify the ownership that results from activities. Thus she is proposing to establish an *episode* involving only herself and Kevin. That the intelligibility of the proposal is dependent on the existence of the parallel activity of the others indicates that this other activity is interpreted by Vanessa as an episode in which she is not a participant.

The mechanics of making obvious to the participants and to outsiders that an episode is in progress and that ownership has therefore been established is the topic of the next two sections.

The Mechanics of Making Episodes Public

Recent descriptions of young children's verbal interaction (Garvey, 1974; Keenan, 1974) have stressed its rhythmic and repetitive nature. Analyzing the relationship between turns, Keenan has noted the repetitive quality of the conversations of 33-month-old twins who were videotaped while alone in their bedroom. Examining the dialogues that were not "sound play" or nursery rhyme routines, she found that coherence was achieved by the children's repetition of the previous turn but with various kinds of modifications. Some constituent from the previous turn may be repeated alone, syntactically expanded, or embedded in a larger construction. A constituent may be repeated with an alteration in intonation or voice quality, or the same utterance may be repeated with a new constituent substituted for the original. Keenan emphasizes the essentially social nature of repetitive verbal interaction. While similar modification functions have been used to characterize the sequence of utterances in a monologue, Keenan suggests that her study indicates "that the production of such sequences can be a cooperative enterprise and a means by which young children achieve a dialogue" (p. 179). Keenan also suggests that repetition functions to acknowledge the previous turn, and she provides evidence that the twins generally expected to be acknowledged, e.g., they would persist in repeating their own utterance until it was repeated or elaborated on by the other.

Garvey has shown that ritual play between dyads (aged 3½ to 5½) while alone in a playroom can be analyzed as the repetition of "rounds" composed of two or more turns each. For example:

A Bye, Mommy.
B Bye, Daddy.
A Bye, Mommy.
B Bye, Daddy.

is the repetition of a round which itself contains two turns (p. 166). When, in the repetition of a round of ritual play, the turns constituting the next round are modifications of the first turns, the next round as a whole often retains the rhythmic quality of the first. Referring to the children's repetition and elaboration of each other, Garvey notes (following Sacks, 1967) "that 'doing the same thing' in adult conversation provides a way of tacitly acknowledging the intent of the speaker's gesture by advancing and elaborating the meaning of that gesture" (p. 177).

In light of the proposals that repetition can function to maintain engagement by recognizing or acknowledging the previous conversational turn, the beginning of the episode can be examined more closely.

(12) S: To build something. We have to *build* something *new*.
(13) D: Yeah, we have to build something *newer*.

Don's repetition of Steven's initial formulation of the joint project both stresses and elaborates "new." Thus the repetition acknowledges the intent of Steven's utterance which was to ignore previous claims and start anew. But Don is not simply agreeing with what Steven said. He is also engaging him in dialogue as they attend to the work. The "doing the same thing" in words has the activities as its topic. The engagement resulting from repetition demonstrates to the participants that they are "doing the same thing" in their activities.

To be effective in maintaining engagement, the utterances need not have any obvious literal significance, e.g.,

(15) S: We are moving, right?
(16) D: . . . We are moving it.

accompanied gathering and placing planks on the boxes as a roof. While the talk is not always irrelevant to the planning of the ongoing activities (and some explicit directives also occur), it is clear that repetition functions to maintain contact and a sense that the work is a project jointly undertaken.

Repetition is a pervasive feature of the children's verbal engagements. The following examples illustrate some of the skills involved in elaborative repetition.

(23) D: . . . now there are a whole *bunch* of guns.
(24) K: A whole *bunch* of guns.
(25) D: I have a whole bunch of guns too, ah ha ha ha ha, I got wh-
(26) K: *Whole bunch of guns*.
(27) D: I got a *whole bunch of guns*.

Here Don formulates a topic for their joint activity. Kevin's role appears less creative since he only repeats a constituent from Don's utterance, although he changes the intonation in (26) and this is picked up by Don in (27). In contrast, each of Don's three utterances embed the constituent in a different matrix. Inasmuch as Kevin repeats Don with little elaboration, he might be seen simply as a tagger-along.

Don and Kevin's dialogue can be compared with a later one between Don and Steven.

(66) D: There, we need a *lot more tools*.
(67) S: We'll need a *lot* of tools.
(68) D: Yeah, we might need a *lot* of them.
(69) S: And we need a *lot* of *screws*.
(70) D: Thanks, Vanessa, we need a *lot* more tools, right?
         We need a *lot more. New.*

Here the boys are considerably more elaborate in their repetition of
each other than were Don and Kevin. For example, here, Don's "we
need" is changed to "we'll need" by Steven then to "we might need' by
Don.

In a setting such as a nursery school with' more than two inter-
locutors, repetition between any two can be heard not only by the
participants but by any others in the vicinity. It seems likely that if
repetition is a way for two children to engage each other in dialogue
or in play, then the fact that they are engaged would be clear not only
to the participants but to those who are simply attending to the interaction. If this is the case, then two children "doing the same thing"
will be heard by others as engaged in "doing the same thing" as
coparticipants, i.e., as forming a social unit. The following examples
display some consequences of this assumption.

In utterance (2), Kevin not only shows himself to be in agreement
with Don but by doing so places himself next to Don in opposition to
Steven. Don's "yeah" in the same way not only acknowledges Kevin
but demonstrates to Steven his solidarity with Kevin. Making solidarity evident through repetition also can be seen clearly in Steven's and
Don's later complaints directed toward Kevin (90–97).

The intricacy of the communication to a third party through repetition can be seen in the following example. While Kevin is off
getting a plank following Vanessa's proposal to him, Don takes Vanessa's box and puts it next to the others. Steven moves toward Vanessa
to take her plank, looks at the plank not at her, and says:

(15) S: We are moving, right?

At that moment, while Steven begins a tug-of-war with Vanessa over
the plank, Kevin returns with his plank and begins sawing. Don, without looking up from the boxes, produces utterance (16) which has
three parts. First in (a) he acknowledges that Kevin has brought a
plank; then during (b) he takes the plank with which Kevin is sawing;
and during (c), which is a repetition of Steven, he places Kevin's plank
next to the other planks which form part of a roof on the boxes.

(16) D: (a) Okay. (b) No. (c) We are moving it.

Don's repetition of Steven in (16c) not only maintains his participation with Steven, who is off struggling with Vanessa, but is a communication to Kevin that his objection to Kevin's sawing and his act of placing the plank (simultaneous with the repetition) is a step in an already established activity between himself and Steven.

Re-establishing and Directing Episodes

In this section procedures for re-establishing an episode, for maintaining contact, and for modifying the topical content of play are examined. The verbal exchanges among the participants can be viewed as an ongoing negotiation. These exchanges not only maintain publicly displayed engagement but also maintain, or attempt to maintain, agreement among the participants about what they are doing together. Several examples of lapses in the episode illustrate some verbal procedures and their properties as negotiations.

An episode that has lapsed can be re-established. But, interestingly, the negotiation that results in starting an episode up again may not simply remind participants of what they had been doing, but may retrospectively reinterpret what they are doing to make the past consistent with resumption of the episode under present circumstances. This rewriting of history is illustrated in the following example.

After Don takes Kevin's plank during (16), Kevin stands back and
· watches until Steven and Don complete the "new house." (The final product is three boxes arranged, open side up, so that the center dividers form two compartments. Planks form a roof over one of the compartments.) Just as the house is completed, the teacher calls Vanessa to do a test and the three boys follow out of curiosity and do not return to the boxes when the teacher reminds them that the test is only for Vanessa. Thus, the "new" episode appears to be over. Don and Kevin go to a corner where Don empties onto the floor a bag of construction pieces: girders, screws, wheels, tools, etc. Steven kneels on a chair idly looking off at some other events. Don and then Kevin begin picking up some of the girders which they call "guns." As (26) is spoken, Don gets up and Kevin follows him back toward the boxes. Steven gets off his chair and meets them as they arrive.

(26) K: *Whole bunch of guns.*
(27) D: I got a *whole bunch* of guns.
(28) S: ⌊*Made this new.*
(29) D: *Yeah* we *all* did it.
(30) K: Yeah.

In (28) Steven reminds them of what had been happening. In doing
so, he can be heard as proposing that the episode be re-established
with himself as a participant as before. It is interesting that he does
not provide a pronoun for the subject. In this case, with Don and
Kevin engaged in dialogue, the reference of "we" would have been
clearly equivocal between the two original participants and the three
now confronting each other. Don acknowledges the episode and
supplies the missing subject, stressing its reference to the three of
them. In clarifying the reference, Don provides for Kevin's participation in this phase of the episode by transforming Kevin's earlier ambiguous contribution of a plank into an act of participation.

Repetition has been proposed as a procedure by which children
can become engaged in episodes of play and by which this engagement can be made public. Repetition or repetitive rounds, however,
are likely to be difficult to manage with more than two participants.
Difficulties in coordinating the exchange of turns may limit the
number of participants in episodes of play. The following examples
illustrate the exchange system for three participants.

In the above sequence (utterances 28–30) the order of speakers is
Steven-Don-Kevin. Steven makes a proposition, Don agrees but qual-
ifies it, then Kevin agrees with Don. In the next three utterances the
speaker order is maintained.

>   (31) S: Now we're going to *fix* it, with our *tools.*
>   (32) D: Yeah, these (our) *tools.*
>   (33) K: These (our) *tools.*

Steven suggests the next activity which is a possible next step given
that the house is complete. Don agrees and transforms the construction pieces into the appropriate implements. Kevin then acknowledges Don by repeating a constituent of his utterance. Thus one way
that turns can be allotted among three is by *chaining* one turn onto the
next. In (30) Kevin does not directly engage Steven but rather his
participation in the group is mediated by Don. In (33) Kevin repeats
without elaboration Don's transformation of a constituent of Steven's
utterance. While Kevin attaches his utterance directly to Don's, he
does it so as to echo Steven as well. A little later the following exchange takes place.

>   (45) S: *Making something* NEW.
>   (46) D: Right.
>   (47) K: Newer.
>   (48) D: New. . . .

Kevin, this time, elaborates a constituent of Steven's utterance. Then Don follows by repeating just the constituent of Steven's utterance that Kevin had elaborated. Thus Don is able, simultaneously, to engage both Kevin and Steven. With chaining the three are not engaged together. It is as if Steven and Don were engaged and Kevin tagging along. In the second exchange, and more so in this last exchange, the three become tied together as a single unit.

Another procedure for maintaining engagement during an activity is *announcements* which occur whenever a participant leaves or returns to the location which is the focus of the activity. For example, as Steven says (31), he gets up and leaves. In this way he indicates to the others that his leaving is related to the activity they are engaged in. That is, he is going on a mission and not simply wandering off. After about 20 seconds Steven returns holding a wrench, then goes off again saying:

(34) S: Okay, I have something now, I'll get some more screws. . . .

Thus he returns just long enough to report on the progress of his mission. While he is gone he says (34) (audible to the others). Kevin says (35) directly to Don as he goes off to join Steven in picking up more items and Don recognizes them both with (36).

(34) S: . . . I'm a get more ⌈screws.
(35) K: ⌊( ) and pegs.
(36) D: Yeah, we're building something . . .

As Kevin and Steven return, Don says:

(37) D: We're making something.

A moment later, Steven announces the purpose of their mission (41) as Kevin and Steven go off again and Don acknowledges (42).

(41) S: We need to have a lot of *tools.*
(42) D: Yeah, I ha, I have tools. . . .

Steven's return is announced in (45) (above) which serves emphatically to reaffirm the previously agreed-upon topic of the episode much as he had done in (28), when faced with an engagement between Don and Kevin in which he was not a participant. By announcing his return in terms of what he is coming back to, Steven both can show that he has been on a relevant mission and can re-establish or reaffirm the episode.

The maintenance of the episode is accomplished verbally through dialogue and announcements which formulate a topic or theme. What is said, however, does not necessarily have to reflect the actions that constitute the physical aspect of the activities. A distinction between how the play activities are formulated and their "physical" nature is possible only insofar as the formulations appear somewhat arbitrary. For example, "carrying guns over to the house" could have been called "carrying tools over to fix the house." The formulation did not appear to be highly constrained by the action of walking and carrying. Without the sound track, an observer may see that activities are being done without having a very good idea as to how they are being described by the children. The lack of constraint of the formulations by the physical actions allows for the possibility that, if nothing were said, the participants could have quite different notions about what they are doing. Thus it may be that constant verbal formulations are necessary for keeping the children on the same track. Only by engaging in dialogue can a consensus be maintained and the coherence of the episode displayed.

The remainder of this section recounts a sequence of events which highlights the primacy of verbal formulations over other aspects of the activities which are described on the basis of the actions the children are seen (on the video) to be doing. These other aspects, in this case, actually appear to contradict the formulations.

Since re-establishing the episode in (28–30) the boys have been collecting construction pieces, screws, tools, etc., and sitting around the boxes, each individually putting the pieces together. The pieces that Don and Kevin brought originally are on the roof, but both boys have some pieces on the floor beside them. When Steven and Kevin return from their first mission, Kevin makes a pile, but Steven drops his tools close by. Kevin tries to keep them separate.

(38) K: NO, *these are* MINE.

Don quickly takes the remaining pieces from the roof for his own pile as Steven moves the pieces that he brought into a separate pile. Now, while separate piles are a *de facto* feature of the play, it is not made a topic of verbal *engagement*. Steven's next utterance as he moves his pieces

(39) S: Making something new.

restates the joint project. His later utterances, (49) and (53), using "we" as the subject, assert the joint needing and having of a single screwdriver and wrench. There seems to be, then, a tension between the individual collection of items and the maintenance of the joint play episode.

That the three boys are engaged in some joint project involving tools is clear to Jeff who has been working at the crafts table all this time. He arrives on the scene carrying some pieces. Although his back is to the camera, he appears to address the group.

(55) J [?]:   Hey, hey can I help?
(56) D: *Noo.*

This is the first instance of a permission request and is appropriate given the status of the activities as an episode. The request presupposes some project to which he could be of assistance. The nature of the activity, however, can be seen to be individual since there is no attempt to coordinate the putting together of the pieces in order to construct a single object. It appears then that Jeff has been attending to the talk among the boys but may or may not have a clear idea of what helping would consist of. The talk can produce an episode recognizable to outsiders in spite of the individual nature of the activities.

Jeff continues to be treated as an outsider in spite of his bargaining for membership. During (57), Jeff shows Don the construction pieces he brought and Don reaches up taking some from him. Jeff drops the rest beside him.

(57) J [D]:   I got some tools here.
(58) D [J]:   Tsk, thanks for the tools.
(59) J [D]:   I'm going to put them down.
(60) D: Thanks, thank, we have more *tools* from *Jeff.*
         [S]:   We have more tools from Jeff to build.

Since Don has unequivocally denied permission to Jeff, it seems unlikely that Jeff is included in the reference of "we." Don's thanking him for the pieces can be heard as contrasting with Steven's "okay" to Don after receiving the wrench a few seconds later.

(61) S [D]:   . . . Let me have, have the wrench. I need the wrench.
(62) D [S]:   Okay, here's the wrench.
(63) S [D]:   Okay.

The wrench, at least, is being treated as a shared object. Since Steven "needed" the wrench, Don, as a coparticipant, might be considered obligated to comply. This transaction would not require a "thank you" but simply an acknowledgment of the cooperative act. As an outsider, however, Jeff is thanked for his contribution. Don takes the contribution himself, then in (60) announces to the group that they all ("we") have more tools. Thus he politely excludes Jeff, reaffirms the episode, and adds to his own supplies at the same time.

The tension between individual tool supplies and the verbal formulation of a joint project finally leads to conflict. While the interaction between Don and Jeff is going on, Kevin begins doing something quite different from what has been going on up to now. He accidentally drops a piece into the open compartment. He looks in, then begins dropping the rest of his pieces in. He does not say anything about what he is doing and the others pay no attention. He goes off, announcing his mission (65) in accord with Don's previous utterance.

(64) D: We need a lot more things, right? Right you guys?
(65) K: I'm a get *more* tools.

Kevin's announcement, in its literal sense, is consistent with his going to get more tools either for the group or for himself. However, since it directly follows Don's question, it can be heard by others as an affirmative response, although Kevin does not necessarily intend to express this relationship. It must be noted that Don's utterance, itself, does not literally say "we, as a group, need a lot more things" rather than "we, each individually, need a lot more things." But in his preceding statement to Steven, in utterance (60) above, "we" clearly has the former sense. Don gives us no reason to think he has changed the sense. So that while Kevin's action of putting his tools in the compartment deviates from what has been going on, what he says ties his action of leaving to the episode as it is currently formulated by Don and Steven.

On returning, Kevin throws more tools in. He makes no announcement and says nothing to Jeff who joins him in the new activity of throwing pieces into the open compartment. This activity is not formulated verbally as a new episode, nor is it related to the ongoing episode. Don, apparently excited by the noisy activity, also joins in. In the process Don knocks a roof plank into the compartment. Steven tries to retrieve the plank as Don excitedly throws the other planks in. Steven reconstructs the roof during (71).

(71) S: Don't knock the house down. Hey we need a new house.
(73) S: We're making a new house?
(74) S: We're making a new house?
(75) K: What a yucky mess.
(76) S: (Remember) we're making a new house?
(77) D [S]: Right. We, we, we didn't *remember* we're making a new house.

Steven succeeds in re-establishing the episode when Don finally responds to him in (77). Don and Steven go back to work, but moments later Don leans on the roof accidentally pushing a plank over the side. He continues pushing the rest over, laughing. As he says (78), Steven begins replacing the roof planks but this time over the compartment with Kevin's pieces.

(78) S: UH-oh our house broke. That's where, our- Oh no, that's where we're making a new place to keep all our tools. Right?
(79) D: Yeah, I'm making a new-
(80) K: That's *my* tools, all *my* tools.
(81) S: Put all, all the tools in, cause it's getting ready for-
(82) K: We're (dressing up).
(83) J: Yeah.
(84) S: For, for to ge- *No No* see it's beginning to make-Now we made a new place for our tools.
(85) D: Can't see em.
(86) S: Yeah.
(87) D: Ha ha ha.
   [S]:   I shut it up. Ha ha.
(88) S: Yeah w- . . .

In (78), (81) and (84), Steven clearly sets out the new thing he is doing. In (81) he responds to Kevin's attempt to claim the tools as his own by giving an explanation for what he is doing. The four boys begin throwing more pieces into the "new place to keep all our tools." Jeff responds in (83) to Kevin's formulation, but Steven ignores Kevin's verbal contribution continuing his own previous explanation in (84). Don tries to move one of the planks (during 84), but Steven puts it back, then puts the other planks on, completely covering the tool compartment. He stands back as Don and Steven engage in a complaint.

(94) S: No, now, now we have to *fix* it, 'gain. We don't want to really *fix* it.
(95) D: No, we don't really, don't want, to fix it.

Kevin, apparently angry about not being able to get at "his" tools, pulls the uncovered box away from the other two. Don and Marvin replace the box but in spite of protests which show their solidarity, Kevin pulls it away twice more before wandering off. Because of his verbal insistence, Steven nullifies what it was that Kevin was trying to do in putting his pieces into the compartment. The activity of covering the tools has been formulated consistently with the joint ownership of the construction pieces and Don apparently accepts it in (85) and (87). Kevin's view of his action of throwing pieces into the compartment, on the other hand, had to do with his individual ownership of the pieces, as is finally indicated clearly in (80). However, since the *de facto* individual ownership had never become an explicit aspect of the ongoing episode, the significance of an activity based on it is easily overridden by Steven's formulation of the next step ("making a new place to keep all our tools") which is consistent with the explicit previous steps of the episode. Steven and Don become reunited in opposition to Kevin's willful destruction of the building which followed his being denied access to "his" tools.

The conflict appears to have resulted from differing understandings about the facts of ownership. It seems that Kevin lost out because his definition did not become the one that was publicly shared. The conflict is suggestive of differences among the boys in their abilities to manage and negotiate social activities. An explanation of the events in terms of differences (individual or developmental), however, is beyond the scope of a description of a single episode. On a descriptive level, the episode, as publicly constructed, involved the joint ownership of the objects being played with. The consensus that was made public did not provide for individual ownership of the objects. That is, the episode provided only for a distinction between participants and outsiders.

Permission, Turn-taking, and Ownership

The distinction between participants and outsiders has been shown in (55) to be relevant to permission. As the episode progresses, more evidence can be found for the appropriate use of permission requests.

As Kevin wanders off, Steven picks up a toy food grinder and begins attaching it to the box Kevin had pulled away. As he tightens the clamp, he says:

(101) S: We have to grind it up um so he can't *wreck* it.
Have to *grind* it up. Grind it up with this so-

The ongoing episode now includes only Don and Steven and the activity is explicitly formulated as a defense against Kevin's attacks. The activity involved in this phase of the episode is quite different from the individual playing with construction pieces. Yet what is happening now can be considered a modification of the ongoing episode. A little later the teacher comes by and asks:

(130) T [?]: What are you making?
(131) D: Something new.

Don's answer ties the current events to what was suggested as the beginning of the episode in utterances (12) and (13). Thus the continuity is displayed. Now, however, the focus is on the grinder, a toy with which only one child can play at a time. The activity involves taking turns at turning the handle of the grinder. Now for an outsider who wants to become a participant the problem is to get a turn with the grinder. But participants also have the same problem. Therefore, it may be the case either that the grinder is owned by the participant whose turn it is, or it is owned by the episode-defined participants as a group regardless of whose turn it is. If the episode, as established verbally, is to remain a useful notion in considering the structure of this play sequence, then the latter should be the case. Permission requests, in this case, should be made only by outsiders and some other method of exchanging turns should be in effect between the participants. Unfortunately for this version of the episode hypothesis, of the six permission requests that occurred subsequently, half were made by Steven and Don and half by Kevin and Jeff. On closer examination, however, an interesting difference between two kinds of permission requests is evident.

As Steven is tightening the grinder clamp onto the side of the box, Don reaches with both hands, takes hold of the clamp as Steven withdraws his hand from the clamp, and begins turning the grinder handle. As Don reaches and takes hold of the clamp, he says (112).

(112) D: . . . Could I do this?
(113) S: Yeah.
(114) D: Turn around and a-

By the time Steven answers, he has already released the clamp and is turning the handle. As Don says (114), he displaces Steven's hand from the handle and begins grinding. Don grinds for some time before Steven reaches for the grinder with his right hand, removing Don's hand with his left.

(145) S: Now I, can I, st- do it, a little bit?

By the time he says "it" Steven is already grinding; Don does not answer. About four seconds later, Don reaches for the grinder again, but this time Steven fends him off with his left hand while continuing to grind with his right.

(146) D: Can I do this?
(147) S: No no.

In these cases the requests are being made while the turn is being exchanged. The requester does not wait for the requestee to answer, nor do they address each other directly.

Kevin has returned and he and Jeff have been watching the exchange. Steven is grinding.

(148) K [S &/or D]: Can I try it?
(149) D [K]: *No.*
(150) K [D]: Why?
(151) D [K]: Only two men to do it. *Cos you-*
(152) J [D &/or S]: Can *I* do it?
(153) D: N- now it's my turn
(154) S: Okay.

Neither Kevin nor Jeff make a move toward the grinder as they speak. In addition, they address their requests to the participants. While the outsiders wait for permission, the participants move to take the turn during the course of the request. The last permission request (from Kevin to Steven [179] below) also has the typical outsider to participant form.

During (153) Don secures his turn from Steven. As soon as Steven concedes to Don (154), Kevin, his patience exhausted, lunges across the boxes and tries to grab the grinder from Don.

(155) K: *NO (I WANT TO).*

Don holds him off with his left hand while continuing to grind with his right. Kevin begins pounding on Don's shoulder with his fists. Don manages to push him away as the teacher comes over. Steven removes the grinder from the box and holds it in his hands. He and Don look down at it as the teacher talks with Kevin who is now crying.

(166) K [T]: Why Don have me that?
(167) T [K]: I don't know why. Did you ask him?
(168) K [D]: I want it.
(169) D [K]: No.
(170) K [T]: Yes. He says *Nooo.*
(171) T [K]: Is that the only paper? . . .

In (166) Kevin points to the grinder in Steven's hands. The teacher, not familiar with what the boys are doing, thinks he is pointing to some paper which happens to be between Kevin and the grinder. It takes some questioning by the teacher before she realizes that "that" refers to the grinder in *Steven's* hands. Prompted by the teacher, Kevin now addresses his request to Steven who is holding the grinder.

(178) T [K]: Did you ask Steven?
(179) K [S]: Can I do the gri- that? *Steven.*

Steven hands him the grinder. Kevin apparently does not realize the ambiguity of his pointing and the teacher asks (178) with a slightly puzzled expression. It should not be overlooked that it was Don and not Steven who denied permission to Kevin (149), even though it was Steven who was grinding at the time. The ownership, then, can be seen as attaching to participation in an episode and not a matter of the brute fact of having one's hand on the object.

After Kevin apologizes for having started the fight, the episode continues. Don helps him clamp the grinder back on the box and, now in control, takes a turn at grinding. Don and Kevin engage each other verbally with the following ritual exchange which occurs several other times in the four hours of data:

(192) K [D]: Hi Don.
(193 D [K]: Hi Donnie.

They both laugh. Now a participant in good standing again, Kevin takes his turn by reaching for and grasping the grinder from Don, saying:

(199) K: Now it's *my* turn.

Thus permission requests from one participant to another can be seen as functioning much as the assertions (153) and (199). While the requestee can resist as in (147), the requester does not wait for what he is apparently requesting. While the outsiders wait for the authoritative pronouncement, there is no indication that insiders consider their coparticipants to have any authority.

Summary and Conclusions

The examination of a segment of children's social interaction has shown the children confronted with the particular problem of carrying on play in the midst of a larger group. In this situation, the play group's composition was continually subject to negotiation and dispute. The children's management of these problems consisted of public acts which made their shared understanding explicit for members of the classroom as well as for the investigator. The availability of these acts for observation made it possible to describe both the organization produced and the means of its production.

The analysis of the interactions has shown the children actively constructing, maintaining, re-establishing, and otherwise orienting to a social episode which provided for the classification of the children either as participants or as outsiders. The participants were recognized by all the children as the joint owners of the play objects. Maintaining participation in and directing the course of the episode involved to a great extent the ability to verbally locate the activity as part of the episode. The "physical" actions, which were carried out either cooperatively or individually, were secondary to the episodic organization as formulated in talk. Among the verbal devices that functioned to maintain this organization were elaborative repetitions and announcements of comings and goings. These devices not only contained formulations of what the episode was about (its topic or theme) but served to maintain the recognition of engagement. These functions were also displayed in the more complex three-participant dialogues. Permission requests by the outsiders showed their compliant recognition of ownership of the play objects by the participants.

The illustration of social organization as an ongoing accomplishment argues for viewing language use as, among other things, a constitutive element in the production of organization. This view has two related aspects. It provides a way, on the one hand, of locating instances of organization and analyzing the complexities of the shared understandings and, on the other hand, of attributing to each utterance a function in relation to the ongoing organization. For developmental research, the view implies a further integration of the study of social and language development. Documentation of the social organization that children are able to understand and produce can be achieved by documenting their use of language in communicating their recognitions. The nature of the organization produced, in turn, reflects back on the individual utterances which constitute its production.

The individual acts examined in this study did not fulfill their function entirely by virtue of their grammatical attributes which specify their literal meaning. For example, "announcements" were often, literally, statements of intent. Their functioning as announcements of a mission can be determined only from knowledge of the topic of the episode which makes those particular intents into relevant missions. The relationship of the appropriate characterization of the act performed in an utterance to the complexities of the relevant shared understandings has been demonstrated, for adult conversation, by Turner (1970). Similarly, the present analysis shows that the identification of children's speech acts (e.g., announcements) must take into account the extended episodes of interaction which provide the relevant context.

The occurrence of requests for permission in the same way cannot be reliably identified by their typical grammatical form (roughly a yes-no question using "may" or "can"). Two reasons for this are illustrated by the data. In the first place, the sentence must obviously be accompanied by waiting for an answer, unlike its use by participants. A request is not simply the utterance of a sentence (here a transcript alone would be entirely misleading). In identifying permission requests, the investigator must have evidence that the speaker intends to obtain permission.

The second reason has to do with what Austin (1962) calls "felicity conditions." For the utterance of this kind of sentence to count as a felicitous permission request, the requestee must have some rights over the thing requested. The description of the episode showed that such rights are social facts recognized by the children. That this is the case, however, was not demonstrated independently of the occurrence of permission requests. If these requests had occurred randomly in relation to the other events which constituted the episode, then there would be no reason to believe that such rights existed or that the children were actually requesting permission at all in uttering the typical sentences. That the outsiders consistently asked permission of the participants, itself, is evidence that the construction of the episode was constitutive of those rights, and that the rights were sustained in the maintenance of the episode. The coherence of the events as a whole provides both for the characterization of the episode as one in which rights of ownership are in effect and for the identification of particular utterances as requests for permission. While it may appear somewhat circular for a class of utterances to count as part of the evidence for their own felicity, this state of affairs simply reflects the constructive role of outsiders in complying with the organization they perceive.

The necessity of locating and identifying individual acts with respect to the coherent organization they are helping to produce is not peculiar to the procedure of the present study, which was to examine closely a single continuous segment of data. More systematic methods in which a class of events are selected for study from various data samples must consider episodic organization in identifying exemplars of the class. The location of beginnings, endings, disputes, claims to turns, as well as speech act types, must be sensitive to what the beginning or ending is of, what the dispute is about, what the claim is to, etc. The development of skills for carrying on disputes, for example, is likely to go hand-in-hand with more complex episodic organizations about which to fight. The skills for disputing may be part of what it takes to produce that organization. So as soon as the new skills appear, the problems that they are addressed to also change. In order to say two actions are of the same kind, it is necessary to show that the problems for which the actions represent solutions are also of the same kind. In the same way, for permission requests and other speech act types which have social facts as their felicity conditions and their consequences, qualitative change is likely to be found with development in the nature of these social facts. If the function of a permission request with respect to episode construction is to be determined, the particular kind of "right" to which it is responsive must be explicated. While at an abstract level of description two permission requests may be considered exemplars of the same speech act type, developmental differences may be found between the two if for one the social fact is more complex or sophisticated. This is not to say that every act must be treated as unique. Rather, it is to recommend that the type of social organization to which the act is contributing be considered in identifying the particular instances.

The concept of episode and the method for locating instances of it together provide a framework for studying social interactions not only among children but also between adults and children. The latter interactions may be of considerable interest in that they are probably an important factor in the child's socialization. This process can be conceived of as not just learning rules for proper behavior but learning more complex episodic organization. For example, "free-play time" during which the analyzed segment occurred, is a teacher's category. It is one of the units along with snack time, clean-up time, etc., with which she structures the school session as part of her professional work (Gearhart and Newman, in preparation). These units can be considered social episodes involving the teacher and the children to which, among other things, different rules for ownership apply. In order to know which rules apply at any particular time the children must learn not only the teacher's rules but also her episodic organization. For example, each time the teacher initiates a new episode at the table, she expects the seating to be established anew. On one occasion the teacher had announced an activity and Vanessa found a seat at the table. Kevin, however, wanting to sit in the same chair he had had before, tried to push her off. The teacher said to him: "Nooo sit in a different one, this time . . ." where the indexical expression "this time" refers to the time since her announcement of the episode. The teacher's rule is that during an episode, but not between episodes, the chairs are owned by the first claimant, i.e., first after the announcement. In order for Kevin to understand the teacher's command as based on a rule, he must first understand the teacher's structuring of the session into separate times.

Coming to understand the organizational possibilities of social behavior is a necessary prerequisite for understanding utterances embedded in that organization both for the child and for his investigators. Studying the functions of language cannot be separated from studying the social organization that the use of language is able to create. The present chapter has attempted to demonstrate ways of elucidating both this organization and the role of language in its production.

Notes

For their helpful comments on previous drafts of this chapter, I am grateful to Benzion Chanowitz, Lindsay Churchill, Alison Clarke-Stewart, John Dore, Maryl Gearhart, Joseph Glick, Ray McDermott, Marilyn Shatz, Roy Turner and Virginia Valian. I especially want to thank Maryl Gearhart for generously sharing her understanding of the data with which we have both been working.

Preparation of this chapter was supported in part by grant No. 5-29284 from the Grant Foundation to the Rockefeller University and by fellowship No. W754016 from the Canada Council to the author.

References

Austin, J. *How to Do Things with Words*. New York: Oxford University Press, 1962.

Fillmore, C. May we come in? *Semiotica*, 1973, *9*, 97–116.

Garfinkel, H. *Studies in Ethnomethodology*. Englewood Cliffs, N.J.: Prentice-Hall, 1967.

Garfinkel, H., and Sacks, H. On formal structures of practical actions. In J. McKinney and E. Tiryakian (Eds.), *Theoretical Sociology*. New York: Appleton-Century-Crofts, 1970.

Garvey, C. Some properties of social play. *Merrill-Palmer Quarterly*, 1974, *20*, 163–180.

Garvey, C., and Hogan, R. Social speech and social interaction: Egocentrism revisited. *Child Development*, 1973, *44*, 562–568.

Gearhart, M., and Newman, D. Social plans and nursery-school tasks: A cognitive model of a teacher's work with implications for social development. In preparation.

Goffman, E. *Behavior in Public Places: Notes on the Social Organization of Gatherings*. New York: Free Press, 1963.

Goffman, E. *Frame Analysis: An Essay on the Organization of Experience*. New York: Harper and Row, 1974.

Keenan, E. Conversational competence in children. *Journal of Child Language*, 1974, *1*, 163–183.

Mitchell-Kernan, C., and Ervin-Tripp, S. (Eds.), *Child Discourse*. New York: Academic Press, 1977.

Piaget, J. *The Language and Thought of the Child*. New York: World Publishing, 1955.

Ryan, J. Early language development: Towards a communicational analysis. In M. P. M. Richards (Ed.), *The Integration of a Child into a Social World*. London: Cambridge University Press, 1974.

Sacks, H. Unpublished lecture notes, The University of California at Irvine, 1967.

Searle, J. *Speech Acts: An Essay in the Philosophy of Language*. London: Cambridge University Press, 1969.

Shatz, M., and Gelman, R. The development of communication skills: Modifications in the speech of young children as a function of the listener. *Society for Research in Child Development Monographs*, 1973, *5*, 1–38.

Sudnow, D. (Ed.). *Studies in Social Interaction*. New York: Free Press, 1972.

Turner, R. Words, utterances and activities. In J. Douglas (Ed.) *Understanding Everyday Life*. Chicago: Aldine, 1970.

Turner, R. (Ed.). *Ethnomethodology*. Baltimore: Penguin, 1974.

Appendix: Transcript of Analyzed Segment

This transcript follows the same conventions used in the examples in the text but with the following additions: (1) Nonverbal actions are described within brackets. When a description appears on the same line as an utterance it occurred simultaneously with the utterance. Descriptions appearing on separate lines are not necessarily simultaneous. (2) Numbers appearing in parentheses at the end of a line indicate the approximate number of seconds before the next utterance. These indications are given only when the pause was two seconds or longer. Numbers in parentheses at the end of a bracketed description (and within the brackets) indicate the duration of the events described.

The transcript is slightly abridged. Whenever utterances were omitted a bracketed description (with its duration indication) is given.

[Steven is pulling a plank back and forth across three wooden boxes (see Figure 1) that Don and Kevin had originally pushed together as a choo choo train. He is pretending to saw the boxes with the plank. Vanessa is nearby. Don and Kevin return from doing Easter eggs. Don notices Steven and runs toward the boxes followed by Kevin.]

1. D [S]: Nooo, I, I didn't, ah. We got that for Christmas. (4)
2. K: We got that for Christmas. [S continues sawing.]
3. D: Yeah. I'm going to saw. [D and V pick up planks. V begins to saw.]
4. S [V]: I'm *making* something. No you don't *saw*.
   [D]: I'm I am *sawing*. [D begins to saw.]
5. D [S]: I'm sawing *too*.
6. S [D]: (   ) (have) to saw, we need scr- cracks. We have to saw-

   [S applies his saw to the crack between the boxes, displacing V. D saws other crack.]

7. D: (saw) [S takes over one end of D's plank. They saw together.] (4)
8. S: Crack. There you (through) [The plank falls between the boxes.]
9. D: Hey look at (it). (2)
10. S: Now you're going to build something with that.
11. D: Yeah. [D and S begin moving the boxes.]
12. S: To build something. We have to *build* something *new*.
13. D: Yeah we have to build something *newer*. [D and S bridge two boxes with planks.]

   [Meanwhile, K and V have been talking about using the planks as "skis." Then V begins sawing the third box.]

14. V [K]: Let's do, let's do our own, okay?

   [K walks off to get a plank to join either V or the other boys. D takes V's box, leaving her holding a plank. He places the three boxes open side up so that the center pieces form two compartments. He then places a plank on top as part of a roof over one compartment. S moves toward V to get her plank. (18)]

15. S: We are moving, right?

   [While S begins a tug-of-war with V over the plank, K returns with his plank and begins sawing.]

16. D: Okay. *No*. [D takes K's plank.] We are moving it. [D places K's plank next to others.]

   [Kevin stands back and watches.]

17. S: *Doon't. No* [S pulls plank from V.]
18. D: Put it right there, put it on the (across).

   [S places plank on boxes as D indicated, completing the roof over one compartment. S and D together straighten boxes into better alignment.]

19. S: That's a new *house*.
20. D: Yeah.
21. S: That's a new *house*.
22. D: Yeah.

   [The teacher calls V to do a test and the three boys follow out of curiosity. They do not return to the boxes when T reminds them that the test is only for V. D and K go to a corner where D empties onto the floor a bag of construction pieces: girders, screws, tools, etc. S kneels on a chair idly looking off at some other events. D and then K begin picking up some of the girders which they call "guns." (60)]

23. D: You make now there a whole *bunch* of guns. (3)
24. K: A whole *bunch* of guns.

25. D: I have a whole bunch of guns too. a ha ha ha ha I got wh-
26. K: *Whole bunch of guns.* [D and K go back toward the boxes with the pieces.]
27. D: I got a *whole bunch* ⌈*of guns.* [S also returns to the boxes.]
28. S: ⌊*Made this new.* [S looks at the house.]
29. D: *Yeah* we *all* did it.
30. K: Yeah.
31. S: Now we're going to *fix* it, with our *tools.* [S goes off.]
32. D: Yeah, these (our) *tools.*
33. K: These (our) *tools.*

[D and K kneel on either side of the boxes and place their "tools" on top. (20)]

34. S: Okay I have something now, [S returns holding a wrench.]
        I'll get some more screws. [S goes off again.]
        I'm a get more⌈screws.
35. K: ⌊(   ) and pegs. [K goes off.]
36. D: Yeah, we're building something (   ) build something. (18)

[K and S return with more construction pieces.]

37. D: We're making something.

[K makes a pile by his side. S drops his tools close by.]

38. K: NO, *these are* MINE. [K tries to keep his separate from S's.]

[D quickly takes the remaining pieces from the roof for his own pile.]

39. S: Making something new. [S moves his pieces into a separate pile.]

[S, K, and D are busy with their "tools."]

40. D: (They're) a whole bunch of these things.
41. S: We need to have a lot of *tools.* [S and K go off again.]
42. D: Yeah, I ha, I have tools. All of the rest.
43. K [D]: You have a gun? [K returns holding a piece.]
44. D [K]: Yeah, eh, eh, ya ya but all of you- [D holds up piece.]
45. S: *Making something* NEW. [S returns.]
46. D: Right.
47. K: Newer.
48. D: New. Nobody-
49. S: You know what, we need some screws to screw, this in, and we need a screwdriver, I have one right here. Okay?
50. D: Okay, (4)
51. S: And *screw* it. [S works with screwdriver.]
52. D: *Nope.*
53. S: We're going t- We're making something *new.* And we have a wrench here, here's a wrench and screwdriver. [S holds up tools.]
54. D: *I'll* do it, I'll have both of *these.* [D takes tools from S.]

[Meanwhile, Jeff has just finished at the crafts table. He picks up some construction pieces and approaches S, D. and K.]

55. J: [?]: Hey, hey can I help?
56. D: *Noo.*
57. J [D]: I got some tools here. [J shows D the pieces.]

58. D [J]: Tsk, thanks for the tools. [D takes one piece from J.]
59. J [D]: I'm going to put them down. [J drops other pieces by D and runs off.]
60. D: Thanks, thank, we have more *tools* from *Jeff*.
   [S]: We have more tools from Jeff to build.
61. S: And we have to- [S stands and reaches toward D.]
   [D]: Let me have, have the wrench. I need the wrench.
62. D [S]: Okay, here's the wrench. [D hands wrench to S.]
63. S [D]: Okay.

[J and then V return with more pieces and drop them beside D. Meanwhile K knocks one of his pieces into the open compartment. He looks into the compartment then throws in the rest of his pieces. (13)]

64. D: We need a lot more things, right? Right you guys?
65. K: I'm a get *more* tools. [K goes off and joins J and V picking up pieces.]
66. D: There, we need a *lot more tools*.
67. S: We'll need a *lot* of tools.
68. D: Yeah we might need a *lot* of them.
69. S: And we need a *lot* of screws. (7)

[V returns, dumps pieces in D's pile.]

70. D: Thanks, Vanessa [V leaves to play with Carol.] we need a *lot* more tools, right? We need a *lot more. New.*

[K returns and throws his pieces into the open compartment. J returns and throws his pieces into the compartment with K's. D notices K's and J's throwing activity and begins throwing in some of his pieces but in the process knocks off a roof plank. (12)]

71. S: Don't knock the house down. [S tries to retrieve the plank.] Hey we need a new house.
72. J: *Hey.*
73. S: We're making a new house?

[S replaces planks as D throws others in. S reconstructs the roof.]

74. S: We're making a new house?
75. K: What a yucky mess. (3)
76. S: (Remember) we're making a new house?
77. D [S]: Right. We, we, we didn't *remember* we're making a new house.

[D and S go back to work but moments later D leans on the roof accidentally pushing a plank over the side. He continues pushing the rest over, laughing. S begins replacing the roof planks but this time over the compartment with K's pieces. (42)]

78. S: UH-oh our house broke. That's where, our- Oh no, that's where we're making a new place to keep all our tools. Right?
79. D: Yeah, I'm making a new-
80. K: That's *my* tools, all *my* tools. [K points to partly covered compartment.]
81. S: Put all, all the tools in, cause it's getting ready for-
82. K: We're (dressing) up.
83. J: Yeah.

84. S: For, for to ge- [D begins to move a plank.] *No no* see it's beginning to make- Now we made a new place for our tools. [S covers tool compartment completely.]
85. D: Can't see em.
86. S: Yeah.
87. D: Ha ha ha.
   [S]: I shut it up. Ha ha.
88. S: Yeah w- [K moves a plank to get at tools. A plank falls in.]
   [K]: *No no don't.*
89. K: Ha ha. [J joins K pushing other planks in. K steps back, watches.]
90. S: Now you *wrecked* it.
91. D: Now you *wrecked* it. [S and D begin replacing planks.]
92. K: Now you *wrecked* it.
93. D: No.
94. S: No, now, now we have to *fix* it, 'gain. We don't want to really *fix* it.
95. D: No, we don't really, don't want, to fix it. [S and D finish replacing planks.]

[K pulls the uncovered box away from the two others.]

96. S: *Now*, NOW YOU WRECKED IT EVEN MORE.
97. D: *He wrecked it even more. Now don't* (   ) [S and D replace box.]
98. S: Yeah. [K pulls box away again.] NO. [S, D, and K struggle over box. D replaces it.] (8)
99. S: We have to grind it up. [S picks up a toy meat grinder.]

[K pulls box away for third time.]

100. D: KEY. COME ON. [D retrieves and replaces box. K wanders off.] (4)
101. S: We have to grind it up um so he can't *wreck* it. Have to *grind* it up. Grind it up with this so-

[S attaches grinder to side of uncovered box, begins tightening clamp.]

102. J [D]: Can I put the paper in? [J brings a handful of paper.]
103. D [J]: Nope.
104. J [D]: Then where's the paper go?
105. D [J]: Put it in there. Put it in there. [D points to open compartment.]

[J throws paper in.]

106. S: That's (the) *garbage.*

[D attempts to help S tighten the clamp.]

107. S: [D[: Don't. [S pushes D's hand away.] Need to grind the (chair) up.
   [K comes back to watch.]

108. D [K]: Stop that Kevin or I'll shoot you dead. [D points at K.]
109. T [?]: Aaw shh really? [T is off camera.]
110. D: Yeah, really, [K stands watching S and D.]
111. T [?]: Aaw aaw.
112. D [K]: We're grind this up. Could I do this? [D reaches and takes hold of clamp screw from S.]
113. S: Yeah. [M turns grinder handle.]

114. D: Turn around and a- [D takes over turning the handle.]

[J brings a plank. K kneels down, watching with thumb in mouth.]

115. J: *Need another* BOARD. *Need another* BOARD (4) *to cover up that part*. Do we need to cover up that part? [J indicates the "paper" compartment.]
116. D: No.
117. S: We need to grind it.

[S takes J's plank and moves it close to the grinder.]

118. D: Yeah we need to grind it. [D grinds rapidly.]
119. K [S]: Why? [K has been watching S and D.]
120. D [K]: Because (   ) (took it) *apart*. (2) That's why we're *grinding* it.
121. T [?]: Because why? [T is off camera.]
123. T [?]: What are you grinding?
124. D: A tool thing where tools are. [D indicates closed compartment.] We putted tools in there.
125. J: Yeah, and *paper*. [J points to paper compartment.]
126. D: Yeah, papers go in there. (2)
127. T [?]: What are you⌈making?
128. S: ⌊And tools go in there. [S thumps roof.]
129. D: Tools go in there. We⌈covered them up.
130. T [?]:   ⌊What are you making?
131. D: Something new.
132. T [?]: Really?
133. D: Yeah.
134. T [?]: Sound interesting.
135. J [D or S]: Hey you know, somebody may come and (may) take those out.
136. D [J]: Yeah, we're stayed on it. Stay here. (2)
137. J [D]: Yeah we need another *board*. [J brings another plank.] (4) We need another board?
138. D [J]: No. No I don't need another board.
139. J [D]: Why not? (3) (Someone) come and steal those papers. (2)
140. D [J]: That's all right.
141. S [D]: You know why I have this board here. For my *skis*. [S has plank he took from J.]

[Carol comes over.]

142. C: Why's the paper in there? [C points to paper compartment.]
143. D [C]: Cos we *need* em in there. (3) We keepin everything in there.
144. J: *Yeah.* I'm the (main mansk)

[D is still grinding, kneeling at the end of the boxes with the grinder on the side of the box to his right. S is kneeling at D's right directly in front of the grinder. J is on S's right. K is sitting across from S and to D's left. C has left.]

145. S: Now I, can I, st- do it, a little bit? [S takes hold of grinder.] (4)
146. D: Can I do this? [D reaches for grinder.]
147. S: No no. [S fends off D while continuing to grind.]
148. K [S &/or D]: Can I try it?
149. D [K]: *No.* [S continues to grind.]

150. K [D]: Why?
151. D [K]: Only two men to do it. *Cos you-*
152. J [D &/or S]: Can *I* do it?
153. D: N- now it's my turn. [D reaches with both hands securing the grinder.]
154. S: Okay.
155. K: *NO.* (*I WANT TO*) [K lunges toward the grinder grabbing D's hand.]

   [D holds K off with his left hand still holding the grinder with his right. K pounds D's shoulder with his fists.]

156. J: *Now it's my turn.* [J tries to grab. K continues pounding D.]
157. D: No. [D pushes J's hand away. J withdraws hand.]
158. T [K]: Kevin, *Kevin?*
159. D: *Stop that.* [D continues holding K off.]
160. T [K]: Kevin, talk to⌈him. Kevin.
161. D: ⌊STOP *that Kevin.* STOP IT.
162. T [K]: Kevin, you better watch out (   )
163. D: *And then now you'll have to go away.* [D pushes K away still holding grinder.]

   [K loses his balance. S pushes his plank at K.]

164. K: NO I DON'T. [K pulls plank out of S's hand and bangs it on the roof.] (7)
165. T [K]: I think you do if you hit people, Kevin? Listen. I think if you hit people like that you do have to go away. Better not do that any more y'know. People really don't like it.

   [J runs off. S removes the grinder from the box and holds it in his hands. S and D look down at it as T talks with K who is now crying. (20)]

166. K [T]: Why Don have me that? [K points across the boxes to the grinder.]
167. T [K]: I don't know why. Did you ask him?
168. K [D]: I want it.
169. D [K]: No.
170. K [T]: *Yes.* He says *Nooo.*
171. T [K]: Is that the only paper? [T points to paper compartment.] Get some more paper. Look on the shelf.
172. K [T]: NOOO I don't want to get paper. [K cries.]
173. T [K]: Well, why do you need⌈Don's paper? [T squats down next to K.]
174. K [T]:   ⌊I want that.
175. T [K]: Why do you need Don's paper.
176. K: *That.* [K points to grinder in S's hands. S continues looking down.]
177. T [K]: You mean the grinder?

   [K nods "yes."]

178. T [K]: Did you ask Steven?
179. K [S]: Can I do, the gri- that? *Steven.* [S looks at K.]
180. T [K]: Better take the thumb out it's hard⌈to understand you.
181. K [S]:   ⌊Steven

182. K [S]: I want that. [S glances to T.]
183. S [K]: Okay. [S hands K the grinder.]
184. K: Thank you. [K begins attaching grinder to his side of the box.]
185. T [S]: Thank you Steven.
186. S [D]: We don't need that there right? [S removes J's plank.]
187. D [S]: Yeah. [T leaves.]
        [K]: And after you's going to be my turn, right?
188. K [D]: I'm sorry a do it.
189. D: *Uh-oh* the (   ) off, [D reaches for grinder.] just gonna screw it
        out. [D begins fastening the clamp.]
190. S: I will screw it more. [S grabs for grinder.] No. [D holds on to it.]
        Uhhhhhhh. [D pulls it away and out of S's reach.]
191. D: *Stop it*. [S grabs again as D brings it back.] I'll screw it myself. [D
        turns from S.]
192. K [D]: Hi Don. [K laughs.]
193. D [K]: Hi Donnie. [D laughs.]
194. K: *There* we are.
195. D: Not yet. [D continues screwing clamp.] There we are. Now.
        [K]: Now it's my turn. [D begins grinding. K takes over clamp.]

[S takes K's hand off the clamp and works on it himself. Finally it's attached
to everyone's satisfaction. (40)]

196. S: It goes into the wood, it goes right here (   )
197. D: Yes.
198. S: (   ) on. [K touches clamp.]
199. K: Now it's *my* turn. [K grasps the handle and grinds.]
        [And so it continues.]

7 Interpretation and Summarization: Issues in the Child's Acquisition of Social Structure

AARON V. CICOUREL

The acquisition and use of language and paralinguistic representational systems presume the child is capable of recognizing, receiving, processing, and generating the immediately experienced and stored particulars we call information. The child learns to express aspects of his or her thoughts and experiences from several sensory modalities in socially organized settings. The researcher is faced with similar problems of expression. Language acquisition and use occur in specific interactional settings and require a creative summarization effort by the child if he or she is to manage the routine overload of

The descriptive material reported in this chapter are from research in Mexico City (in 1967–68 by the present author) and Buenos Aires (in 1968–69 by the present author and Eliseo Verón). The research was supported by small grants from the Joint Committee on Latin American Research of the Social Science Research Council and the American Council of Learned Societies. Carmen Cano de Béjar and Carmen Dominguez provided me with helpful advice and assistance with the Mexican families studied. Gladys Ford of Buenos Aires provided me with careful assistance in the study of Argentine families. Pat Murray offered several helpful suggestions that were incorporated into this chapter.

information available. The researcher must also deal with this overload problem. The creative aspects of everyday social interaction are
usually hidden from us because of selective attention that is cognitively and culturally organized in acts of perception. The researcher's
assembly of a data base is also limited by selective perception and the
context of observation. The researcher's study of the child's transition
to adult interactional competence involves similar problems of interpretation and summarization. In this chapter I use some illustrative materials from a larger study of parent-child interaction to discuss
some methodological and theoretical issues that would link the study
of cognitive and linguistic processes to the notion of the child's acquisition of social structure.

Studies of Conversational Exchanges in Natural Settings

Studies of child development and language acquisition have made
use of experimental, quasi-experimental, and natural settings to infer
how children learn to use language as native speakers and how children develop reasoning abilities, personal and social identities, motor
and perceptual control, and a host of capabilities seen as indications of
potential adult status. Socialization studies by sociologists have often
relied on sample surveys to focus on differences in child-rearing practices by social class. Direct observation or study of social interaction by
those investigators is not common. Although there is a strong tradition among some sociologists, following the work of G. H. Mead
(1934), to address issues in the child's development of personal and
social identities, sociologists usually avoid intensive empirical work in
natural settings with only a few families. Sociologists tend to believe it
is methodologically wiser to survey many families with standardized
questionnaires. The idea of searching for invariant processes and
individual differences by extensive work with a few families is rare.
Weak theories and survey data are preferred over a micro-oriented
concern with social structure.

In the present chapter I have followed work by anthropologists
(Whiting, 1963) where a few families are studied for an extensive
period of time. The illustrative materials described below are based
on a small study of families with different social-class backgrounds in
Mexico City and Buenos Aires. This early work generated information based on occasional observations of the family, especially mother
and children, and interviews with the mother, but it especially relies

on tape-recorded materials of mother-child(ren) interactions in the home at different intervals over a period of one year. The materials obtained are in many respects similar to later work by Blount (1972), Corsaro (n.d.), Newport (1976), and Gelman and Shatz (1975). We were concerned with the child's and the mother's interactional competence across social classes.

An important area of investigation in developmental psycholinguistics is the idea that the mother's speech to the child is adjusted in such a way as to take into account the child's competence and the needs of the language learner (Newport, 1976; Phillips, 1973; Remick, 1971; Shipley, Smith, and Gleitman, 1969; Snow, 1972). Newport (1976) has described the speech of mothers to young children ("motherese") as consisting of several factors, including the function of the conversation. She observers that the general processing capacity of the child listener is deficient, resulting in short, repeated utterances and a structural simplicity that often includes well-formed and clearly articulated utterances. She notes that evidence from different studies shows that syntactic simplification is always present because of the necessity of speech adjustment in adult-child communicative interaction and that conversational functions influence the general nature of maternal speech. An important feature of Newport's study is the two-hour recording of the natural conversation of middle-class mother-child pairs on two occasions with an interval of six months between each recording period. She found that most (60%) of the mother's speech to the child consisted of grammatical sentences and that the remainder of the speech consisted of stock expressions ("yes," "no," "thank you") and sentence fragments. Among other findings reported by Newport is that individual utterances by the mother to the child appear to be simple but contain, nevertheless, a range of complex sentence types, and that mothers' utterances to their children contain significantly shorter surface mean length than utterances made to the experimenter.

Some researchers have recently addressed the impact or influence of the social and conversational status of speakers and listeners on the frequency of sentence types in conversation (Blount, 1972). Others have studied the specific features of adult interactive styles with young children (Corsaro, n.d.). Corsaro has focused on what he terms the "clarification request," a situation where the adult consistently asks for more information about the child's prior speech to learn, find, or create a more acceptable grasp of the child's intentions or understanding of the setting, objects, and events. He suggests that the adult's request for clarification helps the child better understand the kinds of subtle cues necessary to keep interaction viable. The child thus learns to recognize that utterances are more obvious to the speaker than they are to the listener. Clarification requests and other adult interactive styles are studied because they expose the child to more abstract rules or norms and thus provide us with a way of tracing the transmission of culture in the context of everyday interaction. A general question of these empirical studies is how adults or parents routinely expose their children to a normative order that goes beyond the confines of the child's limited linguistic and sociocultural environment (Cicourel, 1973).

The work by Gelman and Shatz (1975) shows that children and adults alter the quality of their speech in moving from one conversation to another. The content may remain roughly the same, but the lexicon, the focus, and the number of repetitions, among other conditions, vary with the type of listener that a speaker encounters. Work by Ervin-Tripp (1968, 1973), Labov (1972), and Snow (1972) indicates how adult speakers seem to be capable of modifying various aspects of their speech in different conversational (social) settings. Shatz and Gelman (1973) report that 4-year-olds generate rather simple sentences to 2-year-olds, but produce longer and more complex sentences for adults. These authors ask: What constraints seem to govern the way speakers select utterance types as they experience different conversations? They suggest that rules of conversation enable the child to produce variations in speech that result in certain lexical and syntactic selections. A central aspect of the Shatz and Gelman research is the development of categories of coding "functional meaning-in-conversation," or the way speech is used in the context of social interaction with others. These authors seek to code the speech of children and adults to reveal pragmatic elements of language that mark speaker intentions such as an assertion, request, uncertainty, and attitude. Extra-sentential aspects of speech become central to coding procedures used by Shatz and Gelman in outlining a system of conversational rules and the lexical and syntactic variations that can be found in the speech by young children. They observe that a "purely" sentential grammatical rule system cannot explain the variations they encountered in their studies.

The paper by Shatz and Gelman makes explicit reference to cultural and social conditions that govern conversational exchanges. For example, they discuss how speakers and listeners entertain what Grice (1967) has called the "cooperative principle," and work by Lakoff (1973) where participants to an exchange presume each can be influenced by the other and vice versa. Participants are thus expected to produce informative remarks without being irrelevant, remarks that are believable and that carry some kind of evidence that is tied to the conversation. The implication here is that speakers will conform to some prevailing cultural sense of politeness and regularity in their speech. Shatz and Gelman seek to use conversational rules, the context of language use, and biographical aspects of the speaker-hearer relationship to predict how speech acts can be understood. The idea is to pinpoint the conversational structures presumed to be part of the speaker-hearer's or listener's competence and used to understand particular utterances and settings.

Five functional meaning-in-conversation categories are identified by Shatz and Gelman for long utterances containing "that" or "wh" predicate complement constructions. The paper provides examples of each category and the descriptions of the functions based on how young children spoke to listeners of different ages in two settings. The authors jointly assigned a functional meaning to each target utterance by following several contextual features such as looking at speech preceding a target utterance, observing the listener's responses to an utterance, observing the speaker's subsequent response to the listener's response, observing what participants were doing during the interaction, and identifying topics in the conversation. On other occasions the authors examined the content of the target utterance to assign meaning, using the context to confirm a judgment or intuition. The functional meaning-in-conversation categories suggest a strategy for the analysis of interactional competence or micro aspects of social structure.

Methodological Issues in the Study of Interactional Competence

The analysis of interactional materials described by Shatz and Gelman and Corsaro provide video-taped documentation for assessing the significance of context when assigning functional meaning to conversational data. Without such materials it is difficult to infer the mental state of the speaker or listener, the speaker's confidence in his or her assertions or those of a listener, and the use of gestures, facial expressions, and eye contact. But coding problems remain because the social significance of what is classified by a coder presumes subtle knowledge of normal and taken-for-granted cultural information.

One focus of this chapter is to describe problems created by the researcher's intrusion into the everyday life of those studied. We were not able to use video cameras. The difficulties of attributing meaning to children's or adults' utterances when the researchers presume they have access to the same information as those studied are complicated by our lack of visual data.

Below I have used some of the materials from families studied in Mexico City (1967–68) and Buenos Aires (1968–69). In Mexico City the sample consisted of two upper-middle-income families, three middle-income families, and five low-income families. The two upper-middle-income families were contacted through the director of a private school, while the remainder of the families were chosen from a social-security-sponsored public housing project.

The families studied in Buenos Aires consisted of three cases from upper-income families, five middle- to upper-middle-income families, and six low-income families. The middle- to upper-income families were contacted through personal acquaintances of friends. The lower-income families were contacted through a social worker in an industrial suburb of Buenos Aires.

After contacting the families, we explained that we were interested in studying the "spontaneous" talk between a parent and one or more children in the home setting without the presence of the researchers. The parents were shown a tape recorder (Uher 4000L) placed inside a small attaché case with a hidden microphone. We explained that the attaché case would be left in the house periodically. Independent interviews were conducted with each mother during the first or second visit to obtain details about the child's birth and early development. We were able to obtain families with children between the ages of 12 months and 10 years of age. We tape-recorded the families for three or more occasions during a 10- to 12-month period.

The strategy pursued (by Verón with the assistance of Rosaliá Cortés) was similar to work by Shatz and Gelman and Corsaro and consisted of initially identifying rules that take into account the relationship between the participants' messages in a conversation but not the system of rule that generates the content of each message viewed as a self-contained product. Verón and Cortés (n.d.) have defined a message as an intervention by a communicator regardless of the length of the message. Following earlier work by Bateson (1972), all messages identified in the context of an interaction sequence were assigned a retrospective dimension "toward the past," and a prospective dimension "toward the future." Messages, therefore, are always produced in situations structured by previous messages, especially the last immediate message. The last message is presumed to have normative elements that refer to or are contained in the message that follows, in some implicit or explicit way. For Verón and Cortés, therefore, rules or norms regulate the relationships maintained by family members, and these rules specify the limits of permitted or prohibitive conduct.

Verón used the conversational material between mother and child to illustrate requests for information or to reveal verbal or nonverbal performances that presume the participants know and can successfully follow normative rules. He also used the speaker's intonation to reveal normative rules governing the adequacy and intentions of extra-linguistic behavior. He refers to the use of speech acts that ask for clarification, that correct the expressive form of the utterance, or that ask for additional information. Different speech acts are used to illustrate the identification of a variety of functional units that will reveal aspects of the child's acquisition of normative rules used in social interaction.

The coding of interactional material using functional meanings in context is a valuable and necessary procedure for understanding the interplay of various modalities in social exchanges and their role in providing both adult and child with information not clearly marked by formal communicational systems. We are forced, however, to treat transcriptions as self-evident sources of data about a variety of social practices within which the child's socialization occurs and adult evaluations of competence and success are derived.

We must continuously review the tapes to discover new materials that can alter interpretations based on linguistic sources of information. Listening to the tapes over and over again provides us with paralinguistic information and stimulates our memory of the original settings and our observations of various familial conditions not evident in the tapes. Familiarity with different tapes and our memory of different visits to the home provide retrospective information that alters our interpretation and summarization of the facts available from the transcript.

The researcher's descriptions of the interactional scene are selectively organized despite an attempt to reveal all details of the initial aspects of the audio or video tape. The coding of every utterance provides for considerable systematization of linguistic and psycholinguistic data, but a discussion of functional meaning in conversation forces us to go beyond lexical, phrase structure, and sentence boundaries. Combining information from several modalities forces us to utilize higher-order concepts to summarize the complex inputs that contribute to a description of a social setting. But linguistic, psycholinguistic, and nonverbal data help us to restrict the extent to which we require the reader's indulgence to make judgments about aggressiveness, "benign" gestures, laughter or tears or smiles, an "angry" tone of voice, and the like.

The inevitable idealizations created by the researcher's and subjects' descriptions are integral aspects of information processing. Differences and similarities in coding reveal important contrasts in cultural perspectives and normal problems of abduction (Peirce, 1931–1935), induction, and deduction in information processing. Hence our judgments about the content or meaning of social exchanges must reflect the participants' and researchers' efforts to create remarks or summaries designed for particular audiences. Data from transcripts can reflect concerted effort by the parents and children to create for themselves and the researcher the normative impressions that each seek. These activities, however, do not negate the fact that the specific interactional skills acquired by parents and children create normative displays that simultaneously reveal key aspects of social structure.

The families we study employ different informational particulars to convey acceptable descriptions of mood, fact, personal characteristics, doubt, and the like, to others and to the researcher. The researcher also organizes these and other sources of information to convince readers that different aspects of social organization or child development are evident in the data presented.

Despite the sometimes fragmented and elliptical style of conversational exchanges in family and other intimate settings, key aspects of a question-answer format are maintained. Thus the ideal-normative rule of one speaker at a time may be preserved, especially in middle-income families. Even when ungrammatical utterances appear, it seems safe to assume that native speakers organize their talk by implicit or explicit formal syntactic structures that intend a standardization of the semantic networks used.

The intrusion of a known tape recorder placed inside an attaché case with hidden microphone may, however, impose a formal atmosphere on the interaction of many families. Asking families if we could leave the recorder for 15 minutes to one hour often aroused suspicions in our subjects that are difficult to describe. Having a foreigner ask that the family carry out "routine" conversation influenced various aspects of the exchanges we taped. But we assumed that self-conscious, idealized, normative talk would not be sustained after five to ten minutes. Hence what we call "natural" conversation here or in experimental settings is not easy to define. The existence of unobserved or unreported ethnographic information is always presupposed. Finally, in the study reported briefly here, the transcriptions are not as detailed as they could be despite many hours of listening to each tape. We do not have access to a machine that would slow down the speech without weakening the pitch.

To illustrate the above-stated issues in the study of interactional competence, I use excerpts of materials from the two sets of families observed in Mexico City and Buenos Aires. The low-income families provide good examples of conversational exchanges that were strained by the presence of the researcher or his surrogate, the tape recorder. The middle-income families were easier to tape-record and seemed less preoccupied with the researcher's or machine's presence.

The first family (A) taped yielded intelligible materials and is from an industrialized working-class area of Buenos Aires called Avellaneda. The family consists of the mother and two children, ages 5 1/2 and 8 1/2, living in two small rooms and sharing a detached small kitchen and small bathroom with other families. The father and mother are not legally married and the children seldom see the father. After asking the mother to continue her normal routine, the social worker and I left the house and went for a walk. The opening lines of the discourse recorded begin with remarks by the mother directed to the son (Table 1).

The mother's comments can be interpreted as satisfying the researcher's request to continue a "normal" routine by asking about playing at school and what the child had eaten ("Did you play a lot at school, listen to me, talk, answer me . . ."). The mother seems preoccupied with getting the son to talk for the benefit of the researcher.

Table 1
Initial Dialogue Between Mother and Son
in Case A (Buenos Aires)

	English	*Spanish*
(1) Mo:	Listen to me (pay attention) Jorge, what did you eat at school today, my "little daddy" (pause) eh? (No response, slight pause) Did you play a lot at school? (slight pause) Listen to me (pay attention) talk, answer me (for?) (very slight pause) (why?) what did you eat at school today (pause) eh? Answer me, my "little mommy," (slight pause) answer me (with pleading voice).	Escucháme Jorge, qué comiste en el colegio hoy papito (pause) eh? (No response, slight pause) Jugaste mucho en el colegio? (slight pause) escucháme, hablá, contestáme, por (very slight pause) que comieron en el colegio hoy (pause) eh? Contestáme, mamita, (slight pause) que comieron en el colegio hoy (pause) eh? Contestáme, mamita, (slight pause) contestáme (with pleading voice).

The son does not answer the mothers request for information on what happened in school that morning despite some effort and pleading with the child. The daughter, however, seems more than willing to respond. The son cries throughout the initial taping session and we are not able to infer much about his communicative competence. But the mother speaks to her 5 1/2-year-old son as if the latter is capable of interpreting her questions, and as if he is also capable of providing an adequate description of his activities in school. The mother's remarks and the son's failure to respond may have been created by artificial and strained conditions in the family setting because of the researcher's intrusion. Hence the conversation does not seem to possess a spontaneous quality; the mother begins with a monologue.

The child's refusal to talk can be clarified' if we provide a more elaborate version of the transcript by looking beyond the opening lines. The tape recorder actually picked up a few remarks that were prior to those reported in Table 1, but they are garbled. Further along in the transcript, the mother says, ". . . it won't do anything to you . . ." and "why are you afraid? It won't do anything, it won't do anything to you." The son's talk remains unintelligible, he falters, and seems to be half crying. Perhaps the small attaché case frightened the child. Later in the tape the child seems to be crying all of the time, saying he was hit by his classmates. His sister confirms this to the mother, but the mother doesn't seem to pay much attention to the daughter. Other remarks on the tape might be used to support the view that the child did not like school, was afraid of being hit by his classmates, and was perhaps emotionally troubled independently of the researcher's presence. Whereas we acknowledge that the presence of the researcher and subsequently his tape recorder may create a bias vis-á-vis the information we obtain from the son, the son's crying creates real problems for the mother if she is trying to satisfy the researcher and simultaneously project an image of uncomplicated, "normal" family life. The son not only spoils the projection of ideal-normative conditions that the mother might wish to orchestrate, but his crying suggests an awareness of the control he can exercise over the setting. The mother's terms of endearment ("papito," "mamita") do not tell us if she is restraining herself for the researcher's benefit or simply using a familiar pattern of parental talk under family conditions of a problem child.

Whereas the son was reluctant to speak, the daughter, jumped into the conversation when her brother failed to respond and generated the dialogue with the mother contained in Table 2. The daughter's remarks reveal an answer to the question initially directed to the son

Table 2
Continued Dialogue Between Mother and Daughter
in Case A (Buenos Aires)

		English	Spanish
(2) Da:		He didn't do anything.	No hizo nada.
(3) Mo:		But, pay attention to (listen to me about) something, what did you (both) eat at school today?	Pero, escucháme una cosa, ¿qué comieron en el colegio hoy?
(4) Da:		Noodle(s?).	Fideo(s?).
(5) Mo:		And what else?	¿Y qué más?
(6) Da:		And soup.	Y sopa.
(7) Mo:		And soup (slight pause) and did (all of) you play a lot? (slight pause) Practice a lesson?	Y sopa (slight pause) ¿y jugaron mucho? (slight pause) ¿ensayaron?
(8) Da:		Yes.	Sí.
(9) Mo:		What (work) did you practice?	¿Qué sayaron?
(10) Da:		Eh (pause) I don't know.	Eh (pause) no sé.

on what was done in school. She begins by saying, "He didn't do anything" to show that she observed and remembered the brother's activities at school. But it is the mother who supplies the question frames that permit the child to respond with short but plausible answers. The daughter's replies are summarizations that presume reflexive attention to the mother's past and present remarks. The daughter's summary remark ("He didn't do anything") conveniently cuts off details about the brother's activities and sounds like a confident assertion. But after a few short responses to the mother's more elaborate questions, the daughter (10) reveals uncertainty in her knowledge of school lessons ("Eh, [pause] I don't know").

The mother's remarks reveal routine questions that could be asked of any daughter, but the concern with satisfying the researcher remains a salient issue. The dialogue continues in much the same vein for another 15 minutes. An organized question-answer format remains throughout the conversation, but there are longer utterances and more spontaneity by the daughter in later sections. The son is silent for the most part except when crying and briefly mentioning the fact that his classmates have been hitting him at school. The children are not always able to sustain an idealized conversational format. Truncated expressions are common.

The next case illustrates how field studies may create idealized adultlike conditions of social interaction between adults and children. The transcript reveals how children may become sensitive to idealized normative conditions because of the parent's and/or researcher's demands. But the inability to satisfy adult normative practices and expectations can be indicative of socialization experiences associated with age and social class. The deterioration of ideal conditions for social interaction stemming from the child's inability to sustain or unwillingness to accept the parent's definition of the situation also provokes parental annoyance. The parent is often unable to recognize or accept normal gaps in the child's socialization to adult status. The parent may refuse to recognize the existence of "normal" or adult-created conflicts that give the child temporary power on special occasions when the researcher or "guests" appear. For example the lower-income mothers always asked their children to recite a verse, tell a story, or to solve simple arithmetical problems, while correcting speech or other errors and eliciting the child's knowledge of objects and events. The mothers seemed anxious to reveal the child's social competence.

In Case C the dialogue between mother and child (who was within 6 weeks of completing 8 years of age) seems especially designed for the researcher's consumption. The remarks seem to be rehearsed. The mother appeared apprehensive when I first asked for permission to tape-record her interaction with her daughter. When I arrived with the social worker, the mother's brother was there and he remained in the house throughout the time we recorded. I interpreted the brother's presence as further evidence of the mother's apprehensiveness. When I began to listen to the tape in preparation for a preliminary analysis of the transcript, I noticed something that had been missed by the typist. I found that I could hear whispering embedded in the noise produced by the participants while they moved furniture around the room after we had left the tape recorder. The opening lines of the transcript are presented in Table 3. The dialogue reads like a well-orchestrated exchange between mother and daughter. The question-answer format is preserved without any overlaps and each utterance is well formed. The whispering that I heard sounded like cues: ". . . what should I say?" ("¿que cuento?"). The mother responded with ". . . tell me 'hi mommy'" ("digame 'hola mamita'"). These whispered cues occurred before the "official" dialogue of lines 1–5 in Table 3.

Our visit was thus treated like a special occasion, but depending on what aspects of the transcript are shown to the reader, this specialness may not be evident. The whispering, the opening lines, and the

Table 3
Ideal-Normative Dialogue Between Mother and Daughter
in Case C (Buenos Aires)

	English	*Spanish*
(1) Da:	Hi mommy! (The greeting seems to be embedded in a slightly laughing, embarrassing tone of voice.)	¡Hola mamita!
(2) Mo:	Hi, daughter, how are things? (The voice seems calm and controlled.)	Hola, hija, ¿comó te va?
(3) Da:	Fine, and you? (The voice sounds slightly excited still, as if expectant of something amusing or as if embarassed.)	Bien, ¿y vos?
(4) Mo:	Very well. How did things go at school? (How were things at school?)	Muy bien. ¿Comó te fué el colegio?
(5) Da:	Fine.	Bien.

movement of furniture retrospectively suggested to me that the setting was being prepared for us as a special performance.

When we speak of "natural" conversations, we should specify differences between different taping sessions and independent observations without the presence of a tape recorder or video camera. But the staged dialogue provides us with some boundary conditions for describing conversation under conditions of self-conscious attention to our verbal performances. We need to identify the ideal-normative rules and constraints that are operative when discourse is carried out in formal or official or bureaucratic settings. Variations in the extent to which ideal-normative rules and constrains operate under different conditions of social interaction are necessary if we are to develop a theory of settings.

The dialogue in Case C continues in much the same way as shown in Table 3. The mother and daughter seem to simulate a fresh encounter between them. The greeting in (1) could be viewed as a child returning home from school. The language used exaggerates the content and tone of voice we might expect between a child and her mother in low- and middle-income households. The tape suggests that it was a strain for them to continue. In Table 4 several subtopics related to school work reveal an orderly question-answer format. But the participants' dialogue begins to deteriorate from line 12 to line 20,

Table 4
Further Ideal-Normative Dialogue Between Mother and Daughter in Case C (Buenos Aires)

	English	Spanish
(6) Mo:	What did everyone do today?	¿Qué hicieron hoy?
(7) Da:	Today we did (stated slowly) stories, scales, aaaand numbers.	Hoy hicimos (stated slowly) cuentas, escalas, yiiii múmeras.
(8) Mo:	What else?	¿Qué más?
(9) Da:	That's all.	Nada más.
(10) Mo:	Tomorrow?	¿Mañana?
(11) Da:	Tomorrow we will do, heh, (pause) heh, the division table, the multiplication one, then we will study aand (pause) we will uh (pause uh recite (or practice).	Mañana vamos hacer eh, (pause) eh, la tabla de dividir, la de multiplicar, despue(s) vamo(s) estudiar yii (pause) y vamos a (pause) a ensayar.
(12) Mo:	Very good. And how to you behave?	Muy bien. ¿Y cómo te portás?
(13) Da:	Well.	Bien.
(14) Mo:	Do you obey the teacher?	¿Obedecés a la maestra?
(15) Da:	Yes.	Sí.
(16) Mo:	[and] with your school mates?	¿Con tus compañeritos?
(17) Da:	Yes.	Sí.
(18) Mo:	Is everything going well?	¿Todo va bien?
(19) Da:	Yes.	Sí.
(20) Mo:	Good. (Very long pause with considerable whispering.)	Bueno.

as both encounter difficulty in trying to sustain the conversation's initial topic. The "good" in line 20 is stated in a rather flat voice and sounds as if the mother is bored with the dialogue.

After the remark in line 20, noises could be heard as if chairs were being moved and there is considerable but difficult-to-understand whispering. The improvised "script" seems to have terminated and the mother seems to have whispered again to reorganize the child's performance. When the mother and daughter begin to talk again, the topic has changed to the daughter's remarks about the date of Argentina's independence from Spain, the ninth of July, and a short verse. In Table 4 the daughter begins to experience difficulty when she starts to describe the next day's school activities. There are more pauses than in the opening lines and her responses become single-word sentences. The mother must keep supplying the frame for even a minimal response by the child.

The dialogue on Argentina's independence is exhausted after a few lines that are occasionally embedded in a laughing (perhaps uneasy) tone of voice, followed by the mother closing the exchange and then silence and further whispering and the sound of people moving around. The mother then appeared at the door as if to indicate that they had completed their conversation. We urged them to continue. The mother accepted our request.

The next section of the dialogue sounds even more strained to me as the mother asks the daughter to recite a little verse. The daughter obliges the mother. After the verse the mother describes several activities they will be doing the rest of the afternoon. Then there is further whispering, someone laughs, and the daughter asks if they want her to recite more verses. The mother says she can recite all of the verses she wants. Verses and short, simulated conversations continue with whispering interspersed throughout. The mother and daughter seem to run out of "material" and the whispering resumes. The daughter then begins to read from a book. After a few short passages the daughter finds it difficult to pronounce specific words (first "desempeño" and then "tareas"), and is unable to pronounce the word "prolonged" or "extended." The uncle, for the first time, joins in to help the girl, as does the mother. But the daughter cannot capture the correct pronunciation. A short, whispered exchange takes place. The daughter continues to encounter difficulties while the mother keeps providing corrections and whispered remarks. Finally, the mother (line 40) states the following:

(40) Mo: (In a low voice that sounds exasperated.) Gosh! Maria, Maria, what a mess you're making (pause). "Prolonged" ("extended"). "Look there, there look!"

Ay! Maria, Maria, que papelón que estás haciendo (pause). Prolongado. Mirá ahí, ahí mirá!

The following remark was unintelligible to me but one typist claims to have heard something like: "Are you nervous or what?" The daughter continues to make additional mistakes and the mother provides further corrections in a normal but impatient voice as well as using a low, whispered voice.

The mother's concern with normal appearances seems to be an inference we can make from her whispering and staged dialogue with the child. But this staged effort seemed to break down because of the daughter's mistakes and the mother's reference to the "mess" the daughter was making of her reading. The daughter revealed an ability to simulate normative speech by pursuing topics suggested by the mother, answering questions, and invoking appropriate lexical items and phonological and syntactic constructions. But the daughter's composure began to deteriorate as her ability to read from a book faltered. The mother and the heretofore silent uncle felt they should correct the child's performance. The corrections became more than just casual or routine suggestions. The mother and daughter were unable to continue the staged presentation for the tape recorder (and researcher). The child could not sustain the earlier ideal-normative talk even with the mother's whispered instructions, help, and guidance. The mother's annoyance and exasperation with the daughter's mistakes produced emergent remarks that were like routine, everyday exchanges where emotional factors and nonverbal informational resources combine to produce less than ideal-normative expressions. The mother seemed to react to the daughter's performance as if it were situated (line 40) when she kept correcting the child and finally was thought to have asked: "Are you nervous or what?" We have no additional information that would suggest anything about the daughter's reaction to the mother's remarks. The child's inability to pronounce "prolongado" is not, however, necessarily tied to the presence of the tape recorder.

This episode provides us with a glimpse of the mother's use of adult standards for evaluating the daughter's performance. The daughter's actions shift the mother's attention from a concern with displaying the child's abilities while satisfying the researcher's request, to the child's performance becoming a public display of incompetence. The mother's conceptions of social structure are embedded in both concerns. The continued whispering that was detected through the first taped session reveals an attempt to satisfy the mother's ideas of proper conduct. But she could not stop herself from getting angry with the daughter's performance.

Another example of the mother not being able to pursue a presentation for the benefit of the tape recorder and researcher occurs in Case R of Mexico City. The interaction was extensive and reveals the child's communicative competence under conditions that could be characterized as "natural." The setting is the noon meal and the dialogue is between the mother and her younger 4-year-old son. A young daughter (10 months old) was present, and an older 10-year-old son enters the exchange, but in the part quoted here most of the mother's efforts are directed to the younger son's refusal to eat. This family is from a middle-income group. The father is a technician for the telephone company. The mother teaches in a primary school in the morning, leaving the younger children with a maid.

The dialogue (Table 5) opens with the mother telling the younger son to sit down and eat with a soft or gentle intonation in her voice. The child says he does not want to eat (2) and the mother's voice intonation changes immediately as she says "yes" (3). The mother in line 5 seems to begin to offer the child something if he behaves well, but he cuts her off with a whining "no" (6). From here on the mother

Table 5
Mother-Child Interaction in Case R (Mexico City)

	English	*Spanish*
(1) Mo:	Yes, yes, you are going to eat. Sit down I am going to serve you now. (Said in a soft voice.)	Sí, sí vas a comer. Siéntate ya te voy a servir.
(2) So:	But I don't want to.	Pero no quiero.
(3) Mo:	Yeees. (In a firm voice.)	Siiii.
(4) So:	No.	No.
(5) Mo:	Look, if you behave well (if you are good) . . .	Mira, si tu te portas bien . . .
(6) So:	No, no, no (whining voice)	No, no, no
(7) Mo:	Yees. Look, you must eat. Sit down, sit down. (The mother seems to be getting angry judging from her sharper tone of voice.)	Siii. Mire, tienes que comer. Siéntate.
(8) So:	No. (Crying)	No.
(9) Mo:	Sit down, I'll hit you. (In a scolding voice.)	Siéntate. Te pego.
(10) So:	No. (Crying and yelling.) Don't hit me.	No. No me pegues.
(11) Mo:	Sit down, you have to eat!	¡Siéntate, tienes que comer!
(12) So:	No. (Still crying.)	No.
(13) Mo:	Sit down. Don't you "move" from there. (The mother's voice sounds quite angry at this point.) Sit down, sit down. (The child can be heard weeping followed by a pause.) Sit down. Sit down. You must eat, Jorgito. (The mother then began talking to the maid.) Bring me the chicken from the refrigerator.	Siéntate. No te paras de ahí. Siéntate, siéntate. (Llanto del niño. Pausa.) Siéntate. Tienes que comer Jorgito. (Dirigiéndose a la sirvienta.) Tráeme el pollo del refrigerador.

becomes increasingly angry, her manner becomes brusque and insistent, while the child cries, yells, and weeps. The older son enters and asks about his food, but the mother gives him short replies as she concentrates on the younger son. She keeps telling the younger son not to get off of the chair (13).

As the dialogue continues, the mother returns to a firm but even tone of voice as she mentions specific foods she will give to her son. Perhaps she remembered the presence of the tape recorder. The son, however, keeps saying "no," noting "I don't want rice." The mother becomes angry again and asks, "Then what do you want?" The son responds with a whine, "Nothing, and nothing." The mother asks if the younger son wants a bottle, then quickly adds that he shouldn't be taking a bottle. The son then asks for his bottle. The dialogue continues with the same issues being covered several times. The mother's anger occurs despite later remarks to the older son about the make of the tape recorder and the fact that it is recording.

The dialogue and intonation of the mother and child in family R do not suggest that the family was creating a performance for the researcher even though the mother is aware of the tape recorder. Despite the initial softness of her voice and the use of an affectionate diminutive, the mother is unable to sustain control over the situation. Her remarks suggest that her 4-year-old son should not be using the bottle at his age. The son "skillfully" manages to have his way. We could argue that the presence of the tape recorder may have forced the mother to abandon sterner strategies for handling the son, but the availability of the bottle implies that the child's behavior is typical even if her response was softened by an awareness of the researcher's intrusion. Our interview with the mother confirmed that the younger son is a problem for her and that he never eats anything he doesn't like. The mother's summary-type remarks during the interview that the younger son is difficult to handle may be viewed as documented by the tape of the noon meal. The mother could not control the situation despite knowing she was being "observed" by the tape recorder.

The final case to be presented is a family in Buenos Aires with an upper-middle-income life style. Both parents are college graduates. They lived with their daughters, Pilar, age 27 months, and María, age 4 years, at the time of the study. The materials quoted in Table 6 are based on the fifth visit to the family. Although the mother in this family is also concerned with presenting a "good" image for the researcher's benefit, seeking to engage the child in a dialogue, other aspects of socialization are revealed that are of substantive interest.

This session was taped by an assistant who had remained in the home for a brief stay to generate some conversation with the two daughters and a friend, Daniel, of the older sister. The assistant attempted to control the conversation by shifting the dialogue from a spontaneous outburst about cameras to a book for children. While examining the book, the assistant tried to select Pilar as a speaker on several occasions, only to have María respond virtually every time.

The dialogue continues with the older sister María revealing her ability to express common cultural knowledge about washing the face and her competence in applying this knowledge to a story book by noting how the bear in the story is washing his face with a sponge. The assistant tries to draw Pilar into the exchange, but María again responds for her sister by noting that bears do not brush their teeth after observing that the book reveals a picture of a bear brushing his teeth. María continually demonstrates her adultlike knowledge by talking about someone getting drunk and expressing the idea that a person can become obese if they eat too much. María and Daniel reveal some confusion about how the tape recorder functions. They cannot understand how the tape recorder can operate inside an attaché case. María continues to speak for her sister, but Pilar manages to utter two imitations of "seesaw" and "hammock." The assistant then leaves the apartment and the mother takes over in directing the conversation.

The mother requests information from Pilar in (1) and (3) in table 6 about a refreshment. The response of "tea" is made in (2) which the mother repeats in (3). The remarks of (5) and (6) suggest that María began to touch the tape recorder while repeating the fact that she desired nothing to drink. The mother seems irritated by María's actions, and this irritation is repeated shortly when the mother tries to engage Pilar in a conversation. The mother experiences the same problem as the assistant did; María begins to respond for her sister. María begins a separate conversation with Daniel after this incident.

In (7) María poses a question about the number of matches she perceives and the mother responds in (8) about a recent trip by the father. Daniel jumps in to provide us with his adultlike knowledge of how the buyer of cigarettes is given matches with his purchase. The children continue a pattern of generating unsolicited knowledge that was initiated when the assistant was present; they do not change this pattern when the mother becomes active in the conversation after the assistant has departed.

The mother's false start in (10) to address Pilar is suddenly cut off and, from my interpretation of the mother's voice after listening to

Table 6

**Dialogue Between Mother and Two Daughters of Family S
and Visiting Playmate (Buenos Aires)**

	English	*Spanish*
(1) Mo:	Pili, (P: Mhuh?) what do you want to drink, coffee with milk?	¿Pili, (P: Mhuh?) vos, qué querés tomar, café con leche?
(2) P:	No, tea (diminutive).	No, tesitos.
(3) Mo:	Tea? (diminutive).	¿Tesitos?
(4) P:	Hm.	Hm.
(5) M:	And nothing for me.	Y yo nada.
(6) Mo:	No, no don't touch it, no, no (M: Nothing for me.) but Mar-Mariachi! No!	No, no, no toque lo, no no (M: Yo nada) ¡pero Mar-Mariachi! ¡No!
(7) Mo:	Why are there many matches?	¿Porqué hay muchos fosforos?
(8) Mo:	Because, (P: Maaa) because (P: Maaa) your father brought them from the (his) trip.	Porque (P: Fofo) porque P: Fofo) los trajo tu papá del viaje.
(9) D:	They it, when you buy cigarettes they give them out.	Se log, cuando compra cigarrillos se los regalan.
(10) Mo:	Listen to me Mariachi, eh Pili, (P: Hm.) uh (?)	Escuchame una cosa, Mariachi, eh Pili, (P: Hm.) este (?)

(From the intonation of the mother's voice, it sounded as if she noticed something that had to be attended.)

(11) M:	Pilar, what's Daddy's name, what's his name?	Pilar, ¿cómo se llama papito, cómo se llama?
(12) P:	Miguel.	Miguel.
(13) M:	And mommy, what's mommy's name?	¿Y mamá, cómo se llama, mamá?
(14) P:	María.	María.
(15) M:	And, and, th, and how is this boy called (what is this boy's name)?	¿Y, y, es, y este nene cómo se llama?

Table 6
Dialogue Between Mother and Two Daughters of Family S
and Visiting Playmate (Buenos Aires)
(continued)

		English	*Spanish*
(16) P:		Ande (?)	Ande (?)
(17) D?M:		Nooo (loudly)	Nooo (en vox alta)
(18) M:		How is he called (what is his name)?	¿Cómo se llama?
(19) P:		Daniel	Daniel
(20) M:		V-e-r-y g-o-o-d	M-u-y b-i-e-n
(21) Mo:		V-e-r-y g-o-o-d	M-u-y b-i-e-n
(22) M:		What is the name? (At least two people talking here, including the mother) What is the name? What is the name of Sara's little girl?	¿Cómo se llama? ¿Cómo se llama? . Cómo se llama la nena de Sara?
(23) Mo:		Let her alone, let her alone, let her alone.	Dejála, dejála, dejála.
(24) P:		Gabriela.	Gabriela.
(25) M:		And what is the name of Sara's husband?	¿Y cómo se llama el esposo de Sara?
(26) Mo:		The father.	El papá.
(27) M:		The father.	El papá.
(28) Mo:		Gabriela's father, what is his name?	El papá de Gabriela, ¿cómo se llama?
(29) M:		Maaximo.	Maaximo.
(30) P:		Maax	Maax
(31) M?:		iiimo (Several persons talking simultaneously here.)	iiimo.

the tape several times, I assume she has been distracted momentarily. This observation seems to be confirmed by the way María takes over in (11) and (13) to ask Pilar the names of her father and mother. This line of talk is continued by María (15–18) until both María and the mother say "v-e-r-y g-o-o-d" at the same time (20–21). The mother apparently was listening to Pilar's performance. The mother (23, 26, 28) enters the conversation to clarify the naming of someone after María (22, 25, 27) has resumed this type of request for information to reveal Pilar's knowledge of the names of others. The mother's clarification suggests that Pilar is unable to comprehend different kinship categories (a playmate's mother's husband and the playmate's father) used to designate the same person. This episode indicates the way cultural knowledge can be tested, elicited, and taught to young children.

The same transcript of observed or recorded social interaction between children and between children and adults can provide the data base for studying phonological knowledge that is being expressed or taught. The differences in speech between 2-year-old Pilar and her 4-year-old sister María show language-acquisition features assumed to be common for their ages. Pilar did not use long utterances, did not respond consistently to speech directed at her, imitated her sister's speech, and used truncated utterances with deleted consonants in specific lexical items. It is difficult to say if in Pilar's speech we are observing some combination of a gap in competence or performance difficulties. But Pilar's age alerts us to expect these speech characteristics, just as we expect to find her sister María speaking differently as well as answering questions or remarks directed to her younger sister.

At a higher level of abstraction we can discuss the semantic problems revealed by each child, noting how their speech implies a lack of adult comprehension and referencing ability, or a lack of knowledge. We can suggest obvious differences in the semantic networks developed and note the significance of sibling teaching for understanding socialization practices.

Several aspects of turn-taking activity are revealed in the last family described. Some regularity in the selection of speakers seems clear despite our not having visual information about the setting during the tape recording. Thus we cannot always specify the basis for self-selection with the children in Family S. The significance of the turn-taking is not always clear because we lack more information about the ethnographic context. Was Pilar's performance inhibited by the presence of the assistant? Was María motivated to speak more because of the assistant and the tape recorder? The mother's remarks to María seemed designed to give the daughter a chance to talk (23), but did not clarify if María's behavior was unusual or routine. In other tapes, gathered over the period of a year, María and Pilar engage in spontaneous conversation rather frequently. In the present situation we do not know if María is "helping" her sister when she talks in her place, or if María is trying to obtain more attention for herself.

In all of our tapes it is possible to note differences in mean length of utterances for Pilar and María, and we can identify various occasions where the observations of Gelman and Shatz (1975) on "that" and "wh" predicate complements are confirmed. María, for example, used these constructions fairly often to clarify and describe topics and specific objects and events ("Let's see, how is it called?" and "Isn't it true that he's going to get fat . . ."). María also used adultlike constructions to elicit information from her sister. These constructions reveal Pilar's competence as a partially socialized member of the family. The activities of María and Daniel on the present tape and on other tapes reveal a variety of functions described by Gelman and Shatz (1975) and Shatz and Gelman (1973).

The material from Family S also raises questions about the developmental acquisition of the conventional meaning of words within the perspective of conversational postulates. It is not clear when we can speak of children recognizing or abiding by the idea of a common purpose or set of purposes, or a similar direction to conversations. The cooperative principle described by Grice (1967) is not observed easily despite Daniel's and María's following the assistant's use of the book and the mother's directions. Adults can be said to reveal aspects of the cooperative principle when they organize their talk to children and when they suggest an order, or have the children order their utterances. But this does not mean that the adults will return the cooperation when the children return the favor. In the material from Tables 1–5 the mothers give the children explicit or implicit instructions on how they are to cooperate in the conversation, and also offer the children their assistance when the children do not follow the adult's conception of how the exchange is to proceed.

The study of discourse materials in family settings suggests several more general aspects of socialization.

1. Children generate considerable unsolicited knowledge within a context where the information presented reveals the fact of its possession, and not necessarily because children think others do not have the same information or because children think others would be interested in this information.

2. Older siblings not only simulate the mother's role but also seem to fulfill similar functions in teaching the younger child important cultural information that becomes a necessary part of the child's cultural or social competence in dealing with others in progressively more adultlike exchanges.

3. Children acquire the ability to relate information in complex ways, making use of stored knowledge to generate situationally appropriate remarks, while simultaneously sustaining a sense of social structure vis-à-vis what is happening moment by moment. The differential capabilities of Pilar, versus Daniel and María, suggest how reference and comprehension are achieved, while also revealing how interactional materials can serve as a data base for discovering socialization practices within and across social classes and cultural groups.

4. Continuous attempts are made by adults and older children to elicit utterances from younger children that express and confirm the developmental acquisition of knowledge associated with membership in some group and the transition to adult status in the larger society. This acquisition of membership is a continuous achievement that relies on the tacit but appropriate use of interpretive and summarization principles or procedures. Discourse is an important vehicle for displaying members' competence in the expression and control of knowledge. The attribution of membership in social groups and the differential ranking that can be achieved by or assigned to children is in large part revealed by performances in interactional settings.

Theoretical Discussion

A basic process of communication consists of the ability to link internal representations (a semantic network, auditory and visual images in memory) to external representations organized as grammatical structures and sound patterns. The external representation systems used in discourse must be capable of summarizing experiences and thought. The speaker-hearer (or signer of gestural sign language) must recognize that he or she understands, means, or intends more than is received or expressed orally or manually, and that others make the same assumption.

Recognizing that more information is understood or intended than is received or expressed presumes a reflexive monitoring of information perceived, retrieved from memory, and generated during communicational exchanges with others. We retrieve less information than we have stored for the external representation of a topic or object, and we recognize more information than we can recall and represent. We know little about the extent to which the elaboration of an event, topic, or object is possible because of its dependence on stored information. Our studies tend to focus on recall and summaries of controlled information. We seldom study the elaboration of stored information as a sociocultural reconstruction that is tied to the context of social interaction and the orientation of the participants. But the notion of social structure only makes sense when we recognize the significance of a body of knowledge or social facts in a context of social interaction as an emergent activity constrained by cognitive, linguistic, and sociocultural processes.

Recall and summarization include interpretation. The notion of interpretation presumes that the specification of factual information occurs under conditions of "abduction" (Peirce, 1931–1935). The key point to be stressed here is that the observation of facts is embedded in the particular circumstances at the time of observation. Abduction for Peirce is an inferential step that occurs in first stating and then reflecting on a hypothesis that would choose among several possible explanations of some set of facts. The particular circumstances that exist at the time of observation provide the context for the inferential step of making guesses about what is happening in a social exchange. The observation of facts by participants of social interaction means that communicants perceive a setting in terms of what is assumed to be culturally known in common with others (Cicourel, 1973). New experiences lead to reflection that can elaborate our understanding of these activities and can also mean adding information to our memory of the experiences.

There is a long history behind the notion that social interaction is an emergent activity (Cooley, 1902; Mead, 1934; Peirce, 1931–1935; Schutz, 1971), but the cognitive, linguistic, and sociocultural processes that constrain and shape the emergence of social structure have not always been clearly specified. A major difficulty in specifying the different processes in social interaction is the clarification of how top-down (deductive) and bottom-up (inductive) theories can be integrated.

A basic problem in studies of the child's ability to surpass gradually the limitations of using single lexical items and strings in exchanges with others. Thus the ability to use higher-order predicates presumes a reflexive monitoring of perceived, stored, and expressed information that permits the production of connected strings of discourse, including a sophisticated system of turn-taking in conversation, and the selection of utterance types that can be called conversational rules or the notion of a grammar of discourse (Gelman and Shatz, 1975).

If we are to trace the acquisition of adult interactional competence, we must specify the child's use of executive activities or use of interpretive and summarization procedures while experiencing, producing, or contributing to social interaction. An executive or interpretive process that selects and summarizes immediate and stored experiences presumes an important cognitive process and sociocultural awareness not clearly specified in studies of child development.

The idea of executive monitoring or an organized system of interpretive procedures permits the child to selectively arrange incoming information and representational activities according to idealized or normative rules that are culturally prescribed. The child thus acquires the ability to develop and employ hierarchical systems of knowledge (values, moral principles, laws) and higher-order predicates embedded in complex systems of representation, while being sensitive to local conditions of social interaction.

The abductive strategy outlined by Peirce can be extended to describe how the child is able to link immediate experiences to learned sociocultural rules systems while simulantaneously providing for a creative activity that is tied to the perception of an unfolding scene with problematic features. The child can thus imagine and believe in activities or objects for which no clear normative adult categories exist. The child not only acquires the ability to construct imaginatively and/or remember events and objects, but also learns to recognize that what is abductively perceived in real-time may not stand the test of later reasoning. In a discussion with adults or older children the inductive and deductive procedures used may be divorced from the setting in which the child's original experiences occurred.

The interpretive and summarization activities of the child during social interaction presume an acquisition of normal forms of perception the child assumes are experienced by others. The child learns to assume that he or she shares the same social setting as others. Learning to treat a range of appearances and utterance types or signs as "obvious," despite the possibility of noticeable differences that may be communicated in subtle ways, becomes criterial for adults in deciding that children are becoming more "mature." The assignment of adult status to younger persons presumes the latter are capable of treating appearances in flexible normative ways that will gloss or ignore ambiguous or deviant particulars and thus sustain social interaction despite "problems."

An important consequence of acquiring the ability to recognize and create normal or normative appearances is the child's learning to use standardized and special languages or codes. The child must learn normative constraints about who can speak first or next (Sacks, Schegloff, and Jefferson, 1974), when to stop speaking and listen attentively, and when an interruption is feasible. The attribution of adult status to younger persons is especially marked by the child's or adolescent's ability to distinguish among appropriate topics of conversation that can be called relevant, acceptable, insulting, "odd," distrustful, etc. The acquisition of social structure includes the ability to use appropriate terms and gestures to begin or terminate an exchange and to ignore violations of the normative rule of one speaker at a time, as well as the ability to produce appropriate facial and bodily expressions and voice intonation. The normalization process therefore presumes a continuous, negotiated dialectic between idealized or normatively stored information and actual conduct filtered and organized by interpretive procedures. The child must learn to link present circumstances to stored resources and future possibilities.

A key issue that adults often forget is that subsuming informational particulars under normative categories may not mean that the child (or all adults) can explain the representation used despite the employment of native expressions of a standardized or colloquial variety. The child's ability to comprehend something yet not provide it with a clear normative linguistic representation can create problems for the researcher using controlled study procedures and also relying on the parents' judgments about the child's performances.

Summary

The child's acquisition of conversational or discursive rules is quite developed before he or she enters a formal educational setting where reading of organized textual materials begins to influence the language-learning process. The study of the child's socialization to adulthood therefore requires an understanding of the differences between conversational and textual representations because they provide us with clues about the child's ability to comprehend and manipulate adult conceptions of social structure.

A considerable part of the child's socialization experiences in school is devoted to learning how to use a language he or she already knows. Formal courses on grammar and composition may seem strange and the child's native language may appear unfamiliar to him or her. Continuing through adolescence, the child will express fears about writing his or her "native" language because of not knowing the difference between an adjective and an adverb, or not being able to decide when the subject of the sentence takes a singular or plural verb.

Formal education teaches us to use written summary statements that have a hierarchical structure in which some kind of introduction or topicalization occurs that may include relevant objects, persons, and events to orient the reader. Written summaries seem to have a structure not unlike the organization of folktales told over and over again in an oral tradition (Cicourel, 1975; Rumelhart, 1975). Various themes may be presented after an introduction, followed by a resumé. Summary statements with a hierarchical structure therefore epitomize normative efforts to codify and organize an idealized historical record. The contrast between summarization in conversational settings versus textual displays provides us with clues about the child's socialization to adulthood.

Conversational exchanges between two or more persons include utterance fragments, paralinguistic sounds, gestures, facial expressions, and other appearances involving clothing, body movements, and possible physical contact. Summary statements produced within this conversational context may be marked by these various contextual conditions, thus revealing editing practices over the course of a summary's production. Studies of child language acquisition seek performances by children in settings that are free of noises that make transcription difficult, but the study of interactional competence requires natural settings with all of their noisy and complex qualities to reveal the use and confounding of several communicational modalities. Noisy interactional settings produced by persons on intimate terms require the listener and speaker to add or assume considerable information not marked by transcribed speech. Many aspects of the details assumed by the participants are not questioned on the grounds that they will be clarified over the course of the conversation.

The child's progress to adulthood should be marked by the ability to create narrative summaries with a hierarchical structure amenable to algorithmic modeling and reflecting logical and cognitive relationships and processes (Rumelhart, 1975). The child's ability to tell a story and then write a story about some experience, or to recall (summarize) a story, can be examined for obvious grammatical relationships between subject and predicate. It is difficult, however, to obtain evidence that reveals the truth value of propositions used vis-á-vis their intended indexing of possible social realities. The use of a propositional construction that is hypothesis-driven may be obscured by an inability to substain a control of the language. For example, are grammatical sentences used that facilitate referencing by specifying the roles of various concepts in the sentence? Can participants to an exchange thus find or create the meanings that seem to provide adequate sociocultural sense to their activities? We need to know more about the child's understanding and use of grammatical rules in interactional settings—learning strategies that will be appropriate for particular occasions.

The illustrative materials on family interaction in Mexico City and Buenos Aires were used merely as a vehicle to raise methodological and theoretical issues in our studies of the child's acquisition of social structure. The concern with interpretive and summarization processes underscores the parallel problems researchers share with those being studied. We must make judgments about functional meaning in conversation while using studies of lexical, phrase, and sentential structures assumed to reveal clearly identifiable rules or properties. But the study of social interaction forces the researcher into cognitive problems similar to those faced by the children studied: information overload and simplification of summarizations that must be studied as an interactional process and not simply as structural properties or rules. The child's and researcher's interpretive and summarization practices are resources for the successful creation of social structure. These resources resolve the problem of integrating cross-modal information by a selective orientation to the immediate context and its articulation with stored information. Recording family interaction without the presence of the researcher creates, initially, ideal-normative displays of social structure. Further interaction reveals the emergent aspects of social interaction. Summarization reflects normative conceptions of social structure that presuppose a creative interpretive process.

In all of the families we have recorded the parents were unable to control the conditions of interaction and always revealed aspects of socialization practices. Ideal-normative conditions of conversation or "appropriate" conduct were not always sustained, but their content was always expressed.

Our activities as researchers reveal different sources of information for deciding on the relevance of the information obtained. Our coding procedures consist of references to systematic lexical, phrase structure, sentence, and conversational structures. But we are also dependent, in studies of socialization or sociocultural aspects of child development, on information of the settings as "observed" from the vantage point of a tape recorder or video camera. We obviously need different types of family settings if we are to apply the study of functional meaning in context to the general problem of child development or socialization. Our database should consist of contrasts between settings we can observe by mechanical means, as well as narrative and interview materials from the parents that summarize complex information processing by the use of higher-order predicates. The higher-order predicates can be subjected to further analysis by examining the everyday conditions of family interaction referenced by the summary statements. Hence we must be wary of questionnaire information that cannot be evaluated further by reference to conditions of social interaction.

The assembly of questionnaire material into statistical summaries is often the sole basis for sociological research findings of socialization practices in home and classroom settings. These studies, and others restricted to narrow controlled conditions, can be improved if we recognize that the child's and parent's interpretation and summarization processes are not revealed adequately when the data base consists only of materials that indirectly index socialization or child development. We must also observe and record everyday social interaction.

The illustrative transcripts of family interaction from the studies in Mexico City and Buenos Aires are suggestive in the way they reveal the child's use of unsolicited expressions to display knowledge. These materials also reveal differences in the appropriate or inappropriate use of interpretive and summarization procedures for seeking and satisfying conditions of membership in a group. The families we studied oriented their activities for our benefit but could not avoid displaying behavior typical and indicative of everyday actions.

References

Bateson, G. *Steps to an Ecology of Mind*. New York: Ballantine Books, 1972.

Blount, B. G. Parental speech and language acquisition: Some Luo and Samoan examples. *Anthropological Linguistics*, 1972, *14*, 119–130.

Cicourel, A. V. *Cognitive Sociology*. Middlesex, England: Penguin Books, 1973.

Cicourel, A. V. Discourse and text: Cognitive and linguistic processes in studies of social structure. *Versus: Quadernidi Studi Semiotici*, September-December, 1975, pp. 33–84.

Cooley, C. H. *Human Nature and the Social Order*, (1902). New York: Scribner's 1922.

Corsaro, W. A. Sociolinguistic features of adult interaction styles with young children. Unpublished manuscript, n.d.

Ervin-Tripp, S. An analysis of the interaction of language, topic, and listener. In J. A. Fishman (Ed.), *Readings in the Sociology of Language*. The Hague: Mouton, 1968, pp. 192–211.

Ervin-Tripp, S. Some strategies for the first two years. In T. E. Moore, *Cognitive Development and the Acquisition of Language*. New York: Academic Press, 1973.

Gelman, R., and Shatz, M. Rule-governed variation in children's conversations. Unpublished manuscript, University of Pennsylvania, 1975.

Grice, H. P. Logic and conversation. The William James Lectures, Harvard University, 1967.

Labov, W. The study of language in its social context. In W. Labov, *Sociolinguistic Patterns*. Philadelphia: University of Pennsylvania Press, 1972.

Lakoff, R. The logic of politeness; or, minding your p's and q's. *Papers from the Ninth Regional Meeting of the Chicago Linguistic Society*. Chicago: Linguistics Department, University of Chicago, 1973, pp. 292–305.

Mead, G. H. *Mind, Self and Society*. Chicago: University of Chicago Press, 1934.

Newport, E. L. Motherese: The speech of mothers to young children. In N. J. Castellan, D. B. Pisoni, and G. R. Potts (Eds.), *Cognitive Theory: Vol. II*. Hillsdale, N.J.: Earlbaum Associates, 1976.

Peirce, C. S. *Collected Papers*. Cambridge, Mass.: Harvard University Press, 1931–1935.

Phillips, J. R. Syntax and vocabulary of mothers' speech to young children: Age and sex comparisons. *Child Development*, 1973, *44*, 182–185.

Remick, H. The material environment of linguistic development. Unpublished doctoral thesis, University of California, Davis, 1971.

Rumelhart, D. Notes on a schema for stories. In D. Bobrow and A. Collins (Eds.), *Representation and Understanding: Studies in Cognitive Science*. New York: Academic Press, 1975, pp. 211–236.

Sacks, H., Schegloff, E. A., and Jefferson, G. A simplest systematics for the organization of turn-taking for conversation. *Language*. 1974, *50*, 696–735.

Schutz, A. *Collected Papers. Vol. I. The Problem of Social Reality*. The Hague: Martinus Nijhoff, 1971.

Shatz, M., and Gelman, R. The development of communication skills: Modifications in the speech of young children as a function of listener. *SRCD Monog.*, 1973, *38*, No. 5.

Shipley, E. S., Smith C. S., and Gleitman, L. R. A study in the acquisition of language: Free responses to commands. *Language*. 1969, *45*, 322–42.

Snow, C. E. Mother's speech to children learning language. *Child Development*, 1972, *43*, 549–565.

Verón, E., and Cortés, R. *Interacción Madre-Hijo: Metodologiá Para El Estudio De Las Transacciones Normativas*. Proyecto 39: Instituto Torcuato Di Tella, Buenos Aires, n.d.

Whiting, B. (Ed.), *Six Cultures*. New York: Wiley, 1963.

Index